The Top Ten Secrets to Managing Your Money in the New Millenium

1. **Knowing how your credit applications are scored will help you get credit.** This is one of the biggest secrets of the personal finance world. You'll learn in this book the criteria on which your application is judged—and how you can make the grade.

2. **Fatten your retirement nest egg—invest your money in a tax-deferred account.** By sheltering your investments (and hopefully profits!) from Uncle Sam until you retire, you can earn more in a tax-deferred account than a taxable account. In this book, you'll learn about the options available to you.

3. **Don't get tricked by low-ball interest rates advertised by financial institutions.** When you're shopping for a loan—whether a home equity loan, auto loan, or mortgage loan—don't be dazzled by gimmick rates and freebies. Consider the total cost of the loan, based on how much you borrow, plus the up-front fees and closing costs, where applicable.

4. **Treat yourself like a bill, and pay yourself first.** Write yourself out a check or have an amount electronically withdrawn from your bank account into an investment (you'll learn where in this book). It's a great way to build your wealth.

5. **Pay your insurance premiums annually.** It sounds like a simple strategy, but most folks don't. If you pay your car insurance or homeowner's insurance on an annual basis, you can save up to 20 percent more than if you pay monthly or even semi-annual premiums.

6. **When you buy a new car, avoid dealer financing.** Want to save 1 to 2 percent on your auto loan right off the bat? Avoid dealer financing altogether. Forget independent finance companies, too—their rates are even higher. Go to a bank, thrift, or credit union, obtain a pre-approved loan for the amount you plan to finance—and save money!

7. **Dollar-cost average your way to wealth.** Dollar-cost averaging is simply investing a fixed amount of money on a regular basis, such as in a mutual fund or dividend reinvestment program. By investing with this self-disciplined financial strategy, you can slowly reach your long-term financial goals.

8. **Home equity loans can be dangerous if you're not careful.** Taking out a home equity loan or home equity line of credit can explode in your face if you're not careful. The bottom line? If you don't make your payments, they could take your most valuable asset—your home!

9. **Shop around for a bank account that doesn't nickel-and-dime you to the poor house.** It's no secret that banks and thrifts are slapping fees on everything from talking to a teller on the phone to making a transaction at a rival ATM machine. But not all banks and thrifts do so, and others have fees that are much lower. So shop around and save money!

10. **Do your homework.** It's amazing how many people spend so much time researching a potential vacation hot-spot, yet they won't do their homework for any of their personal finance decisions. The steps in this book will help you along your way.

alpha
books

tear here

Reader Feedback—Your Chance to Sound Off

The authors, Robert K. Heady and Christy Heady, want to know your opinions, thoughts, and comments about *The Complete Idiot's Guide to Managing Your Money, Second Edition*. It will only take you a moment and will help us in writing future books, columns, and articles that will best serve your information needs. (You don't even have to sign your name if you don't want to!) You can e-mail us at Jrnl8888@aol.com, or

Write to us at: Money Answers
                   P.O. Box 14875
                   N. Palm Beach, Florida 33408

Tear out or copy and mail this page to us, or, if you prefer e-mail, simply jot down the question number—e.g., #3—and write the answer beside it.

1. On a 1 to 10 scale, with 0 being the lowest and 10 the highest, I'd give this book a ____.

2. Do you think you can definitely use any of the information in the book? ___No   ___Yes

3. What I liked best about the book was: _____

4. What I liked least was: _____

5. What I'd really like to see you write in your next book is
    a. more about the following: _____
    b. and less about the following:_____

6. Recently, the source I've relied on the most for my personal finance information has been (check one):

    ___Newspapers   ___Internet & online services
    ___Magazines   ___Broker
    ___Television   ___Bank, thrift, or credit union
    ___Radio   ___Seminars
    ___Books   ___Other (please name): _____
    ___Newsletters

7. The information source I'll probably rely on more in the future than in the past is:_____
    because: _____

8. The biggest single question about personal finance that I'd like to ask the experts is this:
    _____
    _____

9. (Optional) From time to time, we like to poll our readers to obtain their reactions to the latest events in the world of money and personal finance. It's a chance to air your opinions. If you'd like to become part of our volunteer panel, please indicate below. We only survey a few times a year, and we'll send all poll results to everyone who participates in the poll.

    a. I'm agreeable to being surveyed by mail. My name and address are:
        _____
        _____
        _____

    b. I'll participate but only anonymously via the Internet. My e-mail address is:
        _____

    c. No thanks.

And, of course, please feel free to write the authors at the P.O. Box given above.

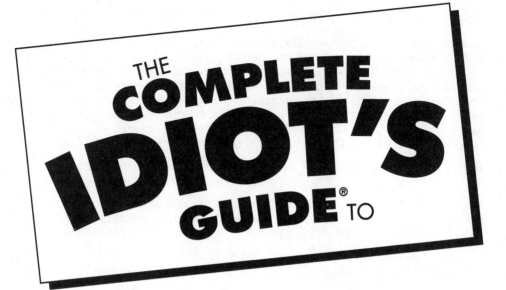

THE COMPLETE IDIOT'S GUIDE® TO

Managing Your Money

Second Edition

by Robert K. Heady and Christy Heady

alpha books

A Division of Macmillan General Reference
A Simon & Schuster Macmillan Company
1633 Broadway, New York, NY 10019-6785

Macmillan Publishing books may be purchased for business or sales promotional use. For information please write: Special Markets Department, Macmillan Publishing USA, 1633 Broadway, New York, NY 10019.

International Standard Book Number: 0-02-862722-9
Library of Congress Catalog Card Number: 98-87594

01 00 99   8 7 6 5 4 3 2

Interpretation of the printing code: the rightmost number of the first series of numbers is the year of the book's printing; the rightmost number of the second series of numbers is the number of the book's printing. For example, a printing code of 99-2 shows that the second printing occurred in 1999.

Printed in the United States of America

Note: This publication contains the opinions and ideas of its author. It is intended to provide helpful and informative material on the subject matter covered. It is sold with the understanding that the author and publisher are not engaged in rendering professional services in the book. If the reader requires personal assistance or advice, a competent professional should be consulted.

Alpha Development Team

Publisher
Kathy Nebenhaus

Editorial Director
Gary M. Krebs

Managing Editor
Bob Shuman

Marketing Brand Manager
Felice Primeau

Development Editors
Nancy Gratton
Phil Kitchel
Amy Zavatto

Production Team

Production Editor
Mark Enochs

Copy Editor
Abby Lyon Herriman

Cover Designer
Mike Freeland

Photo Editor
Richard H. Fox

Cartoonist
Brian Mac Moyer

Designer
Nathan Clement

Indexer
Craig Small

Layout/Proofreading
Angela Calvert
Mary Hunt
Cheryl Moore

Contents at a Glance

Contents

Part 3: Banking Fundamentals   93

8 Top Money-Making Secrets Your Friendly Banker Won't Tell You   95

9 Interest Rates 101   105

Foreword

The nice thing about personal-finance advice is that when you need it, there's plenty of it. For instance:

➤ Are you debating about buying life-insurance coverage for your son? Your friendly insurance salesperson will gladly tell you exactly how large a life-insurance policy a two-year-old needs.

➤ Are looking for a place to park recently inherited money? The customer service rep at your local bank will be more than pleased to recommend a series of mutual funds offered exclusively in your area by her institution.

➤ Credit-card bills finally got you down? A warm voice on a radio commercial reminds you repeatedly about an easy way to consolidate your bills into one low monthly payment.

➤ Do you want the best investment for your regular IRA? The financial planner in the mall can readily show you figures demonstrating that an annuity offered by his parent company is just right for you.

➤ Want to enjoy the good life? An advertisement in the mail details how you can use up to 125 percent of your home equity to finance a new car or a dream vacation.

Does any of this sound familiar? It should. These are real problems and real solutions in today's world. The trouble is, all of this advice is wrong:

➤ Children don't need life-insurance coverage.

➤ Bank-sold mutual funds are the most expensive and often the least rewarding of all fund choices.

➤ Most widely advertised loan-consolidation plans result in the payment of far more interest than is necessary.

➤ An annuity is a tax-protected investment that should never be placed in a regular IRA, which is already tax-protected.

➤ A home-equity loan should not be used to pay for a vacation, car, or any other wasting asset.

In the world of personal finance, a world we all live in, bad advice is easy to find. It abounds. The sad thing is that acting on bad advice has the potential of not only costing you thousands of dollars or more over a lifetime, it can strip away your sweetest opportunities: a decent home, wonderful family vacations, a quality education for your children, a relaxed retirement, and on and on.

Yet good personal-finance advice isn't hidden away. Occasionally, it even comes in bright, clever, easy-to-read packages such as this one.

That's what *The Complete Idiot's Guide to Managing Your Money, Second Edition* is all about: good, practical, dollar-saving advice for a long list of common personal-finance challenges. But more than that, it's a guide to building lifetime financial security. With it, you'll learn how to avoid the self-serving advice that is the hallmark of so much of the personal-finance business, and discover reasonable ways to achieve long-term wealth and the real freedom that comes with it. This book is a treasury of advice and strategies for readers who are willing to admit they need help with a very tough subject.

In your financial life, it's not only *what you know* that counts, it's *who told you what you know*. The *"who"* in this book are Robert and Christy Heady, a unique father and daughter writing team.

Bob is an old pro, a consumer watchdog long before anyone knew what consumer watchdogs were. He's been tougher on banks and other financial institutions than Dillinger ever dreamt of being, and all to and for the benefit of the big institutions' often-captive customers—you and me. Christy is a second-generation personal-finance journalist. Think of what that means: She probably wrote third-grade reports on how to get the highest interest on piggy-bank savings. Together, the Headys describe in fresh, understandable prose time-tested solutions to your financial problems, the ones you wish someone else would handle.

As you read and use the revised second edition of the Headys' book, you'll soon find—like thousands of readers before you—that you no longer have to feel like a complete idiot when it comes to managing your money.

Dennis Fertig

Editor-in-chief, *Your Money*

Introduction

No matter who you are—an ordinary family that's head-over-heels in debt, a senior citizen confused by investment choices, or a college freshman starting to build your credit—there's something valuable here for you. You need practical, down-to-earth help written in plain English...no "blue sky theories"—even that's a confusing subject!

So we're putting the language of money into basic, everyday street language instead of the commonly seen financial mumbo-jumbo that only an accountant can figure out. We want *you* to understand it and to make heads or tails of your personal financial situation.

This is a book written from the trenches, not from an ivory tower. We don't live there, and neither do you. The world of personal finance has become too darn complicated for the average Joe and Jane to understand. Meanwhile, the glut of financial information keeps growing faster than a barrel full of sea monkeys.

So the two of us, father and daughter, are doing this for *you*. We have been inside banks and brokerage firms, the mortgage companies, car dealerships, and the credit bureaus. We've answered thousands of questions from consumers who desperately needed help. We'll show you, chapter by chapter, the most important basics you should know. We'll arm you with tips that will immediately strengthen your personal money situation.

Sure, the cards are stacked against you because of the complex way the money jungle works. But by learning the inside tricks that you'll never read in a newspaper or magazine article (or hear in a 20-second sound bite on TV), you're going to come out dollars ahead. And what else? We're going to take the "I" out of "Idiot" for you by telling it like it is. Just the bare facts, and some tips and tricks to help you along the way.

This book will help you:

➤ Avoid costly mistakes and save a bundle.

➤ Earn more when you invest.

➤ Save more when you borrow.

➤ Cut through the muck before you get trapped in the wrong deal.

➤ Rebuild your credit if it's been injured.

But most importantly, this book will help you *relax* with better financial peace of mind.

If you are looking for a no-nonsense book that will finally help you manage your hard-earned cash, you've come to the right place. Here's how it works:

Part 1, "Getting the Most for Your Money," establishes some basic information about getting started in managing your money. This section will help you learn how to make that first big decision—getting started! Plus, you'll learn secrets about getting out of debt—and how to stay out. You'll also find secrets to cutting costs on everything you buy—from groceries to airline tickets to long-distance telephone service. Chapter 2 tells you how to make effective personal financial planning decisions by learning what to read, what to watch, and who to believe.

Part 2, "The Secrets to Simple, Savvy Investing," explains basic information about the world of investing. You'll learn how to set up investment objectives, which types of investments work best for you and your tolerance for risk, and ten smart money moves that will enable you to reach your financial goals.

Part 3, "Banking Fundamentals," is a section that will surprise many of you with its revealing Chapter 8, "Top Money-Making Secrets Your Friendly Banker Won't Tell You." The entire chapter is devoted to exploring how banks make tons of money from your bank accounts, whether you have $25 or $2,500 sitting in them. But it doesn't stop there. You'll learn how to stop being nickeled-and-dimed to death with bank fees, find out the secrets of CD shopping (and who pays the top rate), and how to spot the key warning signals when it's time to move your account.

Part 4, "Credit and Loans: Getting Money When You Need It," is for everyone who has ever tried to get credit (and didn't), or attempted to cut credit card costs but didn't know how. Additionally, you'll find secrets to car shopping and mortgage shopping, and the biggest tip of all in the credit world: how credit agencies really "score" your application—and what you can do to make the grade.

Part 5, "The Biggest Secrets to Retiring with Enough Money," provides specific investment information to help you plan for the future! You'll learn what you can do to maximize your savings and investments now to guarantee a comfortable life down the road. From establishing a regular savings plan to exploring the confusing world of 401(k) plans, you'll have what you need to create a financially sound future for you and your family.

Part 6, "Getting a Handle on the Rest of Your Money Life," discusses various issues that are imperative to understanding financial planning. You may not come across them often, but when you do—boy, are some of them doozies. This section will show you how to squeeze more out of your paycheck, how to cover your assets and protect your wealth through money-saving insurance strategies, and how to make Uncle Sam your friend by learning up-to-date tips on taxes.

Extras

We know you don't own a secret decoder ring to help you in the confusing world of financial planning—and you shouldn't have to. This book has a few easy-to-recognize signposts that offer tips, tricks, and tidbits to help you along the way. Look for these elements in this book that will point you in the right direction:

The Money Line

These boxes contain extremely useful information that you definitely need to help you make educated decisions in your personal money management. Read them.

Asset Advisory

Want a better and less costly way of managing your money? These tips are some of the biggest secrets you'll ever learn in the personal financial planning world.

Fiscal Facts

The world of financial planning is often confusing, mysterious, and just plain puzzling. Not anymore. These boxes will put you in the know, so you know what you're doing.

Watch Your Wallet

Sometimes making the wrong decision when you manage your money can add up to trouble—and a lot of bucks. Take heed of these warnings to help save yourself some dough.

Online Resources

For those of you who are plugged into the Internet, the Online Resources area will give you immediate Internet addresses of helpful financial information that you can tap into while online.

Acknowledgments

We sincerely acknowledge the following people, companies, and organizations who provided research and assistance for this book:

Dan Pederson, of Savings Bond Informer; National Foundation for Consumer Credit; National Association of Automobile Dealers; *Bank Rate Monitor* and *100 Highest Yields*; American Bankruptcy Institute; Mortgage Bankers Association; Veribanc, Inc. and its founder/research director, Warren Heller; Department of the Treasury, and the Federal Reserve.

Robert K. Heady also acknowledges John Lee, former finance editor of *The New York Times*, who discovered Bank Rate Monitor's value and put its interest rates on the map for millions of readers; Mark Mathes, former editor of Tribune Media Services who marketed Mr. Heady's personal finance column to U.S. newspapers; and, above all, the memory of the late James Vincent O'Gara, executive editor of *Advertising Age*. In the beginning, long ago, Mr. O'Gara and his editor, the late John Crichton, the father of author-director Michael Crichton, made this book possible by taking a chance on a wet-behind-the-ears reporter and teaching him, by example, the meaning of accuracy, integrity, independence and objectivity that make for good journalism. Lastly, we acknowledge that special, rare breed of print and broadcast journalist across America—the reporter who digs for and delivers the kind of urgent, current information that the little guy can use to really help improve himself or herself in his or her personal finances in life.

Christy Heady acknowledges the companies of Morningstar, Bloomberg, the Consumer Bankers Association, Hewitt & Associates, Hulbert Financial Digest, America Online, and Intuit.

Christy Heady would also like to personally acknowledge those people who have made an incredible impact on her journalism career, especially Dennis Fertig and Tom Siedell of *Your Money* magazine, John Wasik of *Consumers Digest*, and all the outstanding people at the CNN Chicago Bureau.

And to her husband, John Andrew Pavela, thank you for your support in the development of yet *another* book.

Dedication

This book is dedicated to Robyn-Jo Brooke Heady, beloved sister of Christy Heady and daughter of Robert K. Heady, who died December 12, 1997 at age 28.

Christy shared her first lessons in reading and writing with Robyn-Jo when they were little girls and loves and misses her more than any words she reads or writes can ever express. Her father especially remembers Robyn-Jo's positive-spirit personality, wonderful sense of humor, the laughter, her deep artistic perception, a devotion to healthy mind, body and soul, her love of little children, and a spiritual evolution and understanding that eventually eclipsed us all. You shall always and forever be our blessed angel.

We also invite our readers to remember Robyn-Jo through a non-profit charity near where she lived, the Children's Health Program, Inc., P.O. Box 30, Great Barrington, Mass. 01230. CHP's program helps low-income families by providing transportation to doctors, nursing and pediatrics aid, food baskets, a clothing exchange, children's health insurance, and even collecting needed items through church groups.

Part 1
Getting the Most for Your Money

Money affects everything we do. It gives us freedom to travel, shop, and live extravagantly. It also determines whether or not we can do these things. And when we plan wisely, money gives us a sense of accomplishment, like that feeling you get when you pay all the bills and have some money left over!

The most important reason to manage your money is to get control. It goes beyond you and your pocketbook or your wallet. Acquiring control over your personal finances can change your future. But in order to get control, you must make the first big decision—getting started!

Once you make the decision to manage your money, this section teaches you how to stop falling behind and get ahead in the world of personal finance (fondly known by many as a "money jungle"). This section gives you the secrets of cutting costs on everything you buy, how to get out of debt and stay there, what to read, what to watch, and who to believe. Knowing these secrets will help you and your future.

Chapter 1

Grab Good Financial Planning by the Tail

In This Chapter

➤ Discover why the first secret to financial planning has nothing to do with money

➤ How you can make financial decisions that are easy to follow —and rewarding!

➤ Learn the simple ways to motivate yourself to wealth

Do you know what the hardest thing about managing your money is? *Making the decision to do it.* That's it. It's a piece of cake after that.

Huh?

We'll explain.

For some of us, it's easier to make life-altering decisions, such as moving our family across the country for a more lucrative job, than it is to decide between a tuna salad or egg salad sandwich for lunch (one of us can attest to this personally). Others may have a difficult time choosing which insurance policy is best for their families or determining which lender they should get their mortgage from.

Life, and especially your financial one, comes down to nothing more than making decisions. Take a moment and think about all the choices you make on a daily basis—what to wear to work, which project to work on, whether or not to put in overtime, what to make for dinner, or what to read the kids before bedtime. Now think about all the "money" decisions you make. Don't think you have many? Guess again.

Everything you do in life involves your wallet—from taking family vacations to bringing your lunch to work, to seeing a new movie, to getting married, or having a new baby. There's a cost to living, and that's why we're here to help.

Because we humans weren't born with a handy-dandy "How-to" Guide, think of this book as your decision-making tool to help make your financial life a better one. This chapter will show you how to get started in creating your customized personal finance plan without talking about money at all.

We're ready, and we know you are, too. Let's go.

Begin Without Even Thinking About Money

Put away your wallets and your pocketbooks, because getting started in financial planning has nothing to do with money. Zip. Nada. It has to do with you and how you make decisions.

Online Resources

The World Wide Web is accelerating a personal finance revolution because you can have an enormous amount of tools at your fingertips. If you have access to the Web, consider some of the following websites as complementary resources to our financial plan. Boot up, log on, and have fun!

FinanceCenter.com: Check out www.financenter.com, which makes personal finance easy to understand with its array of interactive calculators and budgeting tools. You can plug in your personal numbers and decide if now is the right time to refinance your home, whether your spouse should work or not, and what it takes to become a millionaire.

Quicken.com: The mother of all motherloads, Quicken's website offers every how-to article and interactive function (online features you can do stuff with) that can calculate how much you'll need at retirement, how much it will cost to send your child to school, and how much your monthly mortgage payment will be.

MicrosoftMoney Insider: Bill Gates got this one right. Consumers have access to helpful data and interactive tools that allow them to personalize the information they've learned and apply it in real life. Up-to-date rate information and a searchable database of financial advisors nationwide are available.

Achieving success is really the result of making good decisions, and making good financial decisions is based on a long-term focus. That's all. But don't let fear of making mistakes intimidate you: Even a bad decision results in a learning experience.

What happens when you don't make any decisions? Someone else makes them for you. Do you want someone else making the decisions about building your financial security? If planning your financial future is something you've been putting off, ask yourself the following:

➤ Why have I been putting it off?

➤ What do I have to fear by not doing it?

➤ What type of pleasure do I receive by indulging in procrastination?

➤ What will it cost me if I don't do it now?

Take this information and apply it to the following simple steps toward getting started in financial planning:

➤ **Make the decision to *make a decision*.** Sounds silly, huh? Making a decision is often the hardest step. But if you break it up into simple little steps, you'll find decision-making easy and far from intimidating. Just say "okay," and you've done it.

➤ **Make decisions often.** Let's use an analogy. Every year without fail, during the first week of January, memberships and the line for the Stairmaster at your local health club increase. The New Year's diet is in full swing, and every gym rat in the nation has made the decision to do something about his or her health, image, and weight. But this doesn't last very long because these people only make a decision once; they don't decide on a daily basis "I'm going to go to the gym today." If these people made decisions often, perhaps they would reach their fitness goals. If you make the decision to create a personal financial plan, are you going to stick with it just once?

➤ **Be flexible.** You don't live in just a black and white environment. You need to allow for some gray areas—which often disguise themselves as mistakes. Remember, although mistakes come from making the wrong decision, they create experiences you can learn from, and that might help you make the *right* decision next time!

➤ **Enjoy making decisions.** Making decisions can be a blast! For example, if your mistakes help you learn to make better decisions, and the next time you make a decision it turns out to be a great opportunity, wouldn't you enjoy having made that decision? You'll enjoy it more when you create more great opportunities!

➤ **Create short-term and long-term goals.** Many people plan for their financial futures by working so hard today that by the time they reach their long-term goals, they're exhausted and have forgotten why they worked so hard to get there. Long-term goals are important, but so are short-term goals. If you create and meet short-term goals, you won't have to wait 30 years to feel a sense of accomplishment or satisfaction.

➤ **Do your homework.** It'll be more fun than studying for that geometry test you prepared so hard for in high school! Doing your homework in the money world will allow you to make your money work as hard for you as you do for it.

When you work through these secrets, you are shaping your financial destiny. And it all starts with a simple decision!

Why Put Off Today What You Can Do Tomorrow?

Now that you've made the decision to create a plan, your next step is to understand why getting—and staying—in control of your finances is imperative for you and your family. Believe us, we're not into scare tactics. We just report the facts and want you to make better-informed decisions about your money with the knowledge that we share with you.

For example, did you know that most high school seniors are failing finance these days? According to a national survey by the JumpStart Coalition for Personal Financial Literacy, most high school seniors do not have basic personal finance knowledge. Handling credit cards, paying taxes, and even saving for the future are concepts that our future generation in the United States cannot grasp and will, therefore, have trouble managing all of their lives.

But this financial illiteracy doesn't stop at high school students. The Coalition also suggests that many adults lack the skills and knowledge to make sound financial decisions, too.

We've seen it happen with the record 1.6 million bankruptcies filed in the past year, the number of people foreclosing on their homes, and the ten-fold increase in bounced check fees bank accountholders are paying each year for not having sufficient funds in their checking accounts.

But there is a bigger problem. We are living in a society of information overload. Where do you go to get good reliable advice? How can you determine which mechanism to use—your Aunt Stella's broker, your cousin the life insurance agent, the World Wide Web, the bookstore, or free seminars at the library. It's enough to make you scream! No wonder aspirin sales are on the rise these days.

We cannot tell you exactly what to do, but we can help share our knowledge and insight of the world of personal finance (co-author and proud father, Robert, has a few years on his daughter, Christy).

Ignore the Statistics and Stick to Your Plan

The next time you're in a bookstore, look at the first chapter of five other financial planning books. You'll find a common theme: scare tactics from scary statistics—except the authors call them "motivational information." Who do they think they're kidding?

Although the information they report is accurate, it's far from motivating. It's down-right scary. Know them, but don't be bamboozled by them!

➤ Sure, it's true that by the year 2010 it will cost more than $120,000 to get a four-year education at a public university. As for a private university? Egads, our calculators won't go that high!

➤ It's also a fact that if you make a $2,000 purchase on your VISA with 19.8 percent interest and only meet the minimum payments, it will take you more than 30 years to pay off that purchase.

➤ And we've all seen the projections that if you currently make $26,000 a year, you should only expect to receive about $420 a month in Social Security benefits when you retire—that is, if Social Security is still around.

While all of that information is correct, are these scare tactics working? Do they make you get off your duff and start managing your finances? After hearing from thousands of Americans who still have money problems, we didn't think so.

Excuuuuse Me!

We all make excuses to get out of managing our money (no time, not enough extra cash, or retirement is far, far away). One big reason we avoid planning is because of fear. Many people think that if they take a bare-bones look at their finances, they'll have to accept that they're in debt or don't have enough money to pay for their child's college education. Then they may think that they'll wind up old and impoverished. Goodness, why worry about that now? Others simply think managing their money is B-O-R-I-N-G. Save for the future? D-U-L-L. No instant gratification. Why put that extra $100 bucks in a savings account to earn 23 cents?

The Money Line

The statistics on how we relate to managing our money to save for our futures are not encouraging. A Merrill Lynch study concludes that if Americans continue to save at the rate they do now, they may end up with only 36 percent of the money they'll need to maintain their current standard of living. Meaning: They will have only 36 percent of what they need *if they continue to save at their current rate*, independent of Social Security.

Why have we developed such a nonchalant attitude toward the future, anyway? During our childhood, many of our parents gave us a piggy bank and a few pennies and taught us to "save for a rainy day." But few explained *why* we were supposed to do it.

Planning for your future doesn't mean you're expecting something terrible to happen. Buying a life insurance policy doesn't mean you're going to die, does it? Much of your fear will quickly disappear once you realize how easy it is to make your savings grow for retirement. It's never too early to learn—or to start. The whole idea of managing your money is to save a dollar here and there and then take that dollar and build it into two. Believe it or not, it's a concept that you can practice—and you don't need to be a money whiz to do it, either.

Okay, Here's the Money Part

It's time to take the next step in the lessons of financial planning: setting some goals.

If your goal is to win the $100 million Powerball Lottery, you can forget it. Odds are something like 80-million-to-1 to collect all that dough. And, while Las Vegas is quickly becoming a vacation spot of choice for families, don't bet the family farm on those one-arm-bandits for the quickest way to wealth. Cha-ching, it ain't gonna happen.

Winning the lottery or collecting thousands of quarters on a lucky slot machine are possible ways to create instant wealth, but *playing* these games is not. And even if you *do* win the lottery, you'll have enough financial planning burdens to make you go berserk. The tax bite alone is enough to give you a migraine.

Asset Advisory

Here's a little secret that even the wealthiest of the wealthy practice: Pay yourself first. Before your daughter's Girl Scout dues, before the cable bill (yes, it's true!) and even before the mortgage, set aside a small amount of money in an account for yourself. You can begin with ten dollars a week—it's that easy, and at the end of a year, you'll have saved $520!

So let's talk about setting some more practical goals.

Setting goals isn't difficult. It's figuring out how to reach them that gives you a run for your money (no pun intended). You know that you need short-term and long-term goals, so take out two pieces of paper and let's get started. On the first piece of paper, write down any short-term goals you want to accomplish. These may include, but are not limited to, creating an emergency fund and paying off your credit cards and student loans.

Divide the next piece of paper into four time frames: five years, ten years, twenty years, and thirty years. Write down what you want to accomplish in each. For example, in five years you may want to buy a house. Ten years from now you may want to take a vacation to Europe. Twenty years from now you'll have to send the kids to college. And thirty years from now you plan to retire.

On both pieces of paper, write down how much money each goal is going to require. Be honest with yourself; the amount of money you'll need to meet each goal may surprise you. You may have already allocated some of the money that you'll need. If so, good for you. Whether you have or not, most of you are going to have to learn how to manage your money to be able to achieve your goals.

Now total up how much money you're going to need to meet all of your goals. The numbers are astounding, aren't they? But that doesn't mean you have to change your goals. In fact, you can keep those goals and accomplish many of them by following the concepts in this book! This book is designed specifically to help you meet the short-term and long-term goals that you have set for yourself and for your family—and save money in the process.

All it takes is a little knowledge and some self-discipline. Most folks say that knowledge is power. But we disagree. Knowledge is power if—and only if—you put it to use!

The Least You Need to Know

➤ The first step toward managing your money is making the decision to start planning for your financial future.

➤ Don't let mistakes keep you from making more decisions. Think of a mistake as something that will help you make a better decision next time.

➤ Write down your short-term and long-term financial goals and how much money you need to achieve them. Then, read the rest of this book for information on how to reach those goals.

➤ Grabbing good financial planning requires you to do your homework, and you've already learned the first part of homework and research: you are studying this book!

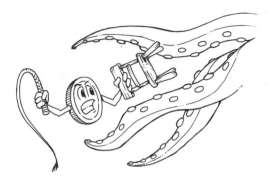

Managing the Debt Monster

Chances are you carry a credit card. From platinum to gold to plain-vanilla plastic, consumers are having a love affair with credit cards. It's powerful, but like Marvel Comics superheroes, you must decide whether to use your plastic for good or evil.

Knowing your credit limit is the key to keeping yourself out of financial trouble and filing for bankruptcy, as 1.2 million Americans did in 1997. Well, superhero, your mission, should you choose to accept it, is to decide how much debt you can afford simply by creating a spending plan and sticking with it. Remember, in order to save for the future, you must pay for the past. This chapter will help you discover top-notch secrets to reduce your debt, ways to measure your financial health, and strategies to reduce your expenses.

Are You in Debt Trouble?

To determine whether you are having problems managing your debts, indicate whether the following statements are true or false:

_____ You use credit cards where you used to pay cash, such as at the grocery store and restaurants.

___ You have depleted your savings—or worse, used cash advances from credit cards—to pay old, past-due bills.

___ You have lost track of how much you owe.

___ You put off paying your telephone and utility bills in order to pay high credit card bills and other debts.

___ You regularly receive letters from collection agencies.

If most of your answers are true, you have a debt problem. Read on to find out what you can do about it.

Measuring Your Financial Health

Checking in with a financial doctor rates right up there with having your teeth cleaned. It's painful (and the taste of rubber gloves is not pleasant), but if you want pearly whites, you've got to go through the torture.

In managing your money, your goal is to get out of debt, right? Once you meet that goal, what do you want to accomplish financially? Do you want to:

Buy a car? (See Chapter 18)

Buy a house? (See Chapter 19)

Retire comfortably? (See Chapter 22)

Insure your health and wealth? (See Chapter 25)

Before you reach those goals, you must figure out how bad the problem is. To do that, you must do three things to measure your financial health. First, compare your assets to your liabilities by completing the worksheets in this chapter. Second, determine what your expenses are. Third, create a budget and trim the financial fat. The best way to begin is to:

Add Up the Pluses and Minuses

There's no greater mess to clean up than unorganized, mismanaged financial affairs, which is why so many people stick to organizing their financial records about as long as they do a New Year's diet. Determining your *assets* (what you own) and *liabilities* (what you owe) gives you a clear picture of what you're worth.

Begin with organized records. These may include, but are not limited to, checkbook registers, recent bank and brokerage statements, copies of your income tax returns (keep these for at least three years), and paycheck stubs. Forget the shoebox theory—keep these and all of your financial records in a well-organized file cabinet for your personal finances.

Once you have all of your information intact, you can fill in the first of three worksheets (taken from *The Complete Idiot's Guide to Making Money on Wall Street*), which is a financial property assets worksheet that includes all the money in your bank accounts, brokerage accounts, and other investments.

Financial Property	Date Purchased	How Much Did You Pay?	Today's Date	What's It Worth Today?
Bonds (type)				
Bond mutual funds (type)				
Certificate of deposit				
Checking accounts				
Coin collections				
Money market accounts				
Pensions & profit sharing plans				
Savings accounts				
Savings bonds				
Stocks				
Stock mutual funds				
Treasury securities				
Other				
Total Financial Property				

A financial property assets worksheet.

Next, by completing your personal property worksheet—which is also an asset—you'll assess how much your physical property is worth. For example, your home is probably the largest (in physical size and financial size) asset you own. Write in when you bought your home, what the price was, and how much it's worth today. If you're not sure—and want to make more than an educated guess—contact an appraiser to be certain.

13

Personal Property	Date Purchased	How Much Did You Pay?	What's It Worth Today?
Appliances (washer & dryer, etc.)			
Automobiles			
Boats, campers			
Computers			
Furniture			
Fur coats			
Home			
Home furnishings			
—curtains			
—rugs			
—tableware (glasses, dishes)			
—blankets			
—lamps			
—silverware			
Jewelry			
Paintings			
Stereos			
Televisions			
Miscellaneous			
Total Personal Property			

A personal property assets worksheet.

Finally, calculate your *liabilities*—all the things you owe. The main thrust of this worksheet deals with loans, such as auto loans, student loans, and your mortgage, but remember to put down ALL of your outstanding credit card balances (yes, ALL of them). Your liabilities show how much debt you carry.

What You Owe	To Whom	Interest Rate %	When Is It Due?	How Much Do You Owe?
Bills, bills, bills				
—electric				
—gas				
—retail stores				
—telephone				
—other				
Loans to family				
Loans to friends				
Automobile loans				
Bank loans				
Credit cards				
—credit card #1				
—credit card #2				
—credit card #3				
Furniture loans				
Student loans				
Mortgage				
Home equity loans				
Miscellaneous				
Total Liabilities				

A liabilities worksheet.

Two kinds of debt traditionally exist, although we're going to add a third: good debt, bad debt, and you-just-have-to-pay-it-to-live debt. This last type of debt would include electric bills, gas bills, and telephone bills. More often, they're referred to as expenses, although they are "owed" debts.

The single largest component of good debt would be your mortgage loan because your mortgage is for your house, which is an *asset* (hopefully an appreciating one!). You must report your mortgage loan on your liabilities worksheet.

Bad debt makes up the bulk of the liabilities worksheet. It is what siphons most consumers' paychecks.

Americans have long been battling a war to reduce bad debt. Bad debt is what you still owe on your car, your credit cards, your unsecured personal loans, and even your student loans. Obviously, the name of the game is to have as few "bad-debt" liabilities as possible and to increase your wealth substantially.

Bad debt works *against* you, although Americans are too happy living moment to moment to realize this. They relish the ability to "buy now and pay later." Credit cards, the biggest enticers, have lured many consumers into vulnerability and higher-status credit cards, such as platinum cards. In 1998, approximately 15 million Americans have a platinum card, up from 3 million in 1996.

Watch Your Wallet

Stay away from anyone who promises to help you with your debt trouble for a "small fee." These people work for places known as *recovery houses*, and they're preying on everyone—especially the elderly. Contact the FTC [(202) 326-3650] to report any wrongdoing. The best organization to help you manage your debt is your local Consumer Credit Counseling Service office. But the only person who can get you *out* of debt is *you*!

Meet Mr. Minimum—Ouch!

Paying only your minimum card balance will result in a much larger debt than your original purchases were worth. Let's say your balance on an 18 percent credit card is $3,000 and that each month you make the minimum payment of two percent on the balance, with a $10 minimum. It will take you 36 years and two months to pay off the card. The total interest you'll pay on the $3,000 will be a staggering $7,587.

Here's another example. Suppose you buy a leather couch for $1,500 and put it on your MasterCard. You can't pay the entire bill this month, but that's no problem! You only have to make a minimum payment to remain in the issuer's good graces. However, as other debts start adding up, you only meet the minimum payment for the next year or so, or at least until you get out of the hole with your other bills. Then, one year later, a friend drops her cigarette on the couch. Now it's torched, and you need a new couch. You get rid of the couch, but you're still paying for it on your credit card. "Surely I've paid it off by now," you think. Well, think again.

How long does it take to pay off such a debt? If you *only* meet the minimum monthly payments, and your credit card has an average annual percentage rate (APR) of, let's say, 19.8 percent interest, it will take you more than 22 years to pay off that $1,500 couch. This is a classic example of how bad debt can work against you. The more debt you are burdened with, the longer it will take to dig yourself out of a hole. Therefore, your first priority should be to eliminate non-productive debt.

Motivate Your Mind to Kick the Habit

There aren't any self-hypnotic tapes to help cure overspending (maybe there should be). However, your personal motivation and goal setting can surely help. Picture this: You have no debt and an investment account worth $75,000. How does it feel? Many psychological experts urge consumers to use their imaginations instead of their wallets to help with their finances.

Once you have the proper motivation, try the strategies discussed in the following sections to reduce your debt.

> **Watch Your Wallet**
>
> Warning: Cash advances are a big no-no. Watch out for those enticing checks lenders are sending because you are such a good credit risk. If you fill them out, many zap you not only with a higher cash advance rate (we've seen 32 percent!) but you also could pay a transaction fee. With no grace period, it's a definite loser strategy.

Use Your Savings

Before you use your savings to pay off the budgetary fat, determine your debt-to-equity ratio. Oooh, all those numbers sound intimidating, huh? It's simple! All you have to do is answer one question: How much of your paycheck goes to pay your debts? The smaller the percent of your monthly pay allocated to credit cards (as well as other loans and debt), the better.

The rule of thumb is this: *current assets should be approximately two times greater than current liabilities.* Keep in mind, then, that your monthly debt should not exceed 36 percent of your monthly income.

So, lump together all of your assets (what you own) and your liabilities (what you owe). If you have socked away a ton of cash in your bank account and you have revolving debt on your credit cards, it's time to pay those off. Why not use your savings? It'll be in your best interest, since you won't be paying any more than you have to!

Go on a Money Diet

Is that extra ten dollars burning a hole in your pocket? Do you feel compelled to spend it? Even if you are deluged with pre-approved credit card offers in the mail, it doesn't mean you should take them. It is not wise to buy now and pay later.

Since there aren't any nutrition labels that warn consumers whether or not they're getting a good deal, it's up to you to spend your money wisely. You can look at where your money goes to see where you can trim the fat.

Here are 10 ways *not* to spend money...starting today:

➤ Never buy extended warranties or service contracts. Buy products that come with good warranties from retailers who stand behind what they sell. Since many service contracts generate high profits for businesses, some experts agree they're generally not a good deal for consumers.

➤ Are speed dialing, caller ID, and three-way calling really necessary? The services cost approximately $2 to $6 extra per month, but that adds up to hundreds of dollars over a few years. Stick with basic telephone coverage.

➤ If you're in the market for a new car, make sure you read the tips and tricks offered in Chapter 18 carefully. Many consumers see a flashy new car as an investment, but it's not! When you drive a new car off the lot, it immediately loses a certain percentage of its value—typically 20 percent! If you do your homework, you can buy a used car that's next to new for a fraction of the original sticker price.

➤ One of the most superfluous items that Americans buy—and don't use—is new exercise equipment. If you sell the treadmill and exercise bike that are collecting dust, you probably could pay off one of your credit card bills.

➤ Never go shopping when you're bored, down in the dumps, or hungry. That's recreational shopping, and it can cost you plenty! You'll probably buy things you don't need and probably can't afford just to make yourself feel better. Think of an alternative: exercise, play with the dog, or make your spouse a romantic dinner.

➤ Most consumers don't realize that everything goes on sale eventually. Wait for the sale. (You'll learn more about shopping tricks in the next chapter.)

➤ The biggest mistake consumers make is carrying more than one credit card. The more plastic you own, the more chance you'll lose track of your spending. One major credit card is enough. (You'll find a list of the best credit card deals in Chapter 17.)

➤ Here's a great way to cut costs on expensive water-heating bills: reduce your water-heater temperature from 145°F to 120°F, and you'll save 10 to 15 percent on your next bill.

➤ Go to matinees instead of evening movies. They're often discounted. In some cities, matinee prices are as much as 50 percent less than regular evening prices. You can also buy movie theater "fun-pack" tickets at reduced prices.

Asset Advisory

If you're knee-deep in debt, you could liquidate some—but not all—of your assets to help pay the bills. Which ones you liquidate will be up to you. If one of them is an investment that will give you a huge capital gain to pay a lot of taxes on, however, consider other alternatives. For example, selling old items at a garage sale (really!).

➤ Better yet (for all you movie buffs out there), save the $7.75-per-movie charge and wait for the flick to come out on video. They always do, don't they?

These are specific examples of how you can immediately start saving on some of your expenses, which ultimately reduces your debt.

Get Outside Help

If you're having trouble implementing these strategies to resolve your debt crisis, it may be time to seek outside help. Contact your local credit counseling office through the national number (800) 388-CCCS.

Another available resource is the National Center for Financial Education, P.O. Box 34070, San Diego, CA 92163, which provides support services for cardholders who need assistance managing credit.

It's a Budget to Your Rescue!

Unless we light a firecracker and place it under your chair, the only way we can motivate you to keep track of where your money goes is to scare you. So here goes.

If you don't track where all your money goes, what will happen? Over time, the following things will happen: you'll wind up in the cold month of January wondering how the heck you spent $2,769 on Christmas presents for the family, you'll know your banker better than you'd like because you'll probably bounce checks all over town as a result of mismanaging your finances, and someday you'll live on a monthly Social Security benefit check of $455 (that's it!) because you piddled all your money down the drain when you were young. Does that scare you? It should!

"Budget" is a scary word; it's too constrictive for some folks. What you need to understand, however, is that everybody needs to have a daily record of where all his or her money goes. Accept it and motivate yourself toward the feeling of accomplishment. The true reward of having a budget is something all Americans want: control. Imagine having control over *all* of your finances. Once you do, you can reach your dreams and financial goals even faster!

What Do You Spend Money On?

First, you need to figure out where your money goes. Create your expense categories and fill in the amount you spend on a monthly basis for each category. To get a more accurate picture, you may want to check all your receipts from the past several months. Your categories can include but are not limited to:

➤ **Auto expenses:** Car payments, auto insurance, maintenance, gas (save your receipts!)

➤ **Clothing expenses:** Overgarments, undergarments (all your garments), shoes, and socks

➤ **Dental expenses:** Periodic cleaning, dental work, oral surgery, and so on (not covered by insurance)

➤ **Dining expenses:** Restaurant expenses, even if it's for fast food

➤ **Entertainment:** Movies, plays, concerts, the zoo, whatever

➤ **Education:** School supplies, tuition bills, and so on

➤ **Gifts:** Birthdays, holidays, weddings, Bar Mitzvahs

➤ **Groceries:** Separate into two categories—food and drugstore items—if possible

➤ **Home-based business:** This should be broken down into smaller categories, including equipment, supplies, taxes, and so on

➤ **Household items:** Plants, furniture, dog (just kidding)

➤ **Household expenses:** Items necessary for the upkeep of the house: paint, lawn maintenance, and so on

➤ **Insurance:** Separate your policies into categories, such as life, health, and homeowner's

➤ **Rent/Mortgage:** Your biggest expense (probably); important for tax return purposes

➤ **Taxes:** Real estate and income taxes paid (don't forget income tax refunds as a source of income)

➤ **Utilities:** Phone, electric, gas, water

➤ **Vacations:** Hotel stays, airplane tickets, new luggage, meals, sightseeing tours, souvenirs

There's probably more, but this list gets you started on the right foot.

Trim the Fat!

From the expense categories you create, pick a few expenses you can live without...for good. If the children are stuck on seeing a movie every Friday night, rent a video instead of going to the show.

As another example, set yourself a limit—such as to eat out only twice a month. The second largest component of "where your money goes" is dining out. That nasty habit costs the average American around $5,000 a year. You could pay for Junior's tuition at some state universities with that dough. Keep the following tips in mind to help reduce some of your expenses and save money in the long run:

➤ Establish an emergency fund that equals about three month's worth of basic expenses. Then you won't have to turn to plastic for every unexpected bill.

➤ Lower your tax withholding. Why give the IRS a free loan while you're paying an average 16 percent interest on your debts?

➤ Increase the deductibles on your automobile insurance. Even bumping up a $100 deductible to a $500 deductible could lower your premiums on comprehensive insurance by 25 or 30 percent a year.

Asset Advisory

If you're still swimming in debt and can't make ends meet by reducing your expenses, consider boosting your income—either through a part-time job or odd jobs you can do on weekends. Every little bit helps.

Battling Debt's Biggest Culprit

Americans have been able to *buy now and pay later* since the evolution of the plastic credit card. But this plastic has caused millions of Americans a problem: with enticing credit card offers promising generous credit lines, it has become impossible to climb out of debt.

That's why you should treat your credit card as a tool, not a cure-all. The rule of thumb: If you don't have the cash, don't use the card!

A credit card should be used as a convenience for emergencies; it is nothing more than a tool. Having a credit card or two is a necessity, but becoming laden with $20,000 in credit card debt is a burden—and a very common one. Typical clients of Credit Counseling Centers of America are dual-income families with high incomes. However, they have fallen into the habit of overspending; they have no savings—and up to $20,000 in credit card debt.

To save a few hundred dollars a year on finance charges (and work at maintaining a squeaky-clean credit report), follow the tips listed in Chapter 13 on how to cut your credit card costs in half.

Be a Debt-Buster!

If there's one rule you remember from this chapter, let it be this one: *Pay your bills on time.* Almost all lenders will look at whether you're current or late with your bills. Most lenders are lenient, and will tolerate a maximum of 30 days late. If you are currently behind on your accounts, catch up before you apply. This is how you can make the grade to get credit. You have to fit the profile of the people who pay their bills on time.

Filing for B-A-N-K-R-U-P-T-C-Y

Financial troubles have led millions of Americans to file for bankruptcy, often using the process as an "alternative." How wrong. Filing for bankruptcy is the *last resort* to your financial woes, not a choice. If you are in debt and *need* to file, however, there are pitfalls you can avoid.

Most often, you don't have to file unless it's necessary—declaring yourself bankrupt is not an alternative, it's a necessary solution. One bankruptcy attorney in Chicago claims that he has yet to see a situation where the filing was not required.

If you are having difficulty meeting your rent or mortgage payments, you're completely extended beyond your credit limit, the collection agencies are uncooperative, and you need more than a credit counselor, you may need to file a *Chapter 7* or a *Chapter 13*.

The first thing you should do is seek the advice of an attorney, who will guide you into which bankruptcy proceeding you should file, according to your personal debt situation.

Here's how they work. When you file either Chapter 7 or Chapter 13, you are issued a restraining order by the court, which will protect you from all further proceedings against you until all previous debts are cleared. The restraining order includes protection against wage garnishing, creditor harassment, and foreclosures without a court order.

Chapter 7 is used mainly if you have unsecured debts. For example, if you have furniture or appliances as unpaid collateral, you can return these without paying for them. But if you want to keep these things, you might be allowed a reaffirmation agreement with your creditors. Also, attorneys' fees are set so you can establish an installment plan.

Chapter 13, a wage-earner plan, brings immediate relief by letting you pay your bills rather than letting them go (unlike Chapter 7). You are eligible for an extension plan that allows you to pay back all your bills within a certain period of time, usually 36 to 60 months. Costs incurred by the attorney are added to the total of your other debts and are paid through your payments to the court trustee.

The bright side to filing for bankruptcy is immediate relief. The dark side is a black mark that remains on your credit record to haunt you for 10 years.

But all is not lost. It is still possible to potentially establish a "new" credit record and obtain a credit card, a *secured credit card*. Some companies that offer secured credit cards have guidelines that are a bit more flexible. If you've filed for bankruptcy and need information about applying for a secured credit card, turn to Chapter 17 for details on how to do it.

Fiscal Facts

There are two basic ways of filing for personal bankruptcy. *Chapter 7* gets rid of all debts (except some taxes and maybe alimony payments). *Chapter 13* allows people with steady income to pay off bills over a 36-to-60-month period.

The Least You Need to Know

➤ To measure your financial health, add up the worth of everything you own and compare it to the cost of everything you owe. A financially healthy person should have twice as much in assets as he or she has in liabilities.

➤ To reduce debt, use some of your assets (such as your savings) and reduce expenses so that you can pay more towards the debt.

➤ If you need extra help dealing with your debt problems, contact your local credit counseling office through the national number (800) 388-CCCS.

➤ To keep your spending on track, you need to establish a budget. Budgeting basically involves recording how you currently spend your money and then figuring out how you can change your spending habits in order to achieve your financial goals.

➤ Filing for bankruptcy is not an "alternative" or a "choice." It should be looked upon as a last resort.

Chapter 3

Shop 'Til You Drop—It Really Pays Off!

In This Chapter

➤ Money-saving tips your folks never told you

➤ Learn the steps to control the shopper in you

➤ How to pay less for services you need

There is a four-letter word that, when advertised in a flyer or whispered between the best of friends, sends shock-waves throughout the world, and we promise it's not dirty:

SALE.

Americans have developed a voracious appetite for anything that's a bargain. You may even have discovered that when you see a reduced item—even if you don't need it— you just have to buy it. Digging through sales racks is very Neanderthal. There's a hunt for the goods and when you find 'em, paydirt.

Unfortunately, the trend of saving money has gone beyond the old days of just clipping coupons on a Sunday afternoon. As RuPaul, an eccentric, well-known talk show host(ess) puts it, "You gotta work it, girl."

Today's smart shopper scans newspaper ads for bargains and looks for savings tips in newsletters. Face it, frugality is in.

However, you don't have to be cheap to be frugal. This focus on frugality has forced consumers to become better informed and make better choices. And it doesn't mean that you're a penny-pincher or a tightwad. You're just smart about your money (after all, you work very hard for that paycheck). This chapter will alert you to some pretty interesting money-saving strategies to help you save some dough.

What Supermarkets Don't Tell You

Next time you're at the grocery store, look at all the items on the shelves from top to bottom. Notice anything? Grocery stores usually place the most expensive items at eye level, where they are more likely to be selected on impulse. If you want to be a smart shopper, look at the entire group of products before you decide which to purchase (unless of course you prefer the more expensive brand!).

Don't fall prey to all the "on sale" items at the front of the store. The company that distributes those items actually pays for the space to place the merchandise. You won't really find any bargains until you dig deep inside store aisles.

And finally, make sure you comparison shop. Although the generic brands usually save you money, some house and national brands can actually be cheaper than generic brands.

Well, if you're going shopping, get on out there. But don't forget your coupons!

Watch Your Wallet

Supermarkets don't just try to increase revenues by placing expensive items at eye-level, they also compel consumers to hunt for healthier foods. How? It's the lay of the land. Typically, the most healthy and nutritious foods are located around the perimeter, while the inside aisles are stocked with high-fat, high-sodium (and also high-priced) foods. Hang out on the sidelines—for your wallet —*and* for your health!

Smart Shopping 101

Did you know that a basic pack of razor blades costs $6.80 in Tokyo but only $4.25 in Los Angeles? Lipstick that averages $5.00 a tube in the United States costs five times that much in Brazil—unless you go to a U.S. department store and pay $15 to $20 for your favorite tube. And in Tahiti, a can of ginger ale runs $4.00 and a bag of Doritos goes for $5.00. For those Americans who think U.S. prices are high, know that the average comparison of most selected goods and services costs less in the States than anywhere overseas. However, that doesn't mean we shouldn't practice smart shopping!

And by the way, did you know that every time you use a "preferred-shopper" card to pay for groceries or drugstore items your grocer compiles personal information about you? Sure, you may be using the card for the three or four bucks it saves you right then, but it's actually saving you more than that. What you buy with that card is added to a computer file corresponding with your number. Then, when you receive coupons in the mail, you'll find coupons for similar products that you

Asset Advisory

It's a dog-eat-dog world in the manufacturer's coupon business. The *real* reason companies offer cents off here and there is to get consumers to switch to their brand—and once they switch, to keep them there by offering more coupons. In fact, now there's no need to clip coupons anymore: They're dispensed in machines right in the store. It's a point-of-purchase marketing ploy that has allowed companies to rake in the bucks.

frequently shop for. If you don't mind having someone "watch" your shopping habits, those coupons can help save you money on your groceries in the long run!

If you make a concentrated effort to be a smart shopper, you can develop better spending habits and save money. Whenever you hit the mall or grocery store, keep these tips in mind:

➤ **Use cash—not plastic—if you are buying perishable or depreciating items.** Just because many national-chain grocery stores accept all major credit cards doesn't mean you should whip out your plastic at the check-out counter. Remember how long it takes to pay off that card when you make only minimum payments? Imagine paying off a gallon of milk, a bunch of bananas, two cans of New England clam chowder, and a box of Twinkies for three years.

➤ **Just because an item is on sale doesn't mean the price has hit rock-bottom.** Shopaholics love a sale, but often merchandise (especially clothing) isn't a bargain until it's at least 40 percent off the regular price. When a store takes 10 percent off an item, they're barely paying for your tax in some states; that's no deal.

➤ **Buy only what you can afford.** If you don't have the cash to buy something, don't use a credit card to make the purchase. Carrying a balance on a credit card only requires you to carry debt for months and months.

➤ **Bargain with the merchandiser.** You can't do this at a grocery store (unless the merchandise is damaged), but try it at privately owned stores. How? Above all, be discreet. A store owner will not reduce a price if she thinks your deal will become public information. Likewise, don't roughhouse the owner; instead, be tactful with your approach. Come across as a serious shopper who intends to spend some cash (you'll lose your edge if you use plastic). Select a couple of the items you want to purchase, have the owner add up the entire bill, and then act uncertain. Ask the owner if this is the best price she can give you. It may not always work, but it's worth a shot.

➤ **Don't buy for convenience.** If you want to save money on groceries, don't shop for the convenient items, such as carrots that are already cut up or premixed pancake batter. Even if you have coupons for these items, you'll save more money in the long run if you cut up your own carrots and mix up your own pancake batter. If you do buy for the sake of convenience, at that local 24-hour, all-night corner place with the gas pumps out front, for example, understand that you'll pay extra for those chocolate-covered doughnuts and a gallon of milk. Sometimes you may *have* to pay "convenience store" prices for diapers, cough medicine, or toilet paper—but don't make a habit of it.

➤ **Keep your receipts, and watch for ads featuring the merchandise you already bought.** Some stores will honor your receipts and returns if you buy it at full price one week and it goes on sale the next.

The Money Line

Psychologists now say that sex and shopping are inevitably linked, according to a study done by a lecturer at Lancaster University. The study reports that many people get a physical pleasure from shopping. Two-thirds of those interviewed said they went out to buy something when they felt unhappy. If you think you get a buzz when shopping and don't have a significant other to smooch, do us a favor. Leave the credit cards at home and just browse the racks.

Buying in Bulk

You can save 30, 40, even 50 percent on your next grocery bill if you buy in bulk—and borrow a friend's station wagon to haul it home. But it doesn't always work to your advantage.

The common misconception about buying your groceries in bulk (at a warehouse food club, for example) is that you have to buy the 10-gallon jar of peanut butter in order to get a deal. Not true—unless you *like* a lot of peanut butter. You may have to buy more volume of a certain item, but if you're going to buy that amount in smaller quantities over an extended period of time anyway, you're better off. If you do the math, you can see how much you save on some items.

Asset Advisory

Items such as sugar, flour, milk, eggs, laundry soap, and coffee filters tend to be less expensive at a warehouse supermarket, while other items such as meat tend to cost less at the grocery store. So what's the point? It pays to comparison shop.

For example, a three-gallon tub of laundry soap is $9 at your favorite warehouse supermarket. In your regular supermarket, a one-gallon tub of the same laundry soap is $5, and if you bought three gallons, you would pay $15. So you save six dollars by shopping at a warehouse supermarket. But that's for an item like laundry soap, which won't perish. A 10-pound bag of bananas is a different story.

One thing to consider is that it costs money to join a warehouse supermarket—the membership fee can be as high as $35 a year. Most of these warehouse clubs also require that you be a member of an organization or have an employee membership through your company. If you want to join a warehouse club, see if your church, company, or other organizations participate.

Once you shop one of these places, you'll find that warehouse clubs are fun. Where else can you buy a rack of lamb, a VCR, and a sweat suit all under one roof? But be careful. That doesn't mean you have to buy one of everything. And remember to take your coupons to these warehouse supermarkets to see if they honor them; you could save even more!

The Online Shopping Experience

Remember when they said that the mail-order catalogue business wouldn't work because you can't touch anything like you do when you shop in stores? Yep—online shopping is here to stay.

The whole online shopping experience involves browsing catalogues and viewing merchandise, perhaps in a choice of colors, styles, fabrics—just like you do in a catalogue, except you're using your computer.

Most websites that sell products offer an online shopping cart where you can change items and quantities, place an order, use your credit card right online, and—get this— not pay tax! That's right, as of this writing, there are no taxes on any items you purchase on the Web.

Fiber-Optic Wars

Raise your hand if you've switched long-distance services within the past year.

Now, raise your hand if you understand exactly what features you're getting and know what you're paying.

Those telephone advertising wars make you feel as if you're going in "circles" with your "true friends" no matter how many "one rates" there are, huh?

It's not just the big three—AT&T, MCI, and Sprint—that have armed themselves for combat as they did in 1984 when deregulation of the telephone industry hit. It's the 700 or so other companies that have thrown their fiber-optic hats into the ring to really confuse the hell out of us.

Here's a secret we bet you didn't know. The bottom line is that there is very little difference in the standard rates charged by the big three phone carriers. Mind-boggling, huh? It's when you create your customized plan that the bills and services get as hairy as an ape in the Amazon. Keep the following tips in mind to help alleviate a phone phenomenon:

> ➤ **Choose a plan based on YOU.** Even if all of your friends and your family have MCI, you're not guaranteed to save more money. You need to evaluate your calling patterns. Do you make most of your calls during the day? Are you a chatterbox only from 7:00 to 9:00 p.m. on weekends? Whatever the case, once you log your calling patterns, you'll be able to choose a program that suits your needs—and is easy on the wallet!

29

➤ **Make sure you choose some type of plan.** If you don't specifically request a certain plan, some companies will pick one for you. And, as you learned in Chapter 1, you can't grab good financial planning by the tail if you let someone else make your financial decisions. It's the plan, not the company, that's most important.

➤ **Even if you've picked a plan, re-evaluate your telephone patterns six months from now.** Yes, this gives you more homework, but you want to save money, don't you? If your calling plan has changed dramatically, you'll need to analyze your bills to make sure you're still saving as much as possible.

➤ **Rates shouldn't be the sole factor in your decision.** If one major carrier charges only 22 cents a minute for a long-distance call, and another carrier charges 24 cents a minute but offers you more perks (such as prepaid calling cards), choose the latter. Although you want the best price, you also want the best components.

➤ **If you're still befuddled, contact the Telecommunications Research & Action Center.** Known as TRAC, this organization will send you a copy of its complete Tele-Tips residential rates comparison chart for $3. Write to TRAC, P.O. Box 12038, Washington, DC 20005. Make sure you enclose a self-addressed, stamped envelope. The chart features costs for five-, 10-, 15-, 30-, 50- and 150-calls-per-month scenarios, as well as scenarios for heavy day use, average use, and heavy night and weekend use.

Flying the Friendly Skies on the Cheap

If you want to be a shrewd traveler, you're going to have to do more to save money than travel to vacation spots during the off-peak season. One way to save on traveling is to never ever accept the first fare quoted. Research indicates that half of the time, some other airline has a flight within the same time you want to leave, but it has a special, less-expensive fare.

Online Resource

Check out **www.priceline.com**, a website that acts as an intermediary between you and the airline carriers and enables you to "bid" on air fares. You input your departing and arrival dates and destinations, and put in an offer of the highest fare you'll pay for that route. Priceline.com will get back to you the same day to see if your offer has been accepted—or refused. Every inquiry after your first three requests is $25 each.

One of the best money-saving strategies for travelers is to change your eating habits. Eating every meal out can eat up (forgive the pun) all of your money. To control your food budget, try to eat only twice a day, and if possible, buy your food at a nearby supermarket and eat it in your hotel room. You can save hundreds of dollars by doing this. In fact, some smart travelers opt for a room with a kitchen-ette so they can cook their own meals—a wise decision.

Here's a tip you'll love—although it sounds too good to be true. For both foreign and domestic travelers, if you use International Travel Consult-ants (based in Asheville, North Carolina), you can possibly earn a refund. Individuals who spend anywhere between $1 and $20,000 can receive up to 25 percent of the agency's commission. This commission is paid by airlines, hotels, and so on, so the agency returns a portion of its commissions to travelers who use its services. Rebates are awarded on a quarterly basis. For more informa-tion, call (800) 467-5214, or write to P.O. Box 167, Asheville, NC 28802.

Asset Advisory

If your schedule allows you to, take a "bump" if it's offered. Typically this is when an airline will offer free tickets to volunteers who give up their seats in the event that the airline overbooked the flight. Unless the airline can get you on another flight for the same destination within an hour, you get to fly free. Just remember to bring along a good book to read while you wait.

Lazy Shopping

Suppose it's late at night, and you're flipping channels. All of a sudden you see it—the bargain of a lifetime. A genuine 14k gold bracelet with cubic zirconia diamondelles interlaced with faux emeralds for only $79.95. "Only seven left!" screams the shopping channel host. Panic ensues as you pick up the phone and dial the number so you can buy your dream present. But alas, you're too late. All gone.

Tragedy? No. It would probably be the best thing that could happen to you.

Shopping channels entice millions of Americans to buy more unneeded merchandise than ever. How? Because they're very visual, provoking the "see-it-buy-it" habit. In fact, the most recent figures indicate that in 1993, QVC and the Home Shopping Network raked in more than $1 billion in revenue. Is this merchandise a bargain? No, not when you consider the mistakes people can make when they shop via TV.

For example, you can't send cash or write a check when you purchase an item from a shopping channel. Each time you make a purchase, you must use a credit card, which is a habit you're trying to cut back on. Plus, you have to pay for shipping charges, which often add $10 to $20, depending on where you live.

And what happens if you receive defective merchandise? Good question. Sure, you can send it back, but it's often a troublesome process, and you're stuck with a gadget that looks like it belongs in a Star Trek mausoleum.

The Least You Need to Know

➤ It may be worth the price of joining a warehouse supermarket if you normally buy lots of nonperishable items (and have the room to store them).

➤ Getting the best deal on long distance is easy, simply match your calling habits to one of a company's plans. And remember, you don't have to stick with one of the big three.

➤ Buying stuff you see on TV is usually not a good idea. You have to buy it with a credit card, and it's difficult to return if something is wrong with it.

Chapter 4

Getting Out of the Money Jungle

In This Chapter

➤ Why you can't believe "interest rate experts"

➤ Which key rates give you a clue to the future

➤ What you should read and watch to keep up

➤ How to map your money game plan

➤ Which investments are safe and which ones are not

It's the toughest question: How in heck can you make your money grow in such a complicated environment? Who can possibly understand all the investment gibberish and advice that comes sailing your way from banks, brokers, financial planners, government and news media? It's enough to drive you bonkers. The stock markets and the world economy are all over page one, but millions of average people are just as baffled, mixed up and frustrated by the money jungle as you are. They're panicked about Social Security one day going down the drain, and are afraid they'll have to work into their seventies just to survive.

The guy with $20,000 in cash to stash somewhere doesn't have a guaranteed clue of where to put it, or for how long, or at what interest rate. There are enough confusing options to make his head spin. Yet, he doesn't know whom to trust—whether his broker is telling it to him straight, or how safe his bank is versus parking his money in a mutual fund. Expert advice is hard to come by, and even top economic gurus goof when they predict whether mortgage rates are going up or down. This chapter is the first step toward carving your way through the jungle without going out of your gourd.

Watch Those Conflicting Reports!

Your first lesson is to realize that economic "experts" have a lousy batting average when it comes to reading a crystal ball. On the same day, one oracle swears that the Dow Jones average will go through the roof in the next couple of years, while another pundit across town warns you to dump all your stocks now because the world is teetering on the edge of a depression. Hey, they both can't be right—in fact, they can both be wrong! Instead of listening to all their malarkey—that's mostly what it is—you've got to do some common-sense thinking on your own.

Most people try to keep up by scanning the newspaper business pages, watching money shows on TV, subscribing to a financial newsletter or two, or chatting with their banker, broker, or financial planner. They perk up when a neighbor tells them she has a friend who has a friend who knows somebody named Marvin the Broker who's been helping all the wealthy widows in town make a bundle on their investments. Well, guess how smart is Marvin at giving advice when the economy crashes in Bangladesh? Not very, we assure you.

On your own, you have to sponge up every tip you can, and sort through whatever vital information you come across. But there are a few factors you can watch that will gain you an edge, starting now. Just remember that things are changing faster and faster. The knowledge you go to bed with tonight may be outdated by the time you wake up tomorrow.

Watch the Rates: They're the Big Clue!

More than anything, follow the key interest rates. They're the main clue to how the economy is performing and where the markets are going. Here's what to keep your eye on:

1. **U.S. interest rates.** Especially the Federal Reserve's "discount rate" and "federal funds rate." The Fed is the master controller of all rates. It can raise rates to cool off the economy by making borrowing more expensive, which, in turn, cuts into corporate profits and reduces stock prices. But another big influence has entered the scene.

2. **The health—or weakness—of foreign economies.** For the first time in your life, those economies have a direct influence on your investments, and maybe even your job. It used to be that this country's stock market only reacted to domestic indicators such as jobs, incomes, prices, retail sales, and the gross national product. Now it's a whole new ballgame. When a foreign economy plunges, like what happened in Malaysia, Japan and Russia in 1997 and 1998, the U.S. stock market takes a dive.

   Why? When the value of those countries' currencies tumbled, many U.S. investors pulled their money out of those regions. From then on, it was a domino effect. Because U.S. companies could no longer sell as many goods in those lands, it hurt the companies' profits—and drove down their stock prices. Wall Street isn't dumb. When it sees such a scenario shaping up, possibly even affecting Europe and Latin America as well, it starts selling off those stocks and the Dow falls like a rock.

3. **The banks' "prime rate."** When the Fed changes its rates, the banks immediately chime in by raising or lowering their prime rate by the same margin. The prime affects what banks charge their corporate customers to borrow money, thus affecting their profits. The prime also influences the rates you earn on bank CDs, and what you pay on most credit cards, home equity loans and lines of credit, and auto loans. If the prime goes up by one-half percent, so will the cost of your variable-rate credit card. The Fed's action also affects Treasury bill rates that can determine the interest you pay on an adjustable-rate mortgage.

4. **The U.S. inflation rate.** This is the most critical thing the Fed pays attention to. If it suspects consumer prices and other inflationary signals are in the wind, it will hike its key rates by one-quarter or one-half percent to stave off the threat. Conversely, the Fed may try to stimulate the economy by lowering rates if it believes the economy is weak.

5. **Banks' long-term CD yields.** This is the most unscientific indicator of all, but we've used it to accurately predict a general U.S. rate rise, or drop, in advance. Keep your eye on big banks' five-year CDs. If the institution believes rates will be higher in the months ahead, it may increase long-term CD yields faster than those on short-term accounts, such as six months or one year. The reason is that it's cheaper for them to capture five-year CD business by paying an above-market rate now, than by paying an even higher rate down the road.

Do these tips carry over to your stock and mutual fund investing? Yes, indeed. The stock market is super-sensitive to interest rates for the reasons we just gave. When rates have gone down in recent years, stock prices have gone up; when rates have risen, stock prices have dropped. When interest rates and the rate of inflation remained extremely low between 1995 and 1998, many Wall Street investors enjoyed returns of 20 percent per year and higher on their investments. Meanwhile, all it takes is a rumor—nothing more—that the Fed is going to change its rates—or leave them alone—to make the Dow roar or crash.

Watch Your Wallet

If you think some expert who puts out a newsletter has inside knowledge of a major rate move, forget it. The highway is littered with their bad guesses, and the real problem is, no one keeps track of how awfully wrong those guys have been with their predictions. The honest truth is that the so-called economic wizards and gurus who report on the financial world have had a terrible batting average when it comes to predicting anything.

And the problem can get huge. News reporters often pick up wrong predictions from the "experts," then pass them along to you. For example, a TV financial reporter may warn that "higher rates are around the corner, according to Baxter Busterman at XYZ Financial Corporation, and this will affect your mortgage payments and what you pay on credit cards." Busterman may be all wet. You're better off checking out and comparing several different news sources—especially the in-depth business pages of leading newspapers. These will give you a better, more balanced view of what's happening.

Where You Can Go for All the Good Stuff

You've already learned that the "experts," who try to guide you through the jungle, don't carry a compass. Some people in the media don't really know their way, either. Even if some of them did, you couldn't learn everything you need to know from a 20-second sound bite, could you?

So where can you go? Here's a rundown of just a few of the different sources of information available to you—and what you should be looking for from each one when you do your homework.

Newsworthy Newsletters

There are hundreds and hundreds of newsletters around, eagerly gobbled up by millions of novices and professional investors. *All* those little journals can't be right, can they?

No, not all of them can. Many simply give their opinions and theories without backing them up with good, solid data. Others make a killing by preaching gloom and doom, scaring the pants off readers in hopes they'll want to be better prepared before the world ends. All too often, the publishers who create these newsletters are self-serving—churning out their publications with one hand, and taking your money to manage your investment portfolio with the other. That is downright unethical and deceptive. You want to get your information only from people who do not have a hand in your pocket. It's called independent journalism, and it's the best kind.

Don't waste your time or money on every single newsletter out there. Your subscription bill alone could be thousands of dollars, even before you invested one red cent. And who says the information is any good? Instead, zero in on respected sources who know what they're talking about and have the best track record of picking good investments, giving good advice, and providing the facts and figures to back it all up.

One way to cut through the muck is to follow *The Hulbert Financial Digest* (888/485-2378). This is the newsletter of newsletters! For only $37.50, you get a monthly, five-issue trial subscription, giving you access to the ratings of the top 160 newsletters over a period of 10 years. The *Digest* covers newsletter recommendations and performance based on the following time periods: 1 year, 3 years, 5 years, 8 years, 10 years, and 15 years.

Trying to track down the latest information in the banking industry? Need help locating an out-of-state bank that pays the highest interest rates on its CDs? Subscribe to Bank Rate Monitor's *100 Highest Yields* (800/327-7717) to learn the highest CD rates in the country. Better still, go to BRM's free web site at www.bankrate.com and get all the top yields at no cost. You will also get all the latest national and local rates and averages on CDs, Money Market Accounts, mortgages, credit cards, auto loans and home equity.

If you want thorough updates about the mutual fund industry, look into Sheldon Jacobs' *No-Load Fund Analyst* or *Morningstar's Fund Investor*. Both publications focus on performance information and highlight current events in the mutual fund industry. The *No-Load Fund Analyst* (510/254-9017) is $18.75 for one trial issue plus special reports, or $55 for three consecutive issues plus reports. Morningstar's Fund Investor (312/424-4288) is $79 for a one-year subscription.

Hot Spots on the Internet

There's been an explosion of helpful personal finance information on the Internet in the past couple of years. These sites will definitely help you manage your money in every way, from a dinky checking account to cutting your credit card debt and planning for retirement.

Online Resources

www.Quicken.com was developed by Intuit, the company that develops software to help people with their finances. In fact, Quicken is the main personal banking component for CNN's website (see below).

www.CNNfn.com is the Internet address for CNN's up-to-the-minute financial information, which will keep you posted on everything from Dow-Jones averages to clearly-written articles on all phases of personal finance.

www.MSNBC.com is another web companion to one of television's major business news programs.

www.Bloomberg.com is the Internet presence for Bloomberg Personal Finance magazine, one of America's best-known providers of electronic market data and business news.

www.Worth.com is the site for the personal finance magazine of the same name.

www.Cardtrak.com is where to find the best low-rate credit cards of all types—standard, gold, you-name-it—including cards with no annual fee.

Fast 'Net Calculators Do Your Figuring for You

Want to know whether you should refinance your mortgage now, and how much you'll save? Whether you should lease or buy your next car? Or how long it will take you to pay off your credit card or home equity loan?

Run, do not walk, to use the fantastic (and easy) financial calculators on the Internet. Several website operators offer these super-simple calculators that enable you to figure anything in a jiffy. All you do, on a mortgage loan, for example, is punch in your interest rates and points from different lenders, the amount you're borrowing, and how often you'll be making payments—and bingo—you get all your answers! This is a great way to try several "what-if" scenarios to learn which deal is best for your pocket-book. You'll see it all, including full amortization schedules on your loans, your costs month by month, and over all the years of your loans, how much you've paid against the principal and interest, and how much you still owe.

Online Resources

www.interest.com/calculators.html, the website for Mortgage Market Information Services, is a great tool for new home-buyers and refinancers.

www.bloomberg.com/cgi-bin/ilpc.cgi. Bloomberg's mortgage calculators will tell you how much you can afford to borrow, your monthly payment, benefits of prepaying your loan, and more.

www.homepath.com/calcs.html tells you how much house you can afford, whether now's a good time to refinance, the net cost, and the amount you'll save.

It's on the Boob Tube

Here's a quick rundown of the financial programs on television that report the latest financial market news and business industry changes. By learning the information provided in this book, you'll be able to determine how the stories and reports on these TV programs affect your wallet.

CNN's *Moneyline*, which airs Monday through Friday at 7:00 p.m. EST, is packed with nationwide and worldwide coverage of breaking business news, financial market stories, and straightforward economic reports from Lou Dobbs and financial editor Myron Kandel. CNN's *Business Day*, which airs every morning at 6:00 a.m. EST, also covers newsworthy business reports. CNN's *Your Money*, which airs several times on weekends, gives viewers information about the ins and outs of personal finance.

Nightly Business Report is a daily TV program that airs on PBS stations at 6:30 p.m. EST. Veteran financial journalist Paul Kangas covers the action in the stock market, and interviews many investment experts. A sister program of *NBR*, called *Morning Business Report*, airs daily at 6:00 a.m. EST.

CNBC is angled more toward the sophisticated investor. It covers the financial markets and business news round-the-clock. During the trading day, several stock market tickers crawl at the bottom of the screen. The channel offers many half-hour programs that deal with specific investments, such as mutual funds, real estate, and technology stocks.

Wall Street Journal Report, hosted by Consuelo Mack, airs every Sunday morning. This program—considered the television version of the daily newspaper *The Wall Street Journal*—covers the key financial events of the week and interviews experts in the financial and business fields.

Reading All the Fine Print

One of the most consumer-friendly newspapers is *USA Today*, which offers a "Money" section. This section not only covers the most urgent stories of the day about the financial markets, but also gives information about the nation's top business happenings—and many personal finance stories that affect *you*.

Here's a list of others you may want to take a look at:

Money Magazine (800/633-9970) is a monthly publication that broadly covers areas of personal finance and money management, ranging from investment articles to feature stories. This long-established magazine also carries a special section on where to find high-yield CDs and good deals on credit cards. Check out *Money* on the 'Net at *www.pathfinder.com/money*.

Smart Money (800/444-4204) is a monthly magazine that also reports on a wide scope of personal finance matters. Its investigative articles show which investments will earn the reader top interest, which ones won't, and why. *www.smartmoney,com*.

Kiplinger's *Personal Finance* (800/544-0155) is also a monthly publication geared to the individual's personal financial needs. Articles have an educational tone and cover everything from financial planning to stocks and bonds and other investments. *www.kiplingers.com*.

Your Money Magazine (847/763-9200) is a bimonthly publication geared toward the Main Street investor. This practical, down-to-earth magazine gives a wealth of advice on personal finance issues. It also discusses investment products, insurance planning, and savings and borrowing rates in language you can understand. Articles reveal how you can get more bang for your buck in the personal finance world.

Wall Street Journal (800/568-7625) is one of the most powerful daily business newspapers available. You learn about "Who's Who" and "What's What" in Wall Street. It covers virtually every type of financial market—nationwide and worldwide—and reports world events that have an impact on your money. It's most famous for its "C-section," which lists the critically acclaimed column "Heard on the Street," a great place to find out today what's going on tomorrow. Also, if there's a new trend in CDs, stocks, or bond investing, odds are that *Journal's* ace reporters will cover it. *www.wsj.com*.

Business Week (888/878-5151) gives readers no-holds-barred articles and reports about companies and specific company profiles. Additional stories include performance information, business strategies, personal investing, economic reports, and Wall Street's latest news. The Web address is *www.businessweek.com*. *Business Week* is also available through America Online.

Investor's Business Daily is a daily financial newspaper that has become another relevant source for the inside scoop on national and worldwide business and financial matters. *www.investors.com*.

Understanding the Mumbo-Jumbo

If someone were to pull you off the street and ask you to explain the difference between *rate* and *yield*, what would you say? No need to feel at a loss for words anymore. After you learn what these terms mean, not only will you be able to tell what the difference is between rate and yield, but you could probably educate your banker or broker about the methods of compounding, too.

A **rate** is what you earn on a CD or savings account before compounding (don't worry—that's defined here, too), or the interest you are charged on a loan.

A **yield** is the interest you earn after the savings rate has been compounded.

Compounding simply means more interest being added to the interest you've already earned.

APY stands for *Annual Percentage Yield*. It's the total amount of interest you earn on an account in exactly one year.

APR stands for *Annual Percentage Rate*. Usually associated with loans, the APR is a complex mathematical formula that includes other charges on the loan, in addition to the interest rate.

An **index** is a well-known benchmark, such as the prime rate used by a financial institution to set its interest rates. The rate you earn or pay will move up or down according to changes in the index.

After tracking interest rates and bank, stock, bond, and mutual fund accounts for years—and answering thousands of questions from troubled average Joes and Janes like yourself—we've found some of the basic concepts you need to fight your way through the money jungle.

What Kind of Investor Are You?

You do have a personal financial game plan, don't you? You should have a fairly good idea of what your cash position and costs might be in the early and distant future. (If you need a good review, go back to Chapter 2.)

Ask yourself this question: What does that picture look like today, next month, or next year? Get a pencil and jot it down. How much have you set aside for investing? What are your short-term and long-term debts? What is your likely income over the next couple of years? Your job position? Your age? Your health?

It doesn't stop there. How much will you need to live comfortably when you retire? Are you living off an inheritance left to you by a rich uncle, or are you scraping along with monthly checks from investments that are your lifeline? Are you saving for a little cottage by the sea? Will Junior need beaucoup extra bucks if he decides to go for his master's degree? How much will you need beyond your Social Security and 401(k) plan? What are you going to do about unforeseen medical bills and other emergencies?

Asset Advisory

If you are a conservative investor, keep in mind that CD investments at thrift institutions pay more than CD accounts at banks. Savings accounts at credit unions earn more than accounts at either banks or thrifts. Except for mortgages, whose rates are about the same at all three types of institutions, credit unions also charge a lot less on personal loans, such as new cars and credit cards.

Before you set foot in the money jungle, estimate how much extra money you have to invest, how much more you're shooting for, and when you'll need it. This rule applies whether you're out to make just a few hundred bucks, or are wheeling and dealing in the seven figures. Your number of investment choices is mind-boggling. So, before you set out on your safari with machete in hand, go into a quiet corner and have an honest little chat with yourself to determine what kind of investor you are.

How Willing Are You to Take a Risk?

Are you the super-conservative type who can't—or doesn't want to—risk a penny? For example, do you need an extra-safe, regular, fixed income to make ends meet? If so, your game plan should zero in on federally insured banks, savings and loans (also called *thrift* institutions), credit unions, and Treasury bonds and certificates.

If you're not extremely conservative, you have some money you'd like to speculate with (in case some tipsters told you the stock of New Electronic Widget Company will go through the roof), and you won't miss the money if you lose, you might want to dabble in a slightly more risky investment. You can dabble in the stock and bond markets or stash your cash in mutual funds, if you're feeling a little adventurous.

However, if you're not at all conservative, and you like to fly by the seat of your pants, no-holds-barred, then maybe you should tinker in the commodities markets.

Whichever approach you decide is for you, keep in mind that your goal should be to obtain the greatest reward with the least amount of risk. Once you establish your risk tolerance, you'll be able to find your way through the money jungle a lot easier. Part 2 reviews the different types of investments available to you (no matter what your threshold of pain is), and also tells you smart money moves you should be making now based on your level of risk. For a complete review of how to successfully invest on Wall Street, pick up a copy of *The Complete Idiot's Guide to Making Money on Wall Street*.

Uncle Sam Offers the Best Safety Net

Deposits at banks, thrifts, and credit unions are backed by the full faith and credit of the federal government. That's not just idle talk. Even if you're over 60 and remember the Great Depression, when the banks closed, consider this fact:

> No one ever lost a dime in a federally insured bank, thrift, or credit union for up to the $100,000 insurance limit.

That also takes into account the late 1980s, when hundreds of sick outfits went belly-up. Today, institutions have rebounded like you wouldn't believe, and they're making record profits. So, you can toss aside whatever outdated fears you might still hold. And if you're wondering just how safe Treasury securities are, they are backed by the full faith and credit of the U.S. government.

The Federal Deposit Insurance Corporation (FDIC) protects deposits at banks and thrifts for up to $100,000 per person, including principal and interest, at the same institution. The National Credit Union Administration (NCUA) provides essentially the same protection for depositors at credit unions. However, any amount above the $100,000 figure is not protected, so don't even think about depositing more than that into one account. If you have more than $100,000 to invest, consider opening multiple accounts.

It's possible to insure *more* than $100,000 by creating several different joint accounts and trust accounts, as Table 4.1 shows. You may never have a million bucks at your disposal, but here's how the wealthy beat the system by insuring as much as $1.4 million for a family of four at the same institution.

Table 4.1   A Family of Four with Over a Million Bucks

Account Type	Accounts		Amount
Individual	Husband		$100,000
	Wife		$100,000
	Child 1		$100,000
	Child 2		$100,000
Joint Accounts	Husband & Wife		$100,000
	Husband & Child 1		$100,000
	Wife & Child 2		$100,000
	Child 1 & Child 2		$100,000
Trust Accounts	Husband	Wife	$100,000
	Wife	Husband	$100,000
	Husband	Child 1	$100,000
	Husband	Child 2	$100,000
	Wife	Child 1	$100,000
	Wife	Child 2	$100,000
TOTAL			**$1,400,000**

How Much Money Can You Afford to Lose?

This question doesn't apply to federally insured banks, where you're protected, it only involves the gamble you take with uninsured investments. If, for example, a federally insured bank offers you a yield of 8 percent on a one-year $10,000 CD, you're guaranteed to earn $800 in a year. You'll get back $10,800 on your $10,000 investment. You can't say that about speculative investments such as stocks and bonds, although the gamble may pay off with earnings higher than what you'll earn from a bank.

For example, if, in 1924, you had invested $1,000 in the S&P 500 (a basket of 500 stocks that makes up the Standard & Poor's) and let it ride through the ups and downs of the stock market, you would have more than a half-million bucks today! Does that mean the stock market isn't risky? No, because the stock market could average a negative 10 percent return one year, and a positive 10 percent return the next. It just means that the longer your money is invested and the more diversified your investments are, the more you reduce your risk.

Table 4.2 shows how different types of investments performed against inflation over a 20-year period ending in the mid-1990s. Note, for example, that there was less volatility between the maximum and minimum return on government bonds than there was with stock investments.

Table 4.2   Investments Versus Inflation

	Maximum	Minimum
Common stocks	16.9%	3.1%
Long-term government bonds	9.0	0.7
Intermediate-term government bonds	9.4	1.6
Treasury bills	7.7	0.4
Inflation	6.4	0.1

How Long Can You Be Without the Money?

Fiscal Facts

A *liquid* account means that you may withdraw your money from the account at any time without paying a penalty. For example, there's no penalty when you take any of your funds out of a bank Money Market Account, but there is a penalty if you withdraw money from a bank CD account (see Chapters 11 and 12). The CD account is not as liquid as the Money Market Account.

This is a critical decision lots of people skip over. If you're tempted to succumb to the razzle-dazzle of a stockbroker's pitch, or some super-high rate in a bank ad, before you plunk down your cash, remember this: you might need the money sooner than you think.

If you need your cash six months or a year down the road for an emergency or something else you hadn't planned for, what are you going to do? What if the investment rate picture and other financial factors change and you want to move your money to a higher-earning instrument? What do you do then? If you withdraw your funds early, you'll probably be charged a stiff penalty.

Answering all of these questions helps you figure out what type of *liquidity* you are looking for in an investment. Table 4.3 shows how each investment product is ranked, not only by risk, but also by liquidity—and if there are any penalties for cashing in!

Table 4.3   Liquidity in the Money Jungle

Investment Type	How Quickly Can I Get My Money?	Penalties?
Least Risky		
Federally insured:		
Savings accounts	Immediately	No
Checking accounts	Immediately	No
Certificates of Deposit	At maturity	***

Investment Type	How Quickly Can I Get My Money?	Penalties?
Treasury bills	Five days after selling or wait until maturity	No
U.S. Gov't money funds	Next day	No
Small to Moderate Risk		
Savings bonds	Six months	Loss of interest
Money Market mutual funds	Next day	No
U.S. Gov't securities	Five days after selling or wait until maturity	No
U.S. Federal Agency bond funds	Next day	No
Moderate to Slightly Higher Risk		
Mutual funds	Next day	No
Municipal bonds	Five days after selling or wait until maturity	No
Risky		
Blue-chip stocks	Five days after selling	No
Closed-end mutual funds	Five days after selling	No
Small cap stock mutual funds	Next day	No
Small cap stocks	Five days after selling	No
Corporate bonds	Five days after selling or wait until maturity	No
Convertible bond funds	Next day	No
Very Risky		
Futures/commodities	Depends on contract	Varies
Options	Next day	Varies
Gold	Varies	N/A
Sector funds	Next day	No
Junk bonds	Five days after selling	No

*** *If you liquidate your CD before maturity, you face an early withdrawal penalty of up to six months' worth of interest, and an IRS penalty.*

Which Type of Investment Will Probably Earn Top Dollar?

We don't have a crystal ball, but we can explain how, and where, the laws of the jungle come into play.

The disadvantage of bank investments is that they usually pay less than you could earn with stocks, bonds, or mutual funds. How much you'll earn at the bank depends on current interest rates and where they'll be months or years from now. The advantage is that you won't lose your shirt, because bank deposits are federally insured up to $100,000.

Get out your telescope and look at the jungle through both ends. If you look at it from a narrow viewpoint—just one year, 1997—you'll see that stocks and mutual funds pounded meager bank rates into the ground. On a $10,000 investment in that year:

Common stocks earned $2,500.

Bonds earned $1,150.

A one-year bank CD earned $503.

Gold lost $2,100.

The same thing was true in the first half of 1998. Stock investors earned $1,132 in the first six months, bonds earned $627, and bank CDs returned only $245 on their investment. Even gold topped the CDs at $269.

But just two months later, on the heels of foreign economies coming apart in Asia and other sectors, the stock market plunged and wiped out all the 1998 gains to date. So you can't tell what's likely to happen. When you invest in securities, you're totally at the mercy of a slew of different forces, ranging from foreign governments to unemployment figures, consumer prices, and interest rates.

It used to be that interest rates, especially bank rates, went up and down like a roller coaster. Each up-cycle or down-cycle lasted between 18 and 30 months. So, with a little knowledge, you could time your investment move just right by knowing for how long (or short) a period you should invest. That told you how and when to lock up a CD rate, and for what term.

But no more. Bank rates began flattening and then began wobbling up and down only slightly in 1995. That relatively steady picture—calmer than it had been in decades—kept U.S. inflation low and helped fuel the meteoric rise in stock prices. And as some key global markets weakened, notably Japan and Russia, the experts began steering their worries away from inflation and toward deflation. The big question on everybody's mind became, "Will the U.S. economy slip because of the other countries' weaknesses—bringing about less business, lower prices and lower investment earnings?"

By the time you read this book, you'll have read part of the answer in your newspaper and seen it on television.

Ask the Right Questions—Get the Right Answers!

Failing to ask the right questions is one of the biggest and most common mistakes. It often separates the winners from the losers in investing. The time to pin down your banker, broker, or even your financial planner, is *before* you sign on the dotted line, not afterward. That sounds simple enough, right? Of course. Except very few people know which questions to ask! It's an art in itself, but you can do it.

On bank accounts, study the key questions in Chapters 8, 9, 10, 11, and 12. These cover buying CDs and basic savings accounts, opening a checking account, and figuring out which fees to avoid.

Never—repeat, never—take the word of the average teller or account representative at a bank. They are honest and well-meaning folks, but often they haven't been informed about the bank's latest interest rates or other changes in bank policies. Always ask to speak to an officer.

How bad can it get? One day when we were surveying bank CD rates in a Florida city, ten different employees at five different banks gave us twelve different interest rates on the same account! Believe us, checking and double-checking your information always pays off. As they taught us in journalism school, "If your mother tells you she loves you, check it out."

If you're still confused by all the rates, yields, and gibberish, use the best machete of all. Ask the bank one simple question: "If I give you my money today, how much will I have in my account at the end of one year—*in dollars and cents, not percent*—after subtracting all fees and charges?" It works like a charm, and you'll probably see the bank rep's face turn twelve shades of purple. But don't stop there. Ask the same type of question when you borrow: "How much will my total cost of the loan be in dollars?"

If you're dealing with a full-service broker, tell him that you want discounts on your commissions. Ask him if he will meet with you every three months to review your account. Most brokers do business only by phone, rarely face-to-face.

Ask them the same question: "How many dollars will I have at the end of the year?" It may be difficult to pinpoint an answer since the financial markets fluctuate quite a bit, but if you can nail down the track record and performance history of this broker, you're ahead of the ballgame. Home run!

Lastly, make sure you watch those hidden fees. At first glance, it looks like there are only two big patches of trees in the jungle:

➤ The money you put in

➤ The money you take out

Not so. There's something else lurking out there. Hidden among the jungle's branches and vines are a million fees and charges that can whittle down your cash—without you even noticing it! (See Chapter 12.)

The best way to protect yourself is to shop the fees at several outfits. You'll be amazed at the differences. For example, if you don't generate at least $100 in commissions at Smith Barney Shearson, your account will get slapped with a $50 inactivity fee.

Before you sign any document, ask for a copy of the bank's, or broker's, complete fee schedule. Take it home and study it. When you go back, ask for an explanation of every conceivable charge you could get hit with in the type of account you're opening. Just by following these tips alone, you'll probably get back many times your small investment in this book!

The Least You Need to Know

➤ Take any investment advice you get—whether it's from a neighbor, the paper, or a TV financial "expert" with a grain of salt. Check out the sources and the facts for yourself before you invest a dime in the market.

➤ Keep your eye on key interest rates. They're a big influence on the stock market, bank rates and the general economy.

➤ Step one is to always know what your broad financial goals are, how much money you can play around with, and how much risk you can handle in case the market drops.

➤ Federally insured CDs and Treasury securities are the safest investments, but you can make more money in stocks, bonds, and mutual funds over the long haul. Check out Chapter 11 for more information.

➤ Don't be afraid to ask your banker or broker questions, especially if you don't understand something. Make sure you're aware of all the fees that could be involved when you do business with them.

Part 2
The Secrets to Simple, Savvy Investing

Hello, Wall Street? Meet Main Street.

Years ago, the hot financial topic of conversation in mainstream America had more to do with paying bills and maybe, just maybe, investing in certificates of deposit or savings bonds. Fast-forward to today, and you'll find conversations are turning more toward investment strategies that include stocks, mutual funds, bonds, and options. And, it's not just the brokers on Wall Street trading the lingo. It's people like you and me who work hard for a living but also realize that you should be doing something with your money to make it work hard, too.

The money world is more than just balancing your checkbook and paying the bills. So, we're here to share a few simple investment strategies that will help get you started.

You don't need to be a financial Einstein to understand (and also roll the dice on) Wall Street. In this part, you'll learn how to create a portfolio that can do more than pay the bills, how millionaires become millionaires, and where the yesteryear "safe money" investments belong in today's portfolios.

Are you ready to begin?

Chapter 5

Why You Need Wall Street

In This Chapter

➤ How to create your own investment profile

➤ The pluses and minuses of taking the plunge

➤ The lowdown on stocks, bonds, mutual funds, futures, and options

---

Imagine waking up at six o'clock in the morning, throwing on your Reebok running shoes and Nike sweat outfit, and going into the kitchen to eat some breakfast. While gulping Minute Maid orange juice and eating Kellogg's cereal, you plan your exercise regimen and then quickly head to the gym in your Chevrolet van.

Without even knowing it, you've introduced five elements of Wall Street into your house—and most of America is just getting out of bed. Reebok, Nike, orange juice, Kellogg, and Chevrolet are all companies, or products, that are traded on Wall Street. That's right folks, Wall Street meet Main Street, because YOU are its proprietor.

This chapter will help answer some of the questions you have about profiting from the most talked about street in New York City (well, not literally, unless you collect sewer caps) and ways to create wealth for your future.

Making Sense of It All

When it comes to investing, you probably have millions of questions. Should you invest in stocks? Bonds? What about mutual funds? Should you invest for the long haul, or aim for a short-term horizon? Are you willing to accept a lot of risk for an even greater return? These questions are just the beginning.

Before you can select what you should invest in, you need to know what *type* of investor you are.

Creating Your Investment Profile

If you don't chart a clear course in your financial affairs, you'll face rough seas ahead. So ahoy, mates—time to create your personal investment profile. Keeping it simple, you can figure out your profile based on your risk tolerance, your return needs, your time horizon, and your tax exposure.

To assess your risk tolerance, ask yourself how much you can afford to lose. This factor is extremely important because of the severe consequences of taking on too much risk. If you understand what your risk tolerance is, you won't have to press the panic button because you've got yourself covered. The rule of thumb: If your investments are keeping you up at night, then sell. No investment, especially a risky one, is worth losing sleep over.

To determine what kind of investor you are, picture the worst-case scenario. Ask yourself how much you can afford to lose in a one-year time frame, then match it to one of the profiles below.

➤ You're a *conservative investor* if you can sustain losses of no more than 6 percent over a one-year period. That means if you have $1,000 invested and the markets take a tumble, you could withstand losing up to $60 without reaching for the Pepto-Bismol.

➤ You're a *moderate risk investor* if you can withstand losses in your investment portfolio of no more than 15 percent over a one-year time frame.

➤ You're a *high-tolerance-for-risk investor* if you can generally withstand losing between 15 percent to 26 percent of your portfolio in a span of one year. You fly by the seat of your pants and live moment to moment.

Your return needs make up the other half of the equation in the "risk/reward" profile. Once you determine your risk profile, you'll have a general idea of your reward, which is your return. Unfortunately, there is no investment that allows you to have your cake and eat it too. You can't earn a high return and protect 100 percent of your initial investment (your *principal*) without exposing your cash to the ups and downs of the financial markets. That's where the trade-off comes in. If you want to protect your portfolio as much as possible, you won't earn as much in a reward, unless you implement some defensive money strategies. Socking away a few dollars in a safe-money account, such as a money market account, for emergencies is a good example of such a defensive strategy. Traditionally, six to nine months' worth of living expenses should be earmarked for this account in case of emergency, such as a job layoff or disability of one of the household wage earners.

What are the trade-offs? First of all, if you want to protect your initial investment, you'll typically receive a lower return, usually in the form of a lower annual income (such as interest payments you receive from a bond investment). Secondly, there is a trade-off between income and growth. The more certain you are about your annual payment, the less risky the investment is and the lower the potential return in the form of growth.

Your time horizon directly affects your ability to reduce risk. For example, volatile investments, such as stocks, where prices fluctuate greatly over the short term, are considerably smoother over a longer time horizon. That's why diversification is so important; you're not putting all your eggs in one basket. If your time horizon is short, however, you can't be as effectively diversified across all the different types of markets.

Your time horizon begins when you start investing that first buck in your portfolio. If you are investing to save for a child's education, for example, you have already dictated your time horizon. It ends when you withdraw the money. So, what defines a short-term, intermediate-term, or long-term time horizon? Industry standards say that if you need the money within one to two years, you have a short-term time horizon. Two to five years constitutes an intermediate-term time horizon. And more than five years is long-term.

Finally, consider your tax exposure. It's difficult to figure out what your tax exposure is because the tax laws are constantly changing, as we saw with the Tax Reform Act of 1997. The bottom line in investing is what Uncle Sam says you get as leftovers—or in some cases, what you owe *him*. If you are in a high-income tax bracket, you need to be concerned with tax implications that seem to appear magically when you invest—including some obligations you incur. That's where timing comes into play.

To get a grip on planning your investment portfolio based on these four factors, look at Table 5.1 to see where you fall.

Fiscal Facts

Investing for income is *not* the same as *investing for growth*. When you invest for income, you are seeking a steady stream of payments. On the other hand, when you invest for growth, your aim is to try to have your money grow (sometimes referred to as "appreciate") over a longer time frame.

Table 5.1 Investment Factors at Different Life Stages

	Early Career	Middle Career	Late Career	Early Retirement	Late Retirement
Risk Tolerance	High	High	Moderate	Moderate	Low
Your Return	Growth	Growth	Growth	Growth & Income	Income
Time Horizon	Long	Long	Long	Interm./Long	Short/Interm.
Tax Exposure	Lower	Higher	Higher	Lower	Lower

Source: Adapted from American Association of Individual Investors, March 1993

53

The Pluses and Minuses of Taking the Plunge

You cannot get rich quick, no matter what anyone promises you. You can get rich slowly. That's why making money on Wall Street is all about thinking long-term. By investing in any of Wall Street's products—stocks, bonds, mutual funds, futures, and options—you have the potential to reap great rewards. In exchange for these rewards, you do take on risk. The often-quoted legendary trader Bernard Baruch coined a phrase that we're sure is on every investor's mind, "I'm not so concerned about the return on my money as I am about the return *of* my money!"

Of course, every investor wants the highest, assured return possible. But returns aren't certain—and neither is the future. But, if you keep the following adage in mind, it will get you started in your investment course:

> **Seek out investments that pose the greatest amount of return with the least amount of risk.**

What you consider to be the greatest amount of return depends on your investment profile. For example, you may favor shorting index futures to gain a quick buck and not care that you could lose all your money. On the flipside, your grandpa loses sleep every time there's an announcement that the Federal Reserve Board is meeting to discuss the country's state of the economy. Will they raise or lower short-term interest rates? No wonder grandpa, who doesn't like to bear much risk, keeps his money in safe, conservative money market accounts.

Whatever kind of investor you are, one strategy rings true if you want to spread, and possibly reduce, your exposure to investment risk. It's called asset allocation.

Here's how asset allocation works. Your portfolio's risk can be moderated by mixing stocks and bonds. They are both very different animals. Stocks are actually "claims" against real assets. When you buy stock, you are actually buying a piece (a share) of a company. Bonds, on the other hand, are debt that typically promise fixed returns. Because of their differences, the return on each tend not to follow similar patterns. Consequently, combining stocks and bonds moderates your portfolio's risk.

Of course, stocks and bonds are not the only two financial vehicles that make up an investment portfolio. Adding mutual funds to your portfolio, for example, helps allocate a percentage of your portfolio to another asset class.

The following tips will help you tackle and reduce your exposure to risks that are associated with investing your money:

➤ **Keep an eye on reports of reduced purchasing-power risk.** Simply, this is how much bang you can get for your buck. For example, what you buy for a dollar today will not buy you the same product ten years from now.

➤ **Keep your eye on market risk.** (*Market risk* is just being exposed to the ups and downs in the financial markets.) An increase in the amount of risk that the financial markets and our economy experience will cause any investment to decrease in value.

➤ **Maintain enough liquidity in your investment portfolio.** When an investment is *liquid*, you can easily sell it and get your money out of it. If you don't have enough investments that are fairly liquid, you run the risk of not being able to get at your money without a hassle, penalty, or loss. For example, if the market is topsy-turvy, you could be forced to sell your investment at a significant loss if you need the money immediately. If your investment is in real estate, it might be difficult to sell your house because there are no buyers. Therefore, you're stuck. Your investment is *illiquid*.

➤ **Monitor any type of inflation reports.** The uncertainty over future inflation rates, called *inflation risk*, can eat into your profit—and, in some cases, your principal! An investment that can't keep up with inflation will not be able to grow, leaving you with little purchasing power. The best indicator of inflation is the Consumer Price Index (CPI).

➤ **Watch for any changes in the business sector.** *Industry risk* is based on how the industry you've invested in is doing as a whole. The certainty of a business's ability to pay income, principal, and other returns due to investors may suffer if the company or the industry as a whole is not doing well. Some of the magazines, websites, and financial TV programs listed in Chapter 4 are good resources to monitor changes in the business sector.

Crash Course in Investing in Stocks

Most people think of the stock market when it comes to investing. This is probably because it has been around the longest and is the most talked about, not only on Wall Street, but Main Street. It can also be extremely profitable. Look back to 1987 where, in just one month's time between July and August, the Dow Jones Industrial Average soared 11 percent. Then came Black Monday, October 19, 1987, when the Dow fell more than 500 points, losing more than 22 percent of its value in a single day.

Talk about a "crash" course in investing in stocks.

Market events like this one have traditionally seduced investors to pull their money out of the market. The culprit? Fear. They became afraid to invest, and that is the biggest mistake to make, because if you don't invest in the market, you could be missing out on the opportunity of a lifetime.

Everyone should have some exposure to stocks, even a conservative 70-year-old couple. Historically, the returns on a portfolio of long-term

Fiscal Facts

A **security** is any type of investment product, including notes, stocks, and bonds.

Treasury bonds, those debt obligations issued by Uncle Sam, have been more volatile (that is, riskier) than a portfolio of 90 percent bonds and 10 percent common stocks. Stocks held alone are riskier than bonds held alone (remember the asset allocation, spread the risk around), but through the magic of diversification, you can add some stock to an all-bond portfolio and actually reduce the portfolio's risk.

Since 1926, the volatility of an 80 percent bond and 20 percent stock portfolio has been equal to that of a 100 percent bond portfolio. This helps explain why many investment advisers do not recommend a stock weight of less than 20 percent.

Of course, you cannot just throw caution to the wind and become greedy. That's mistake #2. If you're looking to sink your money into poor-quality stocks on dreams of getting rich overnight, you'll probably pay too much for them and lose your hard-earned savings. Greed is *not* good despite what was said in the '80s. It doesn't work in the '90s, nor will it in the new millennium. What *is* good is *learning as much as you can about your stock investments*—and the best place to begin is right here.

And Now, the Basics

The word *stock* is a shortened form of the phrase *common stock*. Common stock is a security that represents ownership in a company. When you buy stock, you buy *shares*, which represent a proportion of ownership in that company. In order for a company to offer common stock, it has to "go public," which happens when the company needs to raise money. This is known as an *initial public offering*. The next time the company wants to raise money, it conducts a *secondary offering*. Once a company is publicly traded, its stock can be bought through most brokerage and discount brokerage firms.

The Money Line

Shares are usually sold in round lots, *which are groups of 100. Less than that is an* odd lot. *To figure out how much ownership you have, simply take the amount of shares you own and divide it by the number of* shares outstanding, *which is the total amount of shares that the company has issued and are currently traded by the public. For example, if you own 100 shares of XYZ Company and there are 1,000,000 shares outstanding, then you own .0001 or 1/10,000th of the company. It won't get you the CEO's parking spot, but at least it gives you an idea of how common stock refers to ownership. To find out how many shares are outstanding, you can call a broker for a quote and ask for this information, or you can check the financial pages.*

Why invest in stock? The stock market boasts the best returns you can get on your money, if you keep it invested over a long time frame. Sure, there are bumps along the way, but if you average all the ups and downs of the stock market over the past 70 years, stocks have grown at an average 10.67 percent rate of return. Remember, there are ups *and* downs! Many times, investors park their money in stocks to receive dividends. Investors who buy common stock are hoping the company will generate profits so these profits can be distributed to shareholders. These dividends are distributed on a quarterly basis. You should know the four dates in the dividend cycle to ensure what you're entitled to...and when you will get it.

For cash dividends, the process begins with the declaration date, which is the day the board of directors announces that the company will pay a dividend. On this date, the company also declares the amount of the dividend payment and the record date.

Next is the ex-dividend date, which comes four days before the record date. On the ex-dividend date, the investors who purchase the stock for regular way (three-day) settlement are no longer entitled to receive the dividend. If you bought the stock on the ex-dividend day, you will not show up on the company's books as a shareholder until the day *after* the record date. Instead, the dividend is mailed to the previous owner. Typically, the market value of the stock drops by the value of the dividend when it opens for trading on the ex-dividend date.

Then comes the record date, when the company asks the registrar to provide a list of current shareholders so that the company knows who is entitled to the dividend checks. To receive the dividend, you have to be on the company's books as a shareholder as of this date. If you are not, you do not receive the dividend.

It all ends on the payment date, when the company actually cuts the dividend checks. This date is usually about two weeks after the record date, so as to give the company time to generate all the dividend checks.

Understanding this process will help you avoid unpleasant surprises. Of course, there are times when you can have your dividends reinvested, through a company's dividend reinvestment program (DRIP), for example, or in a mutual fund. This allows you to invest your cash dividends back into the security (that is, the stock or mutual fund) to purchase additional, fractional shares.

Asset Advisory

One of the best ways to tell how your investments are doing is to compare them to the *Standard & Poor 500*, which represents a "basket" of the 500 largest blue-chip companies in America. Many portfolio managers use this index, or *benchmark*, as a way to measure their performance.

Enter Uncle Sam

Not only can you receive dividends when you invest in stocks, but you have the potential to make a profit when you sell the stock. This profit is known as a *capital gain*. The difference between the price when you buy the stock and when you sell it is known as your *return*. How do you make a capital gain? *Buy low and sell high!* It's one of Wall Street's oldest and well-proven tricks of the trade.

Finally, the tax benefit comes into play when you invest in stocks. You do not incur a taxable event until you sell the stock. For example, even if you bought 100 shares of XYZ Company stock at $25 a share and it's currently trading at $100 a share, you don't have a profit *until you sell it*. That means you don't have a taxable situation to report to the IRS on your tax return (unless, of course, you receive dividends along the way). Until you do so, it is known as a *paper profit*.

When buying a stock, choose one that is consistent with your investment goals. The three major types of stock are described below:

➤ **Growth stocks**   Growth stocks are touted as one of the easiest ways to make money because the companies that issue them are built for growth. You can define a growth stock company as one that maintained faster-than-average gains in earnings and profits over the last few years and its future looks similar. The only difference within this category is that there are large growth stocks, medium-sized growth stocks, and small-sized growth stocks. Each type depends on company sales. Some examples of growth stocks include Xerox, Abbott Laboratories, McDonalds, and Eastman Kodak. Keep in mind that growth stocks tend to have higher p/e ratios than other stocks!

Fiscal Facts

When searching for a growth stock to invest in, check out the company's **price/earnings ratio** (the p/e). This tells you whether the stock is overvalued or overpriced. It's calculated by taking the price of the stock and dividing it by its earning per share. In mid–summer 1998, the average p/e ratio was 28. The higher the p/e, the more the stock has a potential to be overpriced. *Value Line Investment Survey* is a great resource for this type of information.

Just as growth stocks can increase in value, they can also sink in value. To minimize the risk involved with these volatile stocks, invest in large growth stocks and hold them as part of the long-term section of your investment portfolio. Some growth stocks offer some pretty decent dividends, too.

➤ **Income stocks**   If making a steady income off your investments is more important to you than earning a large capital gain some time down the road, consider investing in income (dividend-paying) stocks. Examples of these stocks include electric, gas, and telephone companies. Although income stocks tend to be less volatile than growth stocks (and don't have as much price appreciation at times), a stock with solid dividend increases can pay more over time than bonds.

➤ **Growth and income stocks**   With these stocks, you can benefit from the price appreciation and also collect income through dividend payments.

Some examples of growth and income stocks include DuPont, Emerson Electric, and Dun & Bradstreet. Growth and income stocks, at times, may not be able to capitulate on as much of a growth rate as some pure growth stocks.

Other types of stocks are available. These include *cyclical* stocks, which are considered to "ride the economic highway" because the companies involved depend on the state of the economy. *Initial public offerings* are another opportunity, though they can often be a bit risky because the company is a new publicly traded stock. There are also *penny stocks*, which trade for $5 a share or less.

The ideal situation would be to enter the stock market when it's rising and exit when it's falling, but it ain't that easy. All too often, small investors bail out after the market has started to fall and jump in after it has started to rise. Because the stock market movements are jerky, investors, particularly new ones, should always plan on investing in stocks for the long-term—no jumping in and out. The bottom line? Unless you have a crystal ball and can predict the future of the market, investing in good, solid growth stocks will typically win hands-down over the long haul.

My Name Is Bond, U.S. Bond

Just as companies issue stock to raise money, they can also issue bonds. Stock, as you know, represents ownership in a company. Bonds, on the other hand, represent an IOU from the company to you. As a bond investor, you are *lending* your money to the corporation or government. This "loan" requires the bond issuer to pay you the amount borrowed plus interest over a stated period of time. Bond investments are also known as fixed-income investments because they typically pay interest to bondholders on a semi-annual basis. This interest is considered income, hence the name.

The following sections explain common bond jargon and the types of bonds available. Before you read on, however, learn the cardinal rule of investing in bonds:

Interest rates and bond prices move in directions opposite to each other.

Watch Your Wallet

To realize a profit from cyclical stocks, you must time your buys and sells carefully (or you can diversify your portfolio to help smooth out the ride). *Buy* cyclical stocks when their well has just about run dry but their situation can't get any worse (buy low), and *sell* cyclical stocks when they are enjoying record profits and everything seems hunky-dory (sell high).

Asset Advisory

There are about a zillion financial newsletters offering stock recommendations and theories from gurus about the financial markets. The Select Information Exchange, (212) 247-7123, gives you a list of more than 50 different financial newsletters to choose from. They offer a package of 20 trial subscriptions for only $11.95.

Understanding Bond Jargon

When you invest in bonds, make sure you know the following:

➤ The *maturity date* is a fixed date when the amount of money borrowed by the company must be paid back to you. Although there is a stated maturity date, you don't have to hold it until maturity. You have a right to sell it whenever you want. (Hint: What you want to do is sell it for a profit. Remember, "Buy low and sell high?")

➤ The amount of the original investment is the *face value* or the *par value*. This amount is equal to the amount of money you agreed to lend to the borrower/company. You can, however, buy bonds that are more than the face value, known as a *premium,* or less than a face value, known as a *discount.*

➤ In exchange for these companies borrowing your money, they promise to pay you back your *principal* plus interest. This interest is based on the bond's *coupon rate*, which is either a fixed rate that pays you the same amount of interest every year (typically every six months) or a floating rate, which fluctuates and is based on some pre-determined index.

You can always buy a bond and wait until maturity to get your money back. Or you can buy a bond and hope to sell it at a price higher than the one at which you bought it, even *before* its maturity date. This is practicing the art of buying low and selling high.

You see, even though bonds have a face value, they also have a *current market value,* which fluctuates. What determines the current market value? The current level of interest rates. Suppose you owned tens of thousands of dollars' worth of 30-year government bonds that were issued in the early 1980s with coupon rates averaging 13 percent—some even as high as 15 percent—that matured in 2010. These specific bonds are still earning that coupon rate/interest today, which makes them pretty attractive, considering the average coupon rate on long-term Treasury securities were below 7 percent as of mid-summer 1998. Because you own these attractive bonds that pay high rates of interest, other investors (like us) would be willing to pay you a higher price for the bonds. Why? Well, as of this writing, we can only go out into the market and get 6.92 percent for the same type of bond. We'll sacrifice our dollars now to get that higher coupon rate.

Whether you practice the strategy of waiting until maturity, or selling your bond out in the market before maturity, you should be aware of the *current yield* of a bond. The current yield is the return (expressed as a percentage) that the bond would earn in the current marketplace. To calculate this percentage, you divide the total market value of the bond by the annual interest payment, and multiply that total by 100.

Let's plug in some numbers. Suppose you bought a bond with a $1,000 face value and a 10 percent coupon rate at a price of 90. This means that you paid 90 percent of the face value of the bond. Because the bond has a face value of $1,000, the current market value is equal to $900 in this example. ($900 is the current market value. Depending on the direction of interest rates, this current value may be different *tomorrow*.) The annual interest paid on this bond is equal to the coupon rate multiplied by the face value, which would be $100 in this case (10% × $1,000). Your finished equation would be ($100 × 900) × 100, which equals a current yield of 11.11 percent. The current market value depends on what interest rates are and the overall bond market.

If you decide to hold onto your bond until maturity, you should concern yourself with another type of yield: the *yield to maturity (YTM)*. This is a measure of the total return you can expect to earn if you hold the bond until maturity. It's difficult to calculate, but you should ask your broker what it is before you invest your money. In a nutshell, it takes compound interest into account.

Uncle Sam and Friends: Bond Types

When the government borrows money, it borrows from *you*, the investor. You invest your money in the debt instruments of the U.S. government, which are known as *Treasury bills, Treasury notes*, and *Treasury bonds*.

Each of these debt instruments has a reputation of being a safe investment because each is backed by the full faith and credit of the U.S. government. No other bond investment (with the exception of Ginnie-Mae securities, which are bonds issued by a government agency that pools mortgages together) can make this claim. In exchange for the degree of safety, Treasury investors receive lower interest rates than those on comparable bonds of different issuers.

Treasury bills are considered a discount security because of how they are issued. T-bills don't pay any interest. You purchase the security at a discount from its face value and at maturity you receive the full face value. The difference between the discount price you paid, and what you receive at maturity, is the interest payment. Treasury notes and bonds are different: They are considered coupon securities, pay interest semi-annually, and pay the face value at maturity. The interest you receive is federally taxable, but exempt from state and local taxes.

Typically, the longer the time until maturity, the higher the coupon rate you will receive. Why? Because in exchange for having the use of your money for a longer period of time, the borrower is willing to pay you a higher rate. Here's how the length of maturities stack up for each Treasury security:

➤ **Treasury bills** are bought in maturity dates of three-month, six-month, and one-year maturities. They are sold by the Treasury department at weekly auctions to all types of purchasers. Three- and six-month T-bills are auctioned

Watch Your Wallet

Although tax-free bonds sound like the best deal for everyone, people in a tax bracket of 28 and 33 percent or more have the most to gain from this investment. If you're in a lower tax bracket, you could make more from corporate bonds. To evaluate the numbers for yourself, check out Chapter 26, "Tackling Your Taxes."

off every Monday, and one-year T-bills are auctioned off every month. The minimum investment is $10,000.

➤ **Treasury notes**, typically issued in two- and five-year increments, are auctioned during the third week of every month. The minimum investment for two- and three-year T-notes is $5,000, although additional increments can be added.

➤ **Treasury bonds** have the longest maturities: Ten years on up. T-bonds are auctioned in February, May, August, and November. The minimum investment is $1,000.

Here's a quick rundown of the other types of bonds:

➤ **Municipal bonds**   The interest payments you receive on these government bonds are exempt from federal taxes. In fact, in some states, they're also exempt from state and local taxes.

➤ **Government agency bonds**   Even though these bond securities are issued by a government agency, they are NOT backed by the full faith and credit of the U.S. Government—just the issuing agency—and carry a "moral obligation." Depending on the agency, most minimum denominations are as high as $25,000 per bond. The three best-known agencies are Freddie Mac, Ginnie Mae, and Fannie Mae. Each was created to pool together a large quantity of mortgages and produce *mortgage-backed securities*. How do they do this? They purchase them from banks and savings and loans. These mortgage-backed securities offer higher yields (and thus more credit risk) than Treasuries. Even though these agencies are borrowing money from investors with the promise to pay them back on the maturity date plus interest, the interest income you receive can fluctuate.

➤ **Zero-coupon bonds**   This type of bond is named such because they are issued with no coupon rate at all. Zero-coupon bonds are issued by the Treasury department (Treasury zeros), corporations, municipalities, and government agencies. You buy these bonds at a deep discount from their face value. You make money off the increase in the bond price as it approaches maturity. Keep in mind, however, that even though you don't receive any semi-annual interest payments, you *are* taxed on these interest payments at all levels.

➤ **Corporate bonds**   The biggest attraction of corporate bonds is the higher yields they offer. You may find that they offer two more percentage points than a Treasury security of the same term. Of course, more risk is involved because they are not backed by the full faith and credit of the U.S. government. Minimum denominations? $1,000 face value per bond and on up.

Asset Advisory

For the best review of the different types of bonds, read *The Complete Idiot's Guide to Making Money on Wall Street*—a definite must for investors!

➤ **Junk bonds** A junk bond is simply a corporate bond that offers a higher yield. Technically, junk bonds pay such high rates of interest that the corporation may not earn enough money—either through sales or bottom-line profits—to cover the interest payments investors should receive every six months. That's why they're often called *high-yield bonds*. Note that you should be wary of credit risk. Follow the ratings given by S&P and Moody's, often quoted in sources like *The Wall Street Journal*. Junk bonds come from issuers who are less credit-worthy. There is a danger they could not repay the principal and interest during tough economic times.

Getting Started with Mutual Funds

Mutual funds allow investors to pool their money into a large fund organized by investment professionals. Investors own shares that represent stocks and bonds in several different companies. The number of shares you own depends on how much money you put in. The more you invest, the more shares you can buy. You don't need a trillion dollars to get started, either. Some mutual fund companies allow you to begin with as little as $50 a month. Plus, you can have access to your money all the time. And you can even invest in mutual funds that don't charge *any* sales charges. Mutual funds also tend to be less risky because they build on the idea of diversification.

Mutual funds come in two basic flavors. *Load funds* are those that charge you a sales commission. (Keep in mind, however, that just because a load is being charged does *not* mean you'll earn a better return.) *No-load funds* do not charge their shareholders any sales commissions, but other expenses are sometimes assessed, such as management fees or advertising expenses.

Table 5.2 shows a payoff comparison on a $1,000 investment in a no-load versus a load mutual fund. Assume a 12 percent return on a no-load fund versus a fund with an 8.5 percent load. As the table demonstrates, no-loads are usually the best way to go.

Table 5.2   No-Load Versus Load

Timing	No-load	Load	Difference
Investment less load	$1,000	$915	$85
Value at one year	$1,120	$1,025	$95
Value at five years	$1,762	$1,613	$149
Value at ten years	$3,106	$2,842	$264
Value at twenty years	$9,646	$8,826	$820

Source: Taken from The Complete Idiot's Guide to Making Money on Wall Street

When a No-Load Isn't a No-load

You know that if you buy a mutual fund through a broker, you will pay a commission—a load. You can buy a mutual fund directly from the company and not pay a load, which is a good, cost-effective move. But, some no-load mutual funds are not *pure* no-load funds; they can hit your pocketbook with some fees and charges. Some of these not-so-obvious fees are:

Watch Your Wallet

If a mutual fund salesperson approaches you to invest in a company's mutual funds, ask what's in it for them. Does he or she receive a commission? Make sure you check out the company's performance history, going back five to ten years if possible.

➤ **12b-1 fees** (also known as *12b-1 plans*) are charges that cover marketing and promotional costs. These fees range anywhere from .25 percent to 1 percent of the fund's total assets each year.

➤ **Expense ratios.** These are typically expressed as a percentage of total investment, which shareholders pay for mutual fund operating expenses.

➤ **Fees for reinvesting your dividends.** These fees can really wallop your wallet. Make sure you ask your shareholder rep if this type of fee is involved. You want to avoid funds that charge it.

➤ **Management fees.** This pays for the portfolio manager of the fund. Typical management fee expenses run about .5 percent.

➤ **Back-end load funds** have been hyped as no-load funds, but they are *not*. Even though all your money goes to work for you in the beginning when you invest, you get nicked with a "penalty load" if you withdraw your money before a certain time. The longer you keep your money invested in the fund, the less of a back-end load is assessed.

Because no-load doesn't always mean no-*fee*, you must be careful. The total cost of fees is deducted from the fund's earnings. One mutual fund company that touts its funds as no-load charges its shareholders up to 1.5 percent of their investments to open an account, stating it's a "portfolio reimbursement fee." Table 5.3 lists some other sneaky fees and the funds that go with them.

Table 5.3   Funds and Fees

Name of Fee	Amount	Funds Assessing Fee
Transaction	1 to 3% of investment	Five Vanguard Funds*
Portfolio transaction	.25% of investment	Vanguard Index Total Stock Market

Name of Fee	Amount	Funds Assessing Fee
Account opening/ close-out	$5 to $75	Approximately 30 funds
Portfolio reimbursement	1.5% of investment	Four DFA funds (foreign funds)

* Vanguard's Emerging Markets portfolio charges 2 percent when you buy into the fund and 1 percent when you sell. Four other Vanguard funds—International Equity Pacific, Extended Market, Small Cap, and International Equity Index—each charge 1 percent up front.

One final note: All this talk about no-load fees may make you believe a broker who tries to tell you that the marketing costs and other expenses associated with the fund are *really* what keep no-loads from being no-loads. Teach the lug something new; explain that *no-load means there are no sales commissions*. And then steer clear of the sales pitch. You can do your own homework and save hundreds of dollars in commissions!

Mutual Fund Selection Secrets

Keep the following factors in mind when selecting a mutual fund:

➤ **Select no-load funds whose objectives coincide with your own.** Are you looking for growth? Income? Or both? You can narrow your mutual fund search by matching the investment objective of mutual funds available to your own investment objectives. For example, if you are a Nervous Nellie who can't sleep a wink because of the ups and downs in the stock market, don't plunk down all your money in an emerging market fund that invests solely in Third-World countries.

➤ **Look for mutual funds that can provide at least a 3- to 5-year track record.** You should be able to select your mutual funds based on performance history. Five-year track records will tell you how well (or poorly) the fund did in a variety of environments—when interest rates were high or low, when the stock market was up or down, and when our economy was in an inflationary period or a recession. For a quick review of economic cycles, look at Chapter 9.

➤ **You don't have to limit yourself to just one type of mutual fund.** Even though a mutual fund offers diversification, you can invest in more than one. Fifty? Well, forget it. The experts would label that as mutual fund overkill. You can diversify your mutual fund portfolio by choosing a growth fund, an income fund, an international fund, and perhaps a bond fund. If you divide your money among three or four different types of stock funds, you'll always have some money invested in the most profitable sector of the market.

➤ **Buying last year's biggest winner is foolish.** Don't even think about it. Maybe the portfolio manager got lucky. Instead, stick with a fund that is a steady performer instead of moving in and out of funds trying to catch the waves.

➤ **Enroll in an automatic investment plan with at least one of your mutual funds.** This program's awareness is increasing in the world of the wee investor. As little as $50 a month can be electronically debited and transferred from your bank account to your mutual fund account. Because you are doing this on a regular basis, you can take advantage of any dips in the share price. This is known as *dollar-cost averaging*.

Where to Go for More Info

If you're in the market to invest in mutual funds, several sources of performance information are available. Only, with more than four thousand mutual funds to choose from, how can you cut through the murk?

One option is to check out *Morningstar Mutual Funds*, a twice-monthly newsletter published by Morningstar, Inc. It is considered to be the most informative and user-friendly survey of mutual fund performance, covering almost 7,000 funds total. *Morningstar* rates each fund with a star rating system on a scale of 0 to 5; five stars is the highest honor given to a mutual fund. Each fund receives a star (or no stars) depending on a combination of past performance and the risks involved. The newsletter is available on a three-month trial basis for $55—and it's free at your local library reference desk. A dozen newsletters are published by Morningstar, so to find one that fits what you're looking for, call toll-free anywhere in the U.S. (800) 876-5005 or write to Morningstar, Inc., 225 W. Wacker Drive, Chicago, IL 60606.

CDA Weisenberger is a rating service that tracks the performance of almost 6,500 funds in its reports *The Mutual Fund Report* and *The Mutual Fund Update*. These reports are updated monthly and are available in a newsletter report format or in a software package. Call (800) 232-2285 or write to CDA Weisenberger, 1355 Piccard Drive, Rockville, MD 20850 for more information.

Asset Advisory

For those cyber-space junkies out there, America Online makes available Morningstar's information on the mutual funds it covers.

The *Value Line Mutual Fund Investment Survey* also tracks performance information on two thousand mutual funds, providing in-depth coverage and analysts' opinions on the equity of each and fixed-income mutual funds for subscribers. This report is also available in your local library, but if you would like more information about subscription rates, call (800) 284-7607.

Standard & Poor/Lipper Mutual Fund Profiles is a quarterly survey, evaluating past performance on the 800 largest load and no-load mutual funds. The cost is $132 for an annual subscription (that's four reports), and additional subscription information is available if you call (212) 208-8000.

One Last Word About Loads

Just when you thought you knew the difference between a load and a no-load fund, a new twist to the load fund industry develops.

Load funds, as you know, average a 4 percent sales fee. But, depending on what load fund it is, the 4 percent load may not be charged at the same time. Many times, when you buy a load fund—and we're not recommending that you necessarily do so—the fund company offers Class A, Class B, and Class C shares. As if the industry wasn't complicated enough!

Class A shares are front-end loads—meaning when you invest $1,000 in a 4 percent load fund, your $40 is automatically taken out before it's invested. The sales fee was charged at the beginning—the "front"—of your investment. Class B shares assess a 1 percent annual charge to your account—that's its sales fee. Class C shares are back-end loads, so the load is charged when you sell.

The bottom line? Stick with no-load funds for the least costly investment strategy.

Futures and Options for High Rollers

When you invest in futures and options, you must be prepared for a bumpy ride. The futures and options market is not for the amateur investor. You can make a lot of money in these financial markets, but you could also lose more than your shirt.

Betting on the Futures

The best way to describe what futures are is to look on the shelves or in the freezer of your neighborhood grocery store. Orange juice, wheat, sugar, and corn, to name a few, make up the products that investors "bet" on in the futures market.

Unlike stocks, bonds, and mutual funds, there is no ownership or IOUs—just exponential rewards if you win big—but you have to know how to play the game. A *future* is simply a contract in which a "pre-selling" of the commodity is taking place at an agreed-upon price today for delivery in the future. Each delivery date is different because they are pre-set by the financial futures exchange. The months in which the contracts expire are known as the *spot months*.

The people who do not own the underlying commodity, but rather, bet on the rise and fall in the commodity prices, are known as *speculators*. As a speculator, you try to achieve a profit from the ups and downs in the price of the contract. Speculators invest in futures contracts either to buy goods they do not want or to sell goods they have no intention of delivering. If you own the underlying commodity (like a farmer who owns his wheat crop and is trying to sell it) you are known as a *hedger*. The floor traders at the exchange are known as *scalpers*.

Watch Your Wallet

Investing in commodity funds takes a big chunk out of your initial investment because of the high commissions that these portfolio managers earn. But that's not all, additional fees—sometimes as high as 6 percent of managed assets—are assessed. That's on top of high commissions, sometimes as much as 10 percent. This type of investment is for high rollers who have the money to invest and don't mind the ups and downs of the futures market.

Even though you are not obligated to come up with a lot of start-up money to invest—usually about 5 to 10 percent of the contract's value—it doesn't make the futures market any less risky. In fact, if your contract is dropping in value, you may have to put up additional money to keep your position—definitely not an investment for the beginner!

If you're interested in the futures market, but don't want to risk as much money, you may want to invest in mutual funds that invest in commodities. These are called *commodity funds* or *futures pools*, and there have been some surprising profits in these. The performance of these pools varies widely from fund to fund and from year to year. Usually, they will do well when the markets move sharply upward or downward and the pools are invested on the side that will profit.

If you want more information about the different commodity funds available to you, contact *Managed Account Reports*, the newsletter that tracks the commodity funds industry. For a sample copy, call (212) 213-6202.

Know Your Options

If you want to protect your investments, consider dabbling in the options market. Options, like futures, have an expiration date and can help protect your portfolio. *Call options* allow investors the right—but not the obligation—to buy the underlying security (typically stock) at a set price (the strike price) for a particular period of time. *Put options*, on the other hand, give you the right—yet not the obligation—to sell the underlying security at a set price for a particular period of time.

Many times put options are used if you are feeling bearish and expect to profit from falling stock prices or to protect your investment portfolio, kind of like insurance. Let's say you own 100 shares of XYZ Company stock. You hear rumors that third-quarter earnings reports are not expected to be all that great, so you're worried about the stock price taking a hit because of the news. Instead of selling all your shares (because, of course, you are investing for *long-term* price appreciation, no matter what bumps happen along the way), you can purchase insurance. The price drop is just short-term, so you don't want to sell your stock, but you still need to protect your shares against any decline.

To protect your position, you could cushion the blow in case XYZ Company stock price drops. Here's how. Assume you bought XYZ Company stock at $25 a share a few years ago. The current price is $36, but you've noticed it starting to pull back a bit. Instead of selling your shares, you can buy a put option (*not* a call option) because it will give you the right to *sell* 100 shares of XYZ stock at whatever the strike price is—no matter what the current trading price is.

Plug in some numbers. If you bought an XYZ put option with a strike price of 30 for $200 (quoted as $2, which is the *premium*) and the XYZ stock price falls to 30 or below, you have two choices:

➤ You have the right to *exercise* (sell) your option by selling your shares of your underlying XYZ stock for $30 a share, no matter what the current stock price is.

➤ You can hold onto your underlying stock and "close the position," meaning, sell your put option. If you did this, you would make a profit because your put option would be *in-the-money*. It has to hit the price of 30 and keep going down for you to be *in-the-money*. If, however, the option never dropped to 30 before expiration, your option would expire worthless. Your loss? The total amount you paid for the option, which is the premium. But it's insurance, so consider yourself protected!

Fiscal Facts

Think of **call** and **put** options this way: Since you buy call options when you think the underlying market is going up, remember call options as "calling up" someone. Buy put options when you think the market is going down, as in "put down" your foot. Call up...put down. Remember that.

The Least You Need to Know

➤ If you want to make money on Wall Street, first you have to know what your investment profile is. Make sure you take into consideration your risk tolerance, your financial goals (and dreams!), your tax exposure, and your time horizon (which is when you need the money).

➤ The way to make money in investing is to buy low and sell high.

➤ If you are investing in stock to receive cash dividends, you must be a shareholder on the record date.

➤ You can make a good return off growth stocks if you invest for the long term.

➤ Interest rates and bond prices move in opposite directions.

➤ Mutual funds usually involve less risk because your investments are diversified. Make sure you look for a no-load fund that doesn't involve a lot of extra fees.

➤ Futures and options are not for the faint of heart.

Secrets of the Investing Rich

In This Chapter

➤ Learning the #1 secret: Pay yourself first

➤ How to make money the old-fashioned way—and keep it!

➤ How millionaires spread their money around

Oh, if you could only win the lottery. Then you would be rich, right?

Wrong.

Sure, a winning lottery ticket, especially if it's a million-dollar Powerball ticket, means instant wealth. But a whole new set of financial issues comes with the package—tax implications (Uncle Sam wants his fair share), relatives you haven't seen in ten years, and a new set of wants and needs that a year ago seemed like a pipe dream. The perception of winning the lottery is that you now have all this money to spend, which is why many lottery winners wind up broke or file bankruptcy because they spend it all.

Spending money may seem like a pastime of the wealthy, but there are always sound financial decisions made prior to each purchase and, of course, a handsome investment portfolio doesn't hurt either.

We cannot deliver you a winning lottery ticket, but we can share with you some of the secrets to getting rich. This chapter will show you a few of the tried-and-true methods to creating wealth for your future.

Call Yourself "Bill"

By now, you have learned how to make the decision to manage your money more effectively, get out of debt and stay there, and set up a personal financial plan that will enable you to reach your financial goals. So what is the common denominator among the three?

You!

You are learning about personal financial planning and investing for yourself—not your neighbor, your Uncle Moe, or your Great Aunt Bertha. You are adapting new— and smart!—financial habits that will help you reach your financial goals. But the most important habit is to pay yourself first.

Treat yourself as if you were a monthly bill. Call it the "Pay Yourself First" category. By doing so, you begin to practice the art of self-discipline. By earmarking your personal "bill," you are creating your financial future without even realizing it.

There is one requirement: Do it before Friday night out with the boys, your daughter's Girl Scout dues, or monthly health club dues. Pay yourself every time you get paid. If you have direct deposit, many employers offer the feature of having a percentage of your paycheck directly deposited to a second bank account if you wish. By implementing this feature, you automatically pay yourself first.

Your New Routine

You can make money the old-fashioned way—no, not by inheriting it, although that doesn't hurt, but rather by dollar-cost averaging your way to wealth.

Dollar-cost averaging is a smart investment strategy. All you do is make fixed, regular investments in a stock or any type of mutual fund, even if the market is rising or falling. This strategy works in your favor, no matter what the market does.

Asset Advisory

The money you pay yourself doesn't have to be a lot. In fact, even if you sock away $10 a week for the next year, you'll have $520 by the end of the year. Over time, and depending on how you invest this money, it can grow into thousands of dollars. You have a number of financial products to invest in, as you learned in Chapter 5.

When you dollar-cost average, you have a variety of choices including all different types of mutual funds and stocks, such as in a dividend reinvestment program. No matter which investments you choose to dollar-cost average your way into, make sure you choose your investment on the basis of your financial goals, your risk-comfort level, and your age.

For example, when you buy shares in an equity mutual fund and the price rises, you buy fewer shares. When the price falls, however, you buy *more* shares. Plus, over the long haul, the average cost of your share will be less than the average price or market price when you sell.

You can start with $100. One hundred dollars a month, invested over a 12-month period, is $1,200. Easy enough. But oh, how it can grow. You'll be amazed at how $200 a month can grow, too. If you want to see how dollar-cost averaging is practiced, look at Table 6.1.

Table 6.1   How to Get There from Here

Time of Investment	Amount of Investment	Price Per Share	How Much Do I Own?
January 15	$200	$10	20.00
February 15	$200	$12.50	36.00
March 15	$200	$14	50.29
April 15	$200	$13	65.67
May 15	$200	$13	81.05
June 15	$200	$9	103.27
July 15	$200	$10	123.27
August 15	$200	$11.25	141.05
September 15	$200	$13.50	155.86
October 15	$200	$15	169.19
November 15	$200	$14.50	182.98
December 15	$200	$14	197.27

Total number of shares:	197.27
Total Investment:	$2,400.00
Total Value of Portfolio:	$2,761.78
Net Profit:	$361.78

And that's just for one year! It's never too late to start an investment program by dollar-cost averaging. And it works! If you dollar-cost averaged your way to wealth by investing in the Dow Jones Industrial Average beginning at its highest peak in 1929 (before the Crash) and purchased at the *highest* price every year until the mid-1960s, you would still be rewarded more than *300 percent* on your money.

You Better Shop Around

Banking is an integral part of your overall financial plan, but, unfortunately, as we consumers push for convenience, banks in turn charge higher fees. It's up to you to shop around for a bank that not only meets your financial needs, but also charges you less for doing so.

It sounds as easy as pie, but few people realize how much money they're paying these rich cats in blue suits. Shop around! Heck, you kick a few tires when you buy a new car—and that's not even an investment (it almost never goes *up* in value)! Why pay a bank an extra charge if you're a left-handed welder or if you wear your hair in a bun? Okay, we're exaggerating. But these tips will help you reduce some of your expenses, and that will enable you to put more of your money to work for you in your investment game plan. For more information about the banking industry, have another look at Part 3.

Keep these points in mind when shopping for a bank:

➤ Look for free checking. It shouldn't have a monthly maintenance fee; there should be no penalty fee if you drop below a certain balance, and no transaction fee—no matter how many checks you write.

➤ Don't go with a bank that charges "foreign" ATM transaction fees. (Not those in Versailles, France, but those at a rival teller across the street.)

➤ Skip the bank that hits your account with an activity fee. Some of us aren't big check writers. Instead, if you write fewer than three checks per month, opt for a Money Market Account. More interest!

➤ Look for low bounced-check fees. This is a killer. Even if you don't bounce any checks, there are times when you may deposit someone *else's* check and it will bounce—and *you'll* get hit with the $22 charge!

They've Done Their Homework

Ask anybody for advice—believe us, they'll give it to you. Everyone loves to hear himself talk, especially if it's about a hot investment he made a bundle on. Asking for advice is okay, but you can't bet the farm on it. What you can do is your homework. That includes subscribing to a few investment newsletters that offer advice from some Wall Street professionals.

The Money Line

For all you online addicts out there, there's a wealth of investment information available for everything from analyses of individual companies to chat rooms where you can get the scoop from other investors. On America Online, you can tap into the Motley Fool, Sage, and theWhiz.com. All provide key investment and personal finance information. You can also join in chats or post your money questions to message boards and have investment gurus respond.

But there's a problem. There are a ZILLION newsletters and even more financial websites out there with editors touting their latest recommendations—and not all of them work. So how can you tell the best from the rest? In Chapter 4, we paved the way through the money jungle to get you started. One recommendation was to follow *The Hulbert Digest*, a monthly compilation of the good, the bad, and the ugly in the newsletter business. But now it's time for a more advanced strategy that will enable you to save a few bucks and sample, sample, sample!

Contact Select Information Exchange at (212) 247-7124; for only $11.95 you get a package of *twenty* different financial newsletters. Once you choose which newsletters you want, call the newsletter company and ask for *next month's* issue as a sample or free copy. If they won't provide one, see how much their trial subscription costs.

Also, review the financial TV programs and magazines listed in Chapter 4 as additional resources for research.

Some Exposure Across the Big Blue Doesn't Hurt

We live in a global economy. Many of the products we buy are imported. Many U.S. companies have more than half of their revenue generated from overseas sales. Socking away a portion of your investment dollars—no matter how old you are—to invest in world financial markets is a common investment strategy in the '90s, and it can be *very* rewarding. But there are some short-term *and* long-term ups and downs.

Citing a short-term example, several years ago, in 1993, international mutual fund investors celebrated an average 40 percent return. But there are also some major blows that world financial markets have dealt to investors. In the 1970s, many funds invested in Mexico lost 75 percent of their value.

Allocating a portion of your investment portfolio to international (non-U.S. companies) or global (both overseas and U.S. companies) investing is a smart move, as long as you do two things:

➤ Understand the biggest risk involved with international and global investing: currency risk.

➤ Maintain a long-term time frame for your international and global investments (at least five years).

It used to be that all the world's currency exchange rates were tied to the U.S. dollar. But that was eliminated in the early 1970s, which created currency risk if you were to invest or exchange your money for local currency abroad. Currency risk is simply the risk involved when you convert foreign currency back into dollars or into other currencies. The reason this is risky is because the rate at which the currency is calculated (converted) is determined by the current state of world economies. If France is in a recession, their francs may be worth more (or less) in U.S. dollars, depending on how our economy is doing and vice-versa.

For example, if you're an American tourist in Japan, you will quickly learn that the number of Japanese yen you get for $1,000 may be different tomorrow than it is today. That's because the currency fluctuates in value, and when put into the conversion process, your end result (how much yen you get for your American dollars) will change.

But that doesn't mean you should keep all of your money in the good ol' USA. It would be a mistake to avoid investing abroad, since so many investments, such as mutual funds, have made it so easy to do so. You should, however, still monitor your international and global investments, and add international or global funds (because of the diversification) to a portfolio of U.S. stock and bond funds. This strategy helps reduce the amount of money the entire portfolio will lose in today's global economy. So before you park your pesos overseas, make sure you do your homework!

Also, stashing your cash in foreign markets is a long-term process. That's why, if you want to iron out the volatility, you should plan for the long haul. Ask yourself how long you can leave that money there. If you need it right away, stick your money into a less aggressive investment. Unless they are highly skilled as day-traders in foreign currency markets, overseas investing is not for short-term investors.

Don't Just Buy—Diversify!

By allocating your money into several different investments, you reduce your risk. Think of it this way: If you put one dozen eggs into one basket, and a few in another, and so on, and then you drop one basket, only a few are cracked and the others are intact.

To see how this theory works with investing, pretend you have $10,000 to invest. You've done your homework and have come up with a beauty of an investment: a company stock that created the gadget that takes the salt out of the ocean. You found they have great management, their good-debt-versus-bad-debt ratio is healthy, and historical performance numbers are appealing. You sink all of your $10,000 into this stock and wait for it to take off.

Watch Your Wallet

The last thing a retired person should be doing is experimenting, especially with growth funds. Only 20 percent should be allocated to that category. You can balance the remaining amount with 20 to 30 percent in growth and income funds and the rest in income funds and money market funds.

And boy, does it! Two years later, the stock has increased by 50 percent. You have roughly $16,000 including reinvested dividends. And then tragedy strikes. The company president jumps ship, the money they lent to that small country off the coast of Chile *won't* be repaid, and earnings estimates are seven times below Wall Street's expectations. The stock drops 25 percent in value in one day, and another 25 percent the next. Your eggs are smashed to pieces!

That's where the beauty of diversification comes in. Financial research shows that if you own 20 to 25 stocks, you won't get burned by one bad investment.

Let's use another example. If you take that $10,000 and split it up among several types of equity mutual funds (growth or aggressive growth), an international equity mutual fund, and maybe a short-term bond fund, you will reduce your risk, especially if one fund zigs while the others zag. This is practicing the art of diversification!

Reduce Your Exposure to Uncle Sam

This may be the biggest, most overlooked secret. Of all the retirement programs available to Americans, only 60 percent of Americans admit to contributing to some type of retirement savings program. Why?

Because they want instant gratification. Save money for the future? B-O-R-I-N-G. Put an extra 100 bucks in a savings account to earn 23 cents? Big deal. Credit cards, however, have cured short-term boredom, enticing men and women to charge now and pay later. Unfortunately, this bad habit dissuades us from socking away any money for the future because we're trying to climb out of debt today.

Turn your thoughts of instant gratification upside down by knowing that money inside a retirement account—such as a 401(k) plan, a company pension plan, or an IRA—grows and compounds *without* getting hit by Uncle Sam. The only time you pay taxes is when you take the money out, which is when you're typically in a lower income-tax bracket anyway.

The benefits? If you save $2,000 a year at six percent for 30 years in a regular savings account, you'll have close to $120,900 after paying taxes. However, if you sheltered your $2,000 each year in your IRA at six percent, your savings increases to almost $168,000 because of the tax-deferred feature.

Build a Portfolio of Mutual Funds

Investing in more than one mutual fund is a great way to diversify your portfolio. But the question always remains: How many mutual funds are too many? Like a nervous five-year-old taking swimming lessons for the very first time, just getting your feet wet is a better beginning than jumping straight into the deep end.

Getting your feet wet doesn't necessarily mean putting all of your money in low-risk mutual funds. That strategy would not be practicing diversification, and you wouldn't be lowering your risk. Low-risk funds may have a lot in cash periodically, which may not be what you want when you diversify. You lower your risk by mixing stock funds, bond funds, U.S. and overseas funds, and money market funds. Diversification offers the idea that a gain in one fund offsets losses in another. In financial mumbo jumbo, you should create a portfolio of funds that have a low "core correlation" with one another.

The first step is to look at your whole investment picture; decide what you're trying to achieve. Make these goals reachable, not astronomical. Next, set parameters to determine how much money you can afford to lose and how much money you plan on keeping "liquid" (safe). This will help you decide how risk-tolerant you are. Sorry, folks, but a lot of the players in the mutual fund industry don't do enough to inform or protect the investor against the risks associated with fund investing. Your goal is to look for the highest return with the lowest risk.

Of course, the higher the reward, the greater the risks. A good way to follow mutual funds to see how they rate on risk is to read *Morningstar Mutual Funds* (800/876-5005). (A three-month trial subscription is $55, but it is probably available in your local library or, if you have access to the Web, log onto their website at www.morningstar.net.) Experts tell us that people should be educated about risk. If you think you're going to lose 100 percent of your money and stick it in a money market fund that earns *less* than inflation, that's just as bad as investing in a fund with a 20 percent fluctuation rate!

Your age will also determine your selection of mutual funds. If you're fairly young, you can be more aggressive in your investment approach. Keep 70 to 80 percent in aggressive investments, such as growth and aggressive-growth mutual funds. Pre-retirees should still maintain a portion of their mutual fund portfolio in growth investments, though they should pull back to allocation percentages around 40 percent. Balance the remaining 60 percent between safer investments—for example, a small percent in money market and some in growth and income funds.

Consider DRIPs

A DRIP stands for *dividend reinvestment program*. Its theory is that if you drop a little bit of money on a steady, consistent basis into stocks—paying little to no commissions—you'll benefit from dollar-cost averaging through a DRIP program.

DRIPs build wealth slowly through accumulating small shares of a stock, enabling you to bypass a stockbroker and high commissions. If the company does charge a fee, it's quite nominal. In fact, around 100 of the 1,200 companies that offer DRIPs offer investors the advantage of purchasing company stock at discounts of three percent to ten percent below the current market price of the stock.

It only takes a few bucks to get you started and as little as $10 for *optional cash payments*, which allow you to purchase additional shares. What if the stock is trading at $60 and you want to send in $30? No problem. You will receive a fraction of a share—in this case, half a share. These fractional shares continue to build, along with your future OCPs, and you receive that fractional part of the dividend.

Typically, you must be a shareholder of record (you must own at least one share) to enroll in a DRIP. This share must be registered in your name, not the brokerage firm's name, and the certificate must be sent to you.

Asset Advisory

If you're thinking about enrolling in a DRIP, buy the single share necessary to start your account through a deep discount brokerage firm. That way you can save almost 70 percent in commissions and avoid full-service brokers.

Once you receive the certificate, contact the shareholder services department at the company that offers the DRIP program (not all companies do) to enroll.

To find out which companies offer DRIPs—and those companies that are now joining the No-Load Stock sector, which allows investors the opportunity to go *directly* to the company, no initial share certificate needed—subscribe to the bible of the DRIP industry, *The Drip Investor*. For more information, call (219) 931-6480.

If You Don't Need the Full-Service, Use a Discount Broker

Full-service brokers will charge you up to $4 just for sending you a trade confirmation. Makes the increase in postal rates look miniscule by comparison, doesn't it? Like banks, full-service brokers may charge you an inactivity fee of close to $50 if you do not generate at least $100 in commissions in one year. And—get this—account holders can get penalized with a $50 maintenance fee just for having the account. That's like paying someone $50 a year just so they can hold onto *your* money. No way, José!

Instead of the full-service broker, opt for a discount broker. You still get research reports, but no advice. And no ghastly fees, either! The dynamic trio of full-service brokerage firms are Quick & Reilly (800/672-7220), Charles Schwab & Company (800/435-5000), and Fidelity Investments (800/544-8888).

Know When to Sell Your Investments

The hardest part about knowing when to invest is knowing when to sell. Typically, when you buy a stock, for example, you should have a target price in mind of when to sell it. After all, why are you buying it in the first place? The only way you can profit is if you sell it at a higher price than you bought it.

Successful investors know that they don't necessarily have to sell their stock if it doubles in price from where they bought it. If a stock doubles in price, who's to say it won't do it again? What you should do is continuously reevaluate your stock using the same reasons you bought it in the first place (good earnings, good management, competitive product, and so on).

The Least You Need to Know

➤ *Pay yourself first!* Before any other financial obligation, allocate a small portion to an investment for yourself and your financial future.

➤ Investing in several different investment products is a good way to reduce your risk. This is called *diversifying your portfolio.* Just make sure the investments coincide with your objectives.

➤ Stay informed about your investments. That means doing your homework!

➤ Investing in retirement accounts will help you plan for tomorrow, as well as reduce your tax exposure. Plus, it's a smart financial strategy because tomorrow will be here before you know it. Just do it!

Investing Safely with Uncle Sam

It's a chancy thing, pumping money into the sometimes-high-flying stock market, or investing in bonds, gold, foreign currencies or windmill farms. There's lots of money to be made—IF the investment performs and doesn't fall on its face. Because if it does, you'll be out the original cash you put up, along with any possible earnings on your money. That's the bottom line in the risk-versus-reward money game; you could make a mint if things go right, or lose your shirt if they don't.

The cautious, conservative crowd doesn't invest that way. They play it safe. They plunk down their money for investments that may not earn nearly as much as the stock market does, but they sleep better at night knowing their money is fully protected by the federal government. Getting only 5 or 6 percent on a bank account, U.S. Savings Bond, or money fund may appear to be a dinky return next to the 15 percent you can get from Amalgamated World's stock shares, but when you wake up in the morning, you know the money's there! This chapter looks at four of the basic investments that are fully backed by Uncle Sam, and explains how to build a 100 percent safe portfolio.

Only Two Choices: Your Money's Safe or It Isn't

Learn this right off the bat, because it's critical: When it comes to how safe your money is, there are, broadly speaking, only two kinds of things to invest in:

1. Investments that are guaranteed and protected by the federal government, such FDIC-insured accounts, and others, such as Treasuries, that are backed by the full faith and credit of Uncle Sam.

2. Investments where you could lose your shirt if things don't pan out the way you hope. That includes stocks, bonds, mutual funds, and a host of other places where you can park your cash. Sure, millions of people have made tons of money from these investments, but there's no guarantee of how they will perform in the future. In other words, it's a risk-versus-reward situation; the riskier an investment is, the more you might make—and vice-versa.

This chapter deals with only the first type of investing (#1, above), where you'll *never* take a financial bath, because you kept your money in one of these four places:

1. Treasuries
2. U.S. Savings Bonds
3. FDIC-insured bank savings and CD accounts
4. Government-only money funds

He Who Laughs Last...

When the economy is great and the stock market is roaring, your friendly broker laughs at anyone who puts his money in a low-paying instrument such as a 4.5 percent bank CD account. The broker pushes you into stocks, bonds, and funds instead. But when the Dow Jones average plunges by 6 percent (as much as 500 points in a day, as happened in mid-1998 when some billionaires lost a couple of billion in 24 hours), the broker doesn't laugh any more. He panics. Suddenly, every business writer in the country begins reporting on how safe U.S. Treasury investments are, by comparison. Investors begin calling high-yielding banks around the country to ask about FDIC-insured CDs and U.S. Savings Bonds.

Ask yourself this question: What would happen if there was a real economic catastrophe around the world, and the market sank by 65 percent with the Dow plunging from, say, 8,000 to 2,800? Some gloom-and-doom prophets think that might happen one day. Millions of people's savings would be wiped out, but any money you had stashed away in a safe, federally-protected account would look like a lifeboat.

Enter the subject of safety. With a safe, U.S.-backed investment, you won't become a millionaire overnight, but you'll sure sleep better.

Many consumers tend to forget that advice, especially when times are good with the economy. But older folks remember when banks closed during the Great Depression in the early 1930s, and all of us are aware that hundreds of savings and loans went belly-up in the late 1980s. Even though the banking industry fully recovered in the '90s and began making record profits, some people are still nervous about whether their institution is safer than the one across the street.

Don't Overdo the Safety Angle

Want to know how foolish some people are? They're creatures of habit, taught as kids to "save in a nice, safe place for a rainy day." So they keep more money in bank passbooks and Money Market Accounts that only pay a measly 2 percent on average, than they keep in CDs paying 4 to 5.5 percent! Why? Because the basic savings account with a little old passbook is what they had when they were young. It's their security blanket.

The Money Line

According to the Federal Reserve, in 1998 consumers had deposited a total of $1.537 trillion in low-paying savings versus $960 billion in higher-paying CDs. By contrast, Americans had $8.5 trillion invested in stocks, $2.83 trillion in bonds and $4.89 trillion in mutual funds.

Solid as the Rock of Gibraltar

If you're looking for a safe way to double your money, consider folding it over once and putting it in your pocket. Of course, you really don't earn a 100 percent return this way, but you can count on keeping all of your principal.

There's another strategy to keeping your money safe: Invest in Uncle Sam. The ol' red, white, and blue puts its full faith and credit in the types of investments its financial arm, the Treasury Department, issues, known as Treasury securities.

The Treasury issues debt instruments (securities) in the form of Treasury bills, Treasury notes, and Treasury bonds to finance its deficit spending. Maturities on these securities range from three-month Treasury bills to five-year notes to 30-year Treasury bonds.

That's right—what Uncle Sam is doing is borrowing money from consumers. So, when you invest in any of these Treasury securities, you are loaning the government your money.

Watch Your Wallet

It's foolish to keep too much money in a 2 percent savings account when you could easily earn 5 to 6 percent in a federally-insured bank CD, Treasury, or U.S. Savings Bond.

Asset Advisory

Treasury bills, notes, and bonds are debt obligations of the U.S. government, issued through the Treasury Department. These securities are auctioned at different times when you can bid on them. You can now buy Treasuries for as little as $1,000, and your investment is super-safe because it is guaranteed by the full faith and credit of the United States of America.

Currently, there are close to five-and-a-half-trillion dollars worth of Treasury securities outstanding. That's what it takes to help fund America's debt.

One of the biggest reasons people invest in Treasury securities is because anyone who invests in them will receive their money back when promised. Guaranteed. There really isn't any credit risk when you invest in Treasury securities. That's why the interest rates paid on Treasuries (remember, they're nothing but loans from consumers to the government) are lower than those on comparable bonds from different issuers, such as a corporation.

Of course, Treasuries do experience a lot of price volatility. When interest rates rise, bond prices fall. That means the value of your bonds fluctuates either higher or lower than the original purchase price, depending on the general direction of interest rates.

Getting a "Discount" or a "Coupon"

Treasury bills are considered a discount security because they don't pay any interest. You purchase the security at a "discount" from its face value, and at maturity (the day that the money you loaned the government has to be paid back) you receive the full face value. The difference between the discount price and the face value received at maturity is the "interest" earned on the investment.

Coupon securities, such as T-notes and T-bonds, pay interest semi-annually and the face value at maturity. The interest payments you receive are federally taxable, but exempt from state and local taxes.

How to Open a "Treasury Direct" Account

Buying Treasury securities directly from the Fed, by setting up what's called a Treasury Direct account, is the easiest and most cost-effective way to purchase them. You don't have to live near the Fed or one of its branches either, but you can go there if it's convenient. Call the Bureau of Public Debt at (202) 874-4000 and punch in 1, then 241 to get your documents. Now people with Treasury Direct accounts can also buy

Treasuries over the Internet at the website we mentioned, or by phone at (800) 943-6864. You can arrange to have the Treasury deduct the cost of your investment electronically from your bank or brokerage account, or mail them a certified or cashier's check.

The Money Line

Treasury bills don't "pay interest." Rather, they're sold at a discount off the face value that appears on the security, such as paying $500 for a $1,000-face-value T-bill that you redeem for that amount at maturity.

Going, Going...

Buying a Treasury is a lot different than buying a CD from a bank. Everything is explained to you in simple English at a good Internet website (www.publicdebt.treas.gov.) maintained by the U.S. Bureau of Public Debt.

These are the basics:

Treasury securities are auctioned off (sold) from the Federal Reserve Bank, or a Fed branch, at more than 150 auctions a year. They're not sold by the Treasury Department in Washington, D.C., but that Department does issue a press release about one week before each auction announcing the auction date, amount to be sold, and other details. The Internet address above gives you all the details about how to get information on the auctions in advance.

To purchase a bill, note, or bond, you put in a non-competitive bid at one of the Treasury auctions, which means you accept whatever average rate you get for the securities you want to buy. After you buy a Treasury, your purchase will be noted as being in book-entry form, which means that you don't receive the certificate, but rather are "on the books" with the Treasury department and your interest payments are sent directly to your home.

Table 7.1 Purchasing T-Bills, T-Bonds, and T-Notes

Three-month and six-month Treasury bills are auctioned every Monday; the one-year T-bill is auctioned every four weeks on Thursday (thirteen times a year).	Minimum amount: $10,000
Two-year and five-year Treasury notes are auctioned toward the end of each month; three-year and seven-year Treasury notes are auctioned quarterly, in early February, May, August, and November.	Minimum amount: $5,000
Treasury bonds with maturities of 10 years and 30 years are auctioned on the second month of each calendar quarter. Note: If you wanted to buy a 25-year T-bond, you would buy a 30-year T-bond that is five years old.	Minimum amount: $1,000

But I Don't Have Ten Grand!

The government has made it easier for small savers to get in on the Treasuries action. Instead of needing $5,000 or $10,000, as in the past, now you only need as little as $1,000 to buy a short-term or intermediate-term Treasury security. Before, longer-term securities of five years or more required only $1,000, but the downside was that some investors didn't want to tie up their money that long.

How much can you earn with Treasuries? Generally, a trifle more than what the average bank will pay you on a CD with a comparable maturity, but not as much as what the highest-paying banks will offer (see Chapter 11).

Asset Advisory

It's easy and inexpensive to buy Treasury securities directly from the Federal Reserve by setting up your own "Treasury Direct" account. The cost of your investments can be deducted electronically from your bank or brokerage account, or you can mail a certified or cashier's check.

Try Treasury Money Funds as an Option

There's another way to chase higher yields and keep your money safe. That's by investing in Treasury-only money funds. Most of them yield up to 5 percent, or about double what the typical bank Money Market Account pays, and $2^1/2$ times what an interest checking account pays. Also, when a Treasury-only money fund yield is quoted, it has already taken into account its fees and expenses—unlike a bank which quotes yields before any fees and charges are assessed. And, you don't pay any commission with your fund.

Other advantages of Treasury-only money funds include exemption from state and local income taxes and check-writing features, although minimum amounts of usually $100 are required for each check. By contrast, your earnings on bank CDs are taxable.

If you're looking for Treasury-only money funds, consider the following:

➤ American Century Capital Preservation Funds, (800) 345-2021, which had a total return of 5.06 percent for the first quarter of 1998, invests exclusively in U.S. Treasury securities with remaining maturities of 13 months or less. Get online and pull up their website at www.americancentury.com.

➤ Fidelity Spartan U.S. Treasury Money Market Fund, (800) 544-8888, is ranked #3 out of a total of 18 Treasury-only money market funds for its 10-year average annual return (5.39 percent). For more information, contact Fidelity's website at www.fidelity.com.

➤ Vanguard Treasury Money Market Portfolio, (800) 662-7447, requires a minimum $3,000 initial investment and if your non-retirement account balance falls below $2,500, the portfolio will deduct a $10 fee—unless you have other Vanguard accounts totalling $50,000 or more. Find them on the web at www.vanguard.com.

➤ Weiss Money Management, a money management firm in Palm Beach Gardens, Fla., touts its Treasury Only Money Market Fund as an alternative to bank checking. The fund offers a minimum initial investment of $1,000 and automatic investment plan with a $50 minimum. For more information, call toll-free (800) 289-8100.

For the latest, highest-yielding Treasury-only money funds, and the basics of how all types of money funds work, check out IBC Financial Data's website at www.ibcdata.com.

Any Savings Bonds Today?

Historically, U.S. Savings Bonds are the most patriotic of all investments. Uncle Sam has sold them through big promotions and publicity to finance previous war efforts, such as during World War II. Parents and grandparents purchase bonds to sock money away for children's college tuition, and in these cases, the interest may be tax-exempt. And the best part is that these conservative investments, though they only pay about what long-term bank CDs offer, are backed by the full faith and credit of Uncle Sam.

The most popular is the Series EE bond. But the newest version is an I-Bond, so-called because the rate is partly tied to the inflation rate, which we describe in this chapter.

Besides safety, a big benefit is that your interest earnings are exempt from state and local taxes. And you can defer paying federal income tax on the interest until you cash the bond, or until it stops earning interest in 30 years. In markets such as Detroit, that have stiff state and local taxes, the savings bond can be an advantageous investment.

How the Rate Formula Works

How Series EE Savings Bond rates are calculated every six months can throw the unknowing investor for a loop, but it's not that difficult.

➤ The rate changes twice a year, on May 1 and November 1.

➤ The rate is based on the average of the six-month Treasury bill for each of the three months before May 1 and November 1, multiplied by 90 percent. In other words: If during the three months prior to the next May 1 rate change, the six-month T-bill was at 5.45 percent, 5.50 percent, and 5.70 percent, respectively, the new savings bond rate would be 4.995 percent. Here's how:

First month T-bill rate	5.45%
Second month T-bill rate	5.50%
Third month T-bill rate	<u>5.70%</u>
	= 16.65
divided by 3 =	5.55% average
	<u>× .90</u>
	= 4.995%

So, when you buy a Savings Bond that earns interest for 30 years, every six months, the rate you get on the bond will change, based on the formula above. You may cash the bond anytime six months after the date you bought it. The amount printed on the bond is its "face value," or denomination. Your purchase price is 50 percent of the face value amount (for instance, a $50 bond will cost you $25) but if you hold the bond until maturity, you'll be paid its face value.

Using the formula we just gave you, we'll show you how Savings Bond rates changed in recent years:

Table 7.2 Savings Bond Rate Changes on May 1

	Old rate	New May 1
Series EE Bonds after May, 1997	5.59%	5.05%
May, 1995–April 1997	4.53	4.47
May, 1994–April 1995	4.00	4.00

Where to Buy Bonds

Series EE is the only type of Savings Bond you can buy for cash. Purchases are usually done through a bank, or in denominations of at least $100 via a payroll savings plan where you work. Don't expect your bank to jump for joy when you tell them you want to buy a Savings Bond. Why? The bonds compete directly with the bank's own CDs. No wonder you never see banks advertising bonds, even though they're every bit as safe as CDs, and why the Treasury Department is puzzled that more consumers aren't aware of them.

The Money Line

Savings Bonds are exempt from state and local taxes, and you can defer paying federal income tax on them until the bonds are cashed. They can be bought through a bank or a payroll savings plan in denominations of at least $100.

Tax Savings for You—IF the Money Is for Junior's College

Here's a tip: The interest you earn on Savings Bonds is eligible for a special federal income tax exclusion when you use the bond redemption proceeds to finance higher education. The bonds must be registered in the name of the taxpayer (or taxpayer and spouse) for whom the child is a dependent. If the bonds are issued in the name of the child, or the child as a co-owner, they're not eligible for the tax exclusion. Also, the cost of the college tuition must be greater than the amount (principal and interest) of the bonds you're redeeming to pay for tuition.

P.S. You can buy up to $30,000 (face amount) worth of bonds in a calendar year.

"I" is for "Inflation"

In 1998, the government gave the average Joe an opportunity to buy a U.S.-guaranteed investment that protected him against inflation. They started selling Savings Bonds indexed to the Consumer Price Index, or CPI, in denominations as low as $50.

I-Bonds, as they're called, have face values of $50, $75, $100, $200, $500, $1,000, $5,000, and $10,000. Instead of bearing the familiar faces of our Founding Fathers, such as George Washington, Thomas Jefferson, and John Adams, they carry the likeness of more modern heroes such as Albert Einstein and Martin Luther King.

The rate you earn on I-Bonds comes in a two-part combination: First, the rate the government pays on the most recent auction of five-year Treasury notes, and second, the rise in the Consumer Price Index adjusted every six months. Another difference is that while Series EE Savings Bonds, as described earlier, are sold at half their face value (for example, a $50 bond costs $25), I-Bonds are sold at their full face value.

But like the Series EE, the interest on I-Bonds is tax-deferred until the bonds are cashed, or if the money is used for college tuition provided the taxpayer meets certain income limits. If you cash in either type of bond within five years after purchasing it, you incur a three-month interest penalty.

The I-Bond's biggest downside? When the U.S. inflation rate isn't rising, neither is the rate on the I-Bond. And when deflation is in the wind, you could earn less as the CPI-tied advantage goes up in smoke.

Where to Go for Information

One expert source on these investments is Savings Bond Informer (800-927-1901), a Detroit-based company run by an ex-Federal Reserve man, Dan Pederson, who offers bond holders a customized report that projects rates, values, dates of changes, and accrued interest over the next two years and five years. Cost ranges from $15 to $69 per report, depending on the number of bonds involved. Savings Bond Informer also has an over-the-phone consultation service, and its descriptive brochure is free.

FDIC Protects Your Bank Deposits Up to 100 Grand

After the big debacle of savings and loans dropping like flies in the late 1980s and early '90s, you'd think that by now, everybody would understand federal insurance protection A through Z. Wrong. There are still a lot of misconceptions about how the Federal Deposit Insurance Corporation (FDIC) works. This will simplify it for you:

The "Rule of 1's": Here's the easy way to remember it: FDIC insurance covers one person at one institution for up to $100,000, including principal and interest. That last part is important. If you deposit $100,000 in a CD earning 6 percent for one year, at the end of the year you'll have $106,000 in the account, right? The $6,000 in interest *won't* be protected because FDIC's insurance limit is $100,000.

But if you deposit only $92,000 at 6 percent interest, the account will earn $5,520, so at the end of the year there will be a total of $97,520 in your account. Every single dollar, including the interest, will be insured because there will be less than $100,000 in one person's name at that bank. *Note*: Credit union deposits also are insured up to $100,000, by the National Credit Union Administration (NCUA).

Which bank products are (or aren't) insured: At FDIC-insured banks and NCUA-insured credit unions, the deposits that are protected include passbook accounts, statement savings accounts, Money Market Accounts, checking accounts, and CD accounts. Mutual funds sold by banks are *not* FDIC-insured, even though some banks may try to deceive you by saying, in the same breath, that they will sell you a mutual fund and that, "We're a member of the FDIC." Repeat: Your mutual fund will not be protected by Uncle Sam.

IRAs are insured separately: Let's say you have several savings and CD accounts at one bank, plus an Individual Retirement Account at the same institution. The IRA is insured separately for $100,000 by the FDIC. So, for insurance purposes, the amount in your IRA won't count toward the money you have in savings and CDs. It will have its own $100,000 protection.

How to beat the $100,000 insurance limit: Believe it or not, by creating different kinds of joint accounts and trust accounts, it's possible for a family of four to have a total of $1.4 million of FDIC-insured protection at the same institution. Read Chapter 4 to see how it's done! *Tip*: Lots of people think the FDIC $100,000 limit applies to a person's total bank investments, regardless of how many institutions they keep their money in. Not so. The key is the $100,000 *per-institution* wording in the "Rule of 1's" (above).

So Really...How Safe ARE Banks?

Compared with a couple of decades ago, most U.S. banks today are almost as strong as Fort Knox, thanks to ringing up record profits (often at your expense through low savings rates, high credit card rates and stiff fees). Way back in the late '80s, as a result of mismanagement and bad loans, 1 bank in 120, and 1 thrift in 200, were going down the tubes. Then things got a whole lot better. There were 13 total failures in 1994, 5 in '96, 1 in '97 and only 4 mid-way through '98.

Recently, the failure rates were as low as 1 in 3,000. In fact, nine out of every 10 banks in the country were given a top three-star safety rating by the respected independent research firm of Veribanc, Inc., Wakefield, Mass. "Today," says Warren Heller, Veribanc's director of research, "so few institutions are having difficulties, those that are in trouble often can hide in anonymity."

But if you're the kind of person who'd rather be safe than sorry, call Veribanc at 800-442-2657 and, for $10, get a safety rating on any bank, savings bank, thrift, or credit union for $10 over the phone. A second outfit's rating costs only $5. You can also get more in-depth reports for $25 or $45, or a list of the top "Blue Ribbon" banks in the country for $35.

Watch Your Wallet

Don't let yourself get lulled into a false sense of security! While it's true that hardly any banks fail any more, that's because the industry has been making money hand over fist through outrageous fees. The banking customer still pays in the end. (See Chapter 12 for ways to avoid some of those fees.)

The Least You Need to Know

➤ You could wind up in the poorhouse if your uninsured investments take an extra-bad turn for the worse.

➤ The higher the potential reward, the greater the risk.

➤ Treasury-only money funds pay double what banks pay you on average Money Market Accounts.

➤ Interest on savings bonds may be tax-exempt if the proceeds are used to finance higher education.

➤ Your FDIC-insured bank deposits are protected up to $100,000 per person at the same institution, and you can insure more savings at a different bank.

Part 3
Banking Fundamentals

Everybody—probably including you—has a bank account. But just about everybody is also frustrated by how banks are gouging their pocketbooks. Low rates on savings. High rates on credit cards. Fees and more fees, on everything from ATMs to talking to a live teller. While you're being nickeled-and-dimed to the poorhouse, the banks are making a ton of profits off your accounts. Ironically it's the little guy who can't afford it, who's getting clobbered the hardest—not the well-heeled customer who maintains big account balances. Meanwhile, the banks continue merging like mad, meaning less personalized service for you as cold, impersonal mega-outfits take over, close branches, and lay off thousands of employees.

This section shows you how to fight back and keep more of your cash in your pocket. It tells how banks set their rates, how to avoid fees and get the best deals on checking accounts, CDs and credit cards. You'll learn how to spot the tricks and traps beforehand, and the key questions to ask before you open an account. But we don't stop with the basic secrets. We tell you how to kick the 2-percent savings habit that millions of people fall into, and where to find safe, federally insured CDs that pay three or four times more!

Most important, you'll learn the danger signals that tell you it's time to kiss your old bank goodbye and find a better place to keep your money.

Chapter 8

Top Money-Making Secrets Your Friendly Banker Won't Tell You

In This Chapter

➤ How banks make a bundle by nickel-and-diming you with fees and charges

➤ How bank mergers give your pocketbook the shaft

➤ Why banks sometimes drag their feet in raising or lowering rates

➤ Why you're being pushed away from tellers and toward ATMs

➤ Why the little guy—not the well-off customer—pays the bills

Bank profits keep going up and up—more than $50 billion a year at last count, including $2 billion in ATM fees alone. So how come they keep slapping you with higher fees and paying you next-to-nothing on your savings? Because the public knows zilch when it comes to understanding how and why banks operate the way they do. They don't know, they don't complain. It's all a person can do to balance a checkbook and hunt for high savings rates and low borrowing rates. There's a method to the banks' madness when they lure you to automatic tellers and charge outrageous interest on credit cards and loans. And they don't bother to tell you how all their big mergers are shorting you on the bottom line.

Banks have to make money to stay alive. But you can keep more of that money in your pocket if you learn some of the banker's innermost secrets. This chapter explains some of the key secrets in simple English.

How Banks Stay in the Black

Banks come out ahead when they rent your money (savings accounts and CDs) at one price, then peddle that same cash to someone else in the form of loans (credit cards, auto loans, and mortgages). Look at the bank as though it were a little one-room building with two doors—one in front, the other in the back. You deposit your savings at the front door, the bank marks it up, then lends the money to folks lined up at the back door to borrow.

One big reason many institutions went bust more than a decade ago was that they loaned money to home buyers at very low rates, such as six or seven percent. They got locked into those cheap loans for years and years. That was okay—as long as they only had to pay their savings customers five percent on savings. The banks pocketed the difference, which is called their "spread." But then, in the early '80s, the federal government started something called "deregulation," which permitted banks to pay whatever rate they wanted on savings accounts.

Boom! By mid-1984 CD rates shot up to 10 percent and higher. Suddenly, it cost banks more to get your money at the front door than what they were earning off those long-term loans at the back door. Banks began to lose their shirts! Economic wizards were predicting that it would cost taxpayers anywhere between $80 billion and $500 billion to bail out the sick industry.

As the country rolled into the 1990s, you heard less and less of that kind of talk. Why? Because bankers went to school, so to speak, learned from their mistakes, and made darn sure they protected themselves in the future. When interest rates began to plunge, banks cut their savings rates faster than they cut loan rates. That's called *managing the spread*. The result was that their profits got bigger and bigger. In addition to financing the enormous banking bailout by paying more taxes, you picked up the tab by earning less on your savings and paying more when you borrowed.

But that's only half the story. Banks began going fee-crazy. They raised virtually all their old fees on accounts, and invented a slew of new fees, which have been driving up their profits even higher.

Asset Advisory

Banks don't advertise this fact, but you *can* negotiate a better deal on fees, and sometimes on your interest rate. The decision about which fees to waive may be up to the branch manager. Competition from mutual funds and brokerages is what has made this wheeling and dealing possible. Credit card fees and rates are a particularly good place to start bargaining; competition in this area is fierce!

Fees and Charges: The Other Money-Makers

Fees and charges have been growing like weeds. These ugly little demons keep taking more and more out of your wallet (see Chapters 9, 10 and 12). How do banks get away with it? Simple. Customers focus mostly on interest rates, not on fees. The bank slips in a higher fee here, a new little charge there, and you hardly notice it.

Thirty bucks to bounce a check in some cities? Yes. Fees have become so important to banks that they're now considered "profit centers" all by themselves. In fact, one banker stood up at a big convention a few years ago and proclaimed that his institution had suddenly discovered they were making money hand-over-fist by charging people whose accounts were overdrawn.

The big secret is this: Today banks use sophisticated new computer techniques to identify which customers are profitable and which ones aren't. The Joe Doaks who maintains a low balance, but keeps pestering live tellers for service, is slapped silly with an extra fee every time he makes a transaction. But Mrs. Gottrocks, who has accounts in the six figures, doesn't pay a dime to do her banking. The name of the game is soak the little guy, and give the freebies to the well-heeled customer on whom the bank makes money.

> **Bank-beater secret:** Ask your bank for a copy of its fee disclosure statement. Match it step-for-step against your personal banking behavior; switch to a low-fee outfit if necessary (see Chapter 12).

Big Bank Mergers: Everybody Wins but You

By now, your bank has certainly been gobbled up one or two times by a big bank merger. Mighty Megabuck swallows Friendly Federal and runs giant ads telling you how great this marriage will be for your pocketbook. "More ATMs, more resources, more branches, two great institutions uniting...blah, blah, blah."

Here's what usually happens, aside from the CEOs of the two banks personally making a few million bucks from the merger:

1. Megabuck, to prevent Friendly Federal's nervous customers from fleeing out the door, dangles a few incentives and freebies to keep them happy temporarily, like a special CD rate or a discount on a loan rate.

2. All the other banks in the area, smelling blood, swoop down on Friendly Federal's customers and offer their own special incentives to steal away that business. Because of this competition, more savings rates in the market go up.

3. A couple months after the merger, Megabuck announces it's closing 80 branches that overlapped with Friendly Federal's locations, and laying off 1,500 employees.

4. Six months after the merger, after the temporary rate competition dies down, Megabuck begins cutting all its CD and Money Market Account rates. It also raises some of its personal loan rates a tad. Since mighty Megabuck is the market leader, other outfits in town do the same thing.

Result: The little guy got stiffed from the big bank marriage, and is worse off now than he was before. The example we gave you may vary by situation, but we've seen it happen enough times to know that there's more truth in it than make-believe.

Bank-beater secret: When you hear your bank is merging, start shopping around for a smaller community bank or credit union, and don't believe all the promises that Megabank will feed you.

How Banks Work the Rates

This section explains some tricks that banks use to make the interest rates work to their advantage.

First, banks often push long-term CDs when interest rates are low, and short-term CDs when interest rates are high. Remember that little front-door/back-door example of how banks make sure they mark up your money to earn their profit spread? Well, there's another sly maneuver. Banks want to rent your savings money at the lowest possible cost (see Chapter 11).

Let's say CD rates have been rising for several months. You're all excited to see a five-year account that used to earn 5 percent interest now paying 6 percent. That's a whole extra 1 percent, right? So you're tempted to grab the deal.

But suppose the bank believes that interest rates will rise over the next year. By then, the five-year CD will be paying maybe 7 percent. If you lock in at 6 percent now, you've bilked yourself out of that extra 1 percent. On a $10,000 five-year CD, you'll lose $500 by not waiting. Here's why: By opening the account now, you'll earn $600 a year for all five years, or a total of $3,000 in interest. But if you buy the CD next year instead, when the rate is up to 7 percent, you'll earn $3,500 on the same $10,000 investment. In other words, you'll earn $500 more.

Keep in mind that the reverse is true when rates are falling. Banks then promote short-term CDs more heavily. If you lock up a long-term account, you'll protect yourself with a high yield for a longer stretch of time.

Fiscal Facts

The **prime rate** is the bank's benchmark rate. Supposedly it's what banks charge their most favored business customers when they borrow. The little mom-and-pop store that doesn't have shiny credit will be charged a higher rate—such as 2 or 3 percent above the prime rate.

Bank-beater secret: Buy short-term CDs when rates are rising; go long only when rates are declining.

Second, banks drag their heels in raising savings rates after they increase their prime rate. The banks' prime goes up or down depending on how well the economy is doing (see chapter 11). That rate influences most of the bank's other interest rates, including savings and personal loans. In a perfect world, you'd expect that if the prime rate increases or decreases by, say, one-half of a percent, then your savings and loans would change by the same amount, right?

Wrong. That's not how it works. What typically happens is this: When the prime jumps by a half-percent, banks boost your CD rates more slowly. It may take months for your CDs to increase by as much as the prime. That way, banks can increase their profit by lending at the higher rate for a while before increasing the amount they have to pay you in savings and CD interest. Score one for the banks.

> **Bank-beater secret:** When the prime rate goes up, take out the loans you need immediately. Go short with CDs until the prime goes down.

Third, banks pay you zip on interest checking, money market accounts, and passbook savings. For some strange reason, millions of Americans keep stashing more than $1 TRILLION in low-paying savings accounts and even lower-interest checking accounts. These naive folks could make a bundle more by shifting to CDs. Chalk that up to old-fashioned American savings habits (see Chapter 11).

Banks are euphoric over that idiotic consumer behavior. They're getting the cheapest money of all through the front door by peddling 2 and 3 percent savings accounts that cost them way less than CDs. Then, they mark up the money and lend it out—often at a rate that's more then ten times what the money cost them!

Here's how banks play the "spread." These are the differences in average rates some banks pay on savings and checking accounts versus personal loans and investments:

Loan	MMA	Int Chkg	New Car
Chase Manhattan Bank, NY	1.95%	0.75%	8.60 %
Wells Fargo, San Francisco	2.02%	1.01%	10.25%
First National, Chicago	2.02%	1.25%	8.00%
Bank of America, San Francisco	1.77%	0.75%	9.50%
PNC Bank, Philadelphia	2.00%	1.00%	9.25%

Source: BANK RATE MONITOR

> **Bank-beater secret:** Don't keep a dime more than you need in low-rate MMAs and passbooks. Figure how much you won't have to touch for *X* length of time; put that money into higher-paying CDs for that period of time.

Why Banks Try to Steer You Toward ATMs

When ATMs first came out, it cost nothing to use them. Then, it cost 25 cents, then 50 cents, then a buck, then $1.50. That's if you used a rival bank's machine; many banks still offered the service free to their own customers. In the mid-1990s, the "double-whammy" ATM charge came along. The rival bank also hit you with a $1.50 fee for using the ATM, so it cost you *a total of $3* to make a machine transaction. In other words, the banks want their cake and want to eat it, too. First you're told not to bother a live teller or you'll get hit by a fee of $1 to $3 at some banks. So you run outside to their machines. But once you get into the ATM habit—wham!—you get nailed there, too. Not once, but twice on the same transaction!

Multiply that by millions of customers using their ATMs three or four times per month, and you get an idea of how much money is involved. The latest estimate is that all those new ATM fees have netted the banks an additional $2 billion a year! And there are a number of new fees, besides. For example, many banks now charge customers $25 an hour for helping to balance their statements or just for digging up one of their old account records.

Gone are the days when your friendly teller handled all your transactions. It's not a conspiracy, exactly, because the whole world—including banks—is becoming more electronic. It helps efficiency and productivity. If some mechanical marvel can replace a human being, the bank saves money. And banks love it. Their tellers have to put up with fewer people acting like pests in front of a long teller line. Some outfits go so far as to charge customers $1 for a live teller transaction.

Watch Your Wallet

Pay attention to your ATM usage. You might think that restricting yourself to withdrawals of $20 at a clip is a way to exercise self control—but, every time you take out $20, the bank socks you with a fee. If you must use the ATM, take out a reasonable sum in a single transaction. Better you get charged once for withdrawing $100, than make five separate withdrawals of $20 each, and get charged for each one.

On special checking accounts for low-balance customers, banks will charge you more for your transactions if they are not through an ATM. You could be clipped with a higher charge if you make a simple balance inquiry through a person instead of a machine. When banks close their doors at 3:00 p.m., they know you'll have to conduct your late business electronically.

The up side of this trend is that you can get fast cash any time of the night from an ATM. Also, as banking becomes more electronic, one day you won't even have to visit an ATM. You'll do your banking from your home computer or telephone while relaxing in your La-Z-Boy chair.

The down side is that some banks charge you extra for the convenience. Here's what some big banks charge for using an ATM card at a point-of-sale location such as a store; for using their machine when you don't have an account at their bank; and for using a rival institution's ATM:

	Point-of-sale fee	ATM surcharge	Using other bank's ATM
Bank of America, San Francisco	N/A	$1.50	$2.00
Wells Fargo, Los Angeles	$1.00	N/A	$2.00
NBD, Detroit	.40	$1.50	$1.50
Wachovia, Norfolk, Va.	.25	$1.50	$1.50

N/A = Does not charge for service

The Money Line

While banks grumble that they need to raise fees to cover their costs of handling customer transactions, a recent study turned up this fact: It costs the average big bank only $1.07 to have a live teller care for a deposit, compared with 27 cents at an ATM.

In other words, just finding out how much of *your* money you have left in their bank can cost you two bucks! And that's not even counting the double-whammy ATM surcharge we discussed earlier in this chapter.

Do banks make money from ATM transactions? You bet. Look at it this way: It can cost a bank tens of thousands of dollars to equip just one branch with an ATM system. But consider how much they save in human labor by having *hundreds* of thousands of transactions handled by machines!

Bank-beater secret: Cut your number of ATM transactions to the bone. Check what each trip to a machine costs. Reduce fees by withdrawing more money all at once, instead of taking out small amounts several times.

The Truth About High Credit Card Rates

How come over the past decade, while your savings rates were jumping up and down like a Mexican jumping bean, banks kept their credit card rates sky-high? On fixed-rate cards, for instance, the rate never went lower than 17.25 percent and was as high as 19 percent. At the same time, savings rates have gyrated between 11 percent and a disgusting two percent. Wouldn't *you* like to borrow money at two percent and lend it out at 18 percent? You could live a nifty life with that scheme!

The banks' "official" explanation is that they need those high card rates to cover their operating costs, and nasty things like card fraud, counterfeiting, bad debt, and so forth. Horsefeathers. A more likely reason is that the banking lobbies fought hard for years to raise state usury laws—the maximum amount banks and other lenders in a state can charge on loans. They wound up getting three out of every four states to pass laws setting the usury ceiling at 18 percent.

Card issuers are now afraid that if they bring their rates down too low, the states might change their laws to something below 18 percent. And if they did, well heck, the banks might not get those high usury ceilings back again. Do you suppose that's why so many of the giant banks have transferred their credit card operations to states such as Delaware and South Dakota, which have *no* usury ceilings? That's why they mail billions of high-rate credit card offers out of those states to your homes. They get away with it because it's legal to do that from those no-usury-limit locations. Don't ever expect the banks to admit any of this to you. They won't. They'll just continue to pull the wool over your eyes and cry about their costs that are caused by Americans' high debt and personal bankruptcy rates.

> **Bank-beater secret:** Get rid of all your credit cards, or carry only one or two at the most—the lowest-rate plastic you can find. Pay the cards off every month. NEVER pay only the minimum amount due (see Chapter 17).

Loan Rates That Jump in the Night

Banks have many tricks when it comes to lending money. One is to promote low introductory rates on loans. The reason that this trick works is that a lot of Americans are just plain suckers for what looks like a cheap deal, and they don't bother to notice the fine print before they sign up at their bank.

Suppose that other outfits peddle a variable-rate credit card at 15 percent, but Megabuck Bank pushes a six percent rate. Sounds good until you read the flyspeck footnote at the bottom of the ad. The rate is only good for six months, after which it rises to the banks' prime rate, plus, maybe nine percentage points. If the prime is at 8.5 percent, the card rate eventually goes to 17.5 percent. On a $3,000 balance, that's a difference of $345 a year in interest.

In another example, Friendly Federal lures you into a home equity loan at four percent, which appears to be a lower interest rate than what other outfits offer. They're out to grab you before you decide to do business across the street. The same thing happens as in the Megabuck card offer. The rate only applies for a few months, and then—bingo—it jumps up like an antelope. In both situations, you definitely could have found a better deal at a different bank and saved hundreds of dollars. Don't get snookered. Remember that nothing is for nothing in this world.

> **Bank-beater secret:** If the deal looks too good to be true, it probably is. Study the fine print before you sign on the dotted line.

One strategy banks use to protect themselves on the money they lend out is *not* to lend you any money unless they think you *don't* need any. It used to happen this way, over and over again: Assume that two guys named Dick and Harry apply to the same institution for a loan. Dick's family is strapped. They got behind in their debts after Dick lost his job, and they've been living off their credit cards and savings accounts, which are almost dry. The family rents a small house, and has no expensive jewels or other collateral to pledge against a loan. Dick and the family go to church every week, have never told a lie, and have a child ready for college. They need $5,000 to tide them over and maybe start a small lawn-maintenance service until Dick gets another regular job. The problem is that Dick and his wife have spotty credit reports, which make them a Grade C risk to the bank.

Harry's situation is different. He's a sterling, Grade A credit risk. The family has $120,000 equity in their home, owns another piece of property, has $85,000 in CDs, $110,000 in stocks, four credit cards, and a car that's paid-off. They want to borrow $50,000.

Question: Which loan application do you think would normally whistle through the bank, and which one would probably be rejected? That's right. Harry gets his money on the spot, but Dick might be rejected.

Surprise! Nowadays more banks and finance companies are making "sub-prime" loans, to people with B or C (and sometimes D) credit scores, but at much higher interest rates. If Harry's interest rate is 9 percent, Dick could get socked with 13 or 14 percent or higher, but he'll get his loan.

> **Bank-beater secret:** Dick should contact Consumer Credit Counseling Services (800-388-2227) and get his credit straightened out. CCCS will do it for little or no fee. The nonprofit organization will contact creditors and help Dick's family set up easier payment plans. Second, Dick and his wife should write out a detailed business plan for their new business and present it to the bank. The plan should include a financial projection of revenues, costs, and profits (see Chapters 16 and 21).

Harry's credit position is A-okay, although nowadays the bank may want his shirt size, blood type, and a promise to name his first-born after the bank's loan officer to get the money!

Try Negotiating—Today It Works!

Once upon a time, banks were as rigid as granite when you wanted them to change a rate or waive a fee. Not any more. Most folks aren't aware of it, but because banks today are being hit from all sides by competition, they'll probably cut your credit card rate right on the spot if you complain loudly enough.

You don't like the fee you've just been hit with after giving the bank your business for the past 10 years? You don't like the interest rate they advertise, especially considering the size of the deposit you're contemplating for a CD account? Think you're being overcharged on the home equity loan that you want to take out?

Stand up and bark and tell the bank you're not satisfied, that you feel you need to consider taking your business elsewhere, by shopping other institutions in the area. This nice little aggressive strategy may not work 100 percent of the time, but the odds are more in your favor today than ever before. We've heard of banks cutting a customer's credit card rate from 18 percent to 9.9 percent on the spot.

Don't be bashful. Give it a try. After all, it's your money—not theirs—and you have every right to complain about any part of a deal you don't like. You just might be surprised by the positive reaction you get.

Bank-beater secret: Don't try the negotiation strategy with a bank teller, account representative or platform personnel. Go straight to the branch manager or another officer—nobody else.

The Least You Need to Know

➤ Banks basically earn their money by renting your money in savings, checking, and CDs at lower rates than they charge to lend it out.

➤ Banks are also making staggering profits by raising all their old fees and inventing new ones. Those who get hit the hardest are low-balance customers who make lots of transactions that involve labor by bank personnel.

➤ Banks often make interest rates work in their favor by pushing long-term CDs when interest rates are low, and short-term CDs when interest rates are high. They wait a while to raise savings rates after they increase their prime rate, as they pay you zip on interest checking, Money Market Accounts, and passbook savings.

➤ To get you to take out a loan, banks offer low-ball introductory rates that suddenly rise after a few months. Increasingly, banks are lending to higher-risk customers, but charging them much higher rates than what good credit risks pay.

Chapter 9

Interest Rates 101

In This Chapter

➤ How banks calculate the interest on your money

➤ In simple English—what "APY" and "APR" mean in rates

➤ The key difference between rate and yield

➤ Bank compounding—explained the *easy* way

➤ How banks play with the numbers

➤ The most important rates you should watch

Let's face it. The average Joe and Jane know zip about how interest rates work. They read tons of page-one stories about rates going up or down. They hear about Wall Street analysts having heart attacks if rates suddenly jump, and they hang on every word that comes out of the mouth of the chairman of the Federal Reserve Board. Meanwhile, across America, guys are hanging over their back fences, asking their neighbor, "What do you think is gonna happen to mortgage rates?"

Today, interest rates run our lives, much less the economy. But people don't have the foggiest about what makes rates behave the way they do, or how they can affect their wallets. Yet, by knowing just the few basics outlined in this chapter, you'll be able to take much of the mystery out of the rate subject. It breaks this complicated subject down into Main Street language that you can easily understand so you can apply it to savings, mortgages, credit cards, and you-name-it.

Banks Are Cashing In on Your Ignorance

How many people do you know who can walk into a bank, discuss opening a new savings account, and figure exactly how their interest rate will be computed? Not many. Banks have been around for hundreds of years, and lately they've been inventing a slew of different, complex formulas for every kind of account they offer.

Few customers ever ask how the numbers work. That gives banks a big advantage. They can sell you an account based on a complicated mathematical computation that really earns you less money than you can earn somewhere else. You may never realize you've been had. As one bank customer complained, "I'm getting smoked by all those numbers."

Even if you have a degree from Harvard or the Wharton School, nobody understands all the account rates. Worse still, the rising tide of fees and charges hits the little guy more than people who maintain big balances. But if you, the average person, take some time to learn the inside tricks of what the banks are up to, we guarantee you'll come out ahead, dollar-wise.

Step One: Learn the Rate Basics and the Lingo

A rate is nothing more than a percentage number. Your bank pays you one rate when it borrows some of your money in the form of a savings account or CD, and it charges another customer a higher rate when that person borrows from the bank. The difference is the bank's profit. Your game plan is to earn as high an interest rate as you can when you save, and pay the lowest possible rate when you take out a mortgage, auto or home equity loan or get a credit card.

Watch Your Wallet

Before you sign up for a bank account of any type, *never* let the bank get away with only quoting you mumbo-jumbo "percentages." Instead, insist that the institution explain the deal in dollars and cents, nothing else. That should apply to both your investing *and* your borrowing.

But as you learn more about what makes rates tick, remember that another big secret to making money at the bank is to pay attention to other critical factors as well. One key is to slash those disgusting fees and charges. Another is to beware of introductory come-on rates that look great, but disappear after a few months. A "fantastic" rate means zilch if it goes POOF in the night and you get pounded by ridiculous extra costs!

Everybody uses the word "rate" when they talk about banking, but that's not 100 percent accurate. By law, your banker also uses a few other words to describe what you earn on savings or pay on loans. These are the key terms:

"Rate" Versus "Yield," and That Thing Called "APR": Knowing the Difference

"APY" is for savings and CD accounts:

➤ A *rate* is what the account earns before any interest is added. In other words, it's just a naked number.

➤ More important, the annual percentage yield (APY) is what the account actually pays you in *one year,* after all the interest is added to your original deposit. The key words are "one year." That's the APY regardless of the CD term—six months, one year, five years or whatever. It's the only way to accurately compare different deals at different banks because it includes the *interest* you earn. You're able to compare apples versus apples without going berserk over a zillion different numbers.

➤ Compounding is the mathematical formula the bank uses to figure your yield based on the rate. It simply means interest added to interest. The more frequently the bank compounds your money, the more interest you earn and the higher the yield. For instance, daily compounding is better than monthly or quarterly compounding (see the following table).

"APR" is for loan accounts:

➤ The percentage rate, the amount you borrow, and the number of years you pay back the loan, influence your monthly payment. The more you borrow and/or the higher your rate, the higher your payment will be. The longer you take to repay the loan, the lower your monthly payment—but the downside is that you'll pay more in total interest.

The Money Line

Which would you rather have? An outright gift of $1 million, or a penny in a savings account that doubles every day for 30 days? Better think this one through before you answer. At the end of the 30 days, the $1 million will still be worth a million bucks, but the penny will have grown to an astounding $5.37 million! That's not a misprint: get out your calculator and check it for yourself.

➤ By law, on many loans such as those for new and used cars, lenders must also show an "annual percentage rate" (APR) in addition to the basic borrowing rate. The APR is always higher than the basic rate because it also includes certain fees and charges on the loan. Hence, it does a better job of revealing the total cost of your loan.

Is the Rate Fixed or Variable?

On all bank accounts, you need to know whether your rate is *fixed* or *variable*. It can make a whale of a difference in what you pay the bank, or what the bank pays you. A fixed rate is fixed, period. It can't ever change over the life of an account. If, say, you lock in a mortgage rate while rates are low, that's all you'll be charged, regardless of how high market rates go in the future. With a variable rate, on the other hand, the bank ties your rate to an index, such as its prime rate, a Treasury bill or another index. If that index rate changes, so does the rate you pay. This is the bank's way of protecting itself in case of violent swings in the market. In the event rates jump sky-high, as they did in the early 1980s, you'll absorb the bank's costs by shelling out more interest on your variable rate loan.

Variable rates aren't as frequent on savings accounts as on loan accounts. You might occasionally run across a Money Market Savings Account (MMA) whose rate is tied to what the average money fund pays, or the latest yield on a Treasury bill—plus an extra fraction of a percentage point to make you think you're earning more than you could with other investments. But with some loans, such as adjustable-rate mortgages, the rate is always variable and is tied to whatever index the lender uses.

Compounding = Interest on Top of Interest

Relax. There aren't 10 guys in your neighborhood that know how bank compounding works. Here's the easy way to understand it: Say you open a new $10,000 savings account that earns 6 percent, with *daily compounding*. On the second day, the bank adds interest of $1.64 (6 percent times 10,000 divided by 365 days in a year). That increases your balance to $10,001.64. The next day, it figures interest the same way on top of the $10,001.64, and continues the same process each day thereafter. Your balance gets bigger and bigger.

With daily compounding, you'd have $10,618 in the account at the end of one year. That's a few more dollars than you would have received if the bank had compounded your money less frequently, such as quarterly or annually (see the following table).

Note that there is no difference in the amounts ($10,600) for "simple interest" and "annual compounding," both of which pay interest at the end of the year. But there *would* be a difference if you left the money in the account for a second year. Here's why: With *annual compounding*, the interest in the second year would be added to the interest in the first year. But under the *simple interest* method, in the second year you'd only earn interest on your original $10,000 investment. In other words, on a multi-year CD, and everything else being equal, annual compounding pays more than simple interest.

Here are the quarter-by-quarter comparisons:

Compound Method	First Quarter	Second Quarter	Third Quarter	Fourth Quarter
Continuous	$10,152	$10,305	$10,460	$10,618
Daily	10,151	10,305	10,460	10,618
Weekly	10,151	10,304	10,460	10,618
Monthly	10,151	10,304	10,459	10,617
Quarterly	10,150	10,302	10,457	10,614
Annual	10,000	10,000	10,000	10,600
Simple interest	10,000	10,000	10,000	10,600

Knowing How Banks Create (and Play with) Their Numbers

Many folks foolishly park their money at a bank without ever knowing how and why one bank's yields are higher than another's, even when everything else about the accounts may look the same. By learning how banks design their rate offers, you can easily earn a lot more in interest on a good-size investment.

Time Is Money

On a savings account, the longer you agree to lock up your money, the higher the interest rate. One-year CDs usually pay more than six-month accounts. Five-year CD yields are higher than those on two-year accounts, and so on. Why do banks do this? Because it's an enticement to keep your cash in their vaults for a longer period. The bank can count on the money staying there, instead of having to replace those deposits every few months or every year.

Banks Use a Crystal Ball

Other factors also influence what banks pay on CDs—such as where they think interest rates might be months or years from now (see Chapter 11). And here's where you can become your own rate expert. Usually, when banks believe interest rates will rise over the next several months or years, they raise their long-term CD yields (such as on five-year accounts) faster than those on short-term accounts (such as six months and one year). Why? Because they would rather start paying you a little more today to lock up a five-year account, than pay you an even higher yield later on.

Supply and Demand Affects Your Rates, too

Banks try to balance their savings-account maturities against their loan maturities. In other words, they might want to match the money in their four-year or five-year CD accounts against their volume of four-year and five-year auto loans. If, for instance, they're super-heavy in auto loans, they'll probably offer a slightly higher rate on five-year CDs to bring their deposit portfolio in line with their loan portfolio.

How Banks Brew Up Their Rates

With all that as a backdrop, let's pretend we're looking in on Megabuck Bank over a typical week, to see how it sets its interest rates. In effect, we'll be peeking into their kitchen to see how they make their soup.

The first thing you should know is that banks typically change CD rates every week, generally on Tuesday or Wednesday. Let's say it's Thursday. When you waltzed into the lobby, you noticed Megabuck's rate numbers on their plastic sign are higher than they were last week. The one-year CD that paid 5 percent last week has edged up to 5.50 percent. How come? Nobody in the bank is going to tell you. Chances are, the bank didn't even explain why to its employees.

What might have happened is that two days ago, on Tuesday, when Megabuck's rate-setting committee met, they noticed that a whole bunch of things occurred since last week:

➤ Treasury rates moved up at the federal government's Monday auction.

➤ Many of the country's biggest banks have been raising rates.

➤ Just before the Tuesday meeting, a Megabuck secretary made cold calls to eight other local banks and found their rates, too, had climbed.

➤ The morning paper says unemployment is down, and consumer prices and housing starts were higher last month than the month before—signals that the economy is getting stronger.

➤ Megabuck's loan officer reports more of the bank's consumer and business customers have been borrowing, which means the bank has to pull in some new money to replace what it has loaned out.

That's why Megabuck's committee raised rates. But had the bank gotten different information, if, for example, consumer prices and housing were down instead of up, and if other banks were dropping their rates, Megabuck also might have lowered its numbers.

What Banks Watch to Set Their Rates

Banks don't set rates in a vacuum. There are key things they watch (which you can easily watch, too) to see which way the numbers will probably go. The average person may not realize it, but certain economic indicators will dictate whether a bank will raise or lower its rates, or leave them alone. It's based on how the Federal Reserve reacts to changes in the economic numbers.

The problem is, unless the average guy knows what to look for, he'll go nuts trying to sift through all the latest rumors by analysts, advisers, brokers and banks themselves. One day some pundit says the Fed might raise rates, the next day another wag swears the Fed is going to lower them. That shows you how confused the "experts" really are. They have a lousy batting average trying to predict rate direction, so you mustn't trust everything they say when you're wondering if CD and mortgage rates will go up, down or sideways.

Here's what you should watch:

The Federal Reserve's two key rates. They are the Fed discount rate (what it charges banks to borrow from the Fed) and the Fed overnight funds rate (what banks charge to borrow money from each other). At its meetings, which happen about once a month or so, the Fed may raise or lower one or both of those rates. If it raises a rate, it means the Fed thinks the economy is getting too hot, and it must, therefore, cool things down to head off inflation. If it lowers a rate, the Fed is trying to stimulate a lagging economy by making it cheaper for businesses to borrow money, thus stimulating business activity. Fed rates don't affect you directly, but they do influence the rates that banks set for your deposits and loans.

Key Economic Indicators. These are the numbers the Fed watches to decide what to do with its key rates. Its economists study every piece of economic information they can get their hands on, especially unemployment figures, wages, producer prices, consumer prices, retail sales, new plant equipment, housing starts, you name it. Even the federal deficit and the soundness of the dollar have an influence on the Fed's decisions. When the data show very strong gains, the economy may be tilting toward inflation. Data suggesting a weaker economy, such as higher unemployment figures and lower housing starts, could lead to a Fed rate cut.

The Prime Rate. When the Fed raises or lowers its key rates, the banks fall in line by increasing, or decreasing, their prime rate by the same margin. For example, a one-quarter percentage point decrease by the Fed would prompt the banks to change the prime from 8.50 percent to 8.25 percent. The prime rate is supposedly what banks charge their most creditworthy business customers to borrow money. When that rate changes, your savings and loan rates do, too. For example, a quarter-point drop in variable-rate credit cards and home equity loans, whose rates are tied to the prime rate, would result in these consumer loan rates also falling. Conversely, when the prime rate rises, so do these loan rates.

Local Savings Rate Direction. In local rate tables that run weekly in your newspaper, pick out five to 10 of the largest area banks to follow. Track their 6-

111

month, 1-year and 5-year CD yields week after week. Note which rates seem to be falling, and which ones appear to be rising, especially on longer-term accounts. That trend is usually a hint of where banks expect rates to be down the road. One thing that influences savings rates in a particular market is the strength of the local economy. If the economy is brisk, banks are lending more money to businesses for growth and expansion. That creates a need to attract new funds to replace those that the banks lend out, meaning they must offer higher rates on Money Market Accounts and CDs.

Watch Your Wallet

What some people don't know: It's the 10-year bond yield, not changes in the prime rate, that directly influences mortgage rates. However, the prime rate is a general indicator of overall rate movement, which can include mortgages.

Long-term bond yields. They'll tell you whether mortgage rates are on the way up or down. Specifically, follow 10-year Treasury bond yields, because that's what the mortgage market uses to set fixed-rate home loans. Why? Because long bond yields are based on what's likely to happen years from now, and that scenario can change by the hour or by the minute. In other words, as dumb as it sounds, the experts are continually making their best guess on the *future*, as opposed to the present or what happened five minutes ago. If some new economic indicator suggests inflation is in the wind—bingo—long bond yields will jump, and so will mortgage rates. But if economic data suggest the economy is slowing down, bond and mortgage numbers will drop.

The Money Line

After the Federal Reserve and the banks raise or lower their rates, it isn't until the next billing cycle, or even later, that consumers start to feel it on their variable-rate loans. But banks play a little game after a prime rate change that gives them an edge. When the prime rate is lowered, savings rates come down first, followed by loan rates. But when the prime rises, the opposite happens; loan rates immediately start following the prime upward, and only after that do savings rates begin to move up. Sneaky, eh? Here's how it works: Typically, when banks boost their prime rate by one-quarter percent, average CD yields rise by about one-tenth to 15-hundredths of a percent over the next eight weeks. So, even after the lag time, you don't get the full benefit of the prime rate increase!

Don't Kid Yourself: What Happens in Tokyo Now Affects You in Peoria

There's an enormous new influence on interest rates in the U.S. It's how well other countries are doing in the global economy. When the economy of one distant country slips, such as Malaysia in 1997, the currencies of other nations in the region start falling like dominos.

Once upon a time, that would have had no effect on America. Not so today. Countries are so economically linked that news 10,000 miles away can have a direct effect on your mortgage rates, as well as your job.

For example, Asian economic markets crumble because of a Japanese bank crisis, or Malaysian revolt. Currencies are devalued. The dollar is worth more than it was a few weeks ago. U.S. manufacturers can't sell their goods in Asia because our prices go up, and those nations cut back on their buying. But Asian countries, to survive, begin exporting more to the U.S. The competition forces U.S. manufacturers to cut prices and it drives up their inventories. Plants lay off employees. America's economy gets weaker, and economists foresee a downturn.

The Federal Reserve cuts interest rates to stimulate business. Savings and loan rates drop. Long-term bond yields also fall on the recessionary news, taking mortgage rates with them. Maybe that won't happen, but America no longer lives in a vacuum. Financially, it's tied to the rest of the world.

Chiseling Gets Down to Pennies

Wait until you hear this one. We all know there are 365 days in a year. Well, not all banks use that many days when they compute your interest. Some work with a 360-day year. That shaves your earnings by only pennies, but it saves the banks millions of dollars a year.

Say you deposit $10,000 in an account that pays seven percent interest. If the bank uses a 365-day calculation method, you earn $709.72 in interest; with a 360-day method, the interest comes to $700 on the same account.

"Indexed" Accounts Protect the Bank More Than They Protect You

Indexed accounts have become the rage in the past decade because they allow the bank to set the rates they pay you on savings or charge you on loans, based on a known benchmark. It can be the bank's prime rate, a U.S. Treasury bill, or some other known index that moves up or down with the economy.

An index gives the banks a predictable, controlled device that protects the bank from swings in interest rates. If their costs rise (such as having to pay you higher interest on

113

CDs when the economy gets stronger), their indexes on rates for credit cards, home equity credit lines, mortgages and other loans will also rise. If banks didn't protect themselves that way, it would cut into their profits.

Key Math Questions You Should Ask

➤ What are the interest rate and the annual percentage yield?

➤ Is the interest rate tied to an index? If so, how often can the index change?

➤ How often is the account compounded?

➤ Based on the compounding method, how much money will I have in the account, in *dollars and cents*, at the end of the first year, or when my CD matures, if the account is less than one year?

The Least You Need to Know

➤ Use the Annual Percentage Yield (APY) to compare CDs of different terms and figure out which really offers you the best deal.

➤ The Annual Percentage Rate (APR) includes the rate and certain fees and charges on loans.

➤ Rates on many loan accounts and a few deposit accounts are variable and are tied to an index. When the index rate goes up or down, so does your rate.

➤ Keep your eye on Fed rates, the banks' prime rate, and long-term bond rates. They dictate the rates banks set on your personal accounts.

➤ The more frequently the bank compounds your money, the more interest you earn. Accounts that compound daily are best.

➤ Always get the bank to explain every deal to you in dollars and cents, instead of percentages.

How to Get the Best Deal on a Checking Account

You may not realize it, but nowhere are you getting clobbered as badly on bank fees as on your checking account. While you've been using your checkbook to pay bills and buy things, banks have been slowly, but steadily, jacking up just about every checking fee you can think of. A checkbook is a basic part of American life; no one wants to be without one, yet few people complain about the rising costs, because they need checking "convenience." In reality, not shopping around for a better checking deal could be costing you $200 to $300 extra per year. You could easily keep that money in your wallet simply by changing banks.

Checking is the account we take for granted the most. This makes it easier for banks to slip in fees and charges that you don't notice. This chapter shows you how to get the most out of your checking by explaining how banks exploit these accounts, how to figure out exactly what kind of account you need, how to locate the best deal in town, and how to avoid those ugly fees.

Checking Account Basics

Ever wonder why banks run so many ads promoting checking deals? They want to get their hands on your checking account because it's "core" business. They figure that if they get your checking, they've also got the best shot at landing your CD, personal loan, and mortgage business. And if you're a *high-balance* checking customer (instead of somebody whose balance consistently runs below $1,000), then all the better for institutions. They have more money to lend out at a profit while they're paying you zip in interest.

Watch Your Wallet

U.S. consumers write about 60 billion checks a year to pay bills, according to the Federal Reserve. Their average annual postage cost to mail the bills is between $38 and $58, says the National Automated Clearing House Association.

The average interest-paying checking account earns only 1.5 percent, while the same bank may be charging you 18 percent on your credit card. That's a heck of a markup! In fact, it would probably be cheaper for you to open a non-interest account, than one that earns that puny 1.5 percent yield or less.

To figure out how much your current checking account is costing you—and how you can get a better deal—you need to do a little homework that will pay off! This section explains the different types of checking accounts, how to figure out fees, and how banks calculate your checking account balance.

Why You're Getting Nickel-and-Dimed to Death

Guess what? While you've been looking the other way, your banker has been working behind the scenes, quietly hiking his checking fees and charges. Studies show that in markets such as South Florida, it's costing the average customer more than $300 per year just to have a regular, non-interest account.

Your banker is getting away with murder, because few checking customers scream or complain about the rising costs. To most folks, carrying a checkbook is as natural as getting up in the morning and brushing their teeth.

The fees creep in so stealthily that you probably don't even notice them—50 cents here, a dollar there. It's not until your monthly statement arrives that you discover strange, new, little costs popping up like measles on your statement.

Also, even if the bank pays you interest on checking, it probably isn't enough to buy you cab fare across town.

Mistakes You Should Avoid from Day One

Chances are that when you walked into a bank and told them you wanted to open a checking account, an account representative sat you down, filled out your application, then asked, "Would you like our Miserbuck Special, where you only have to keep a

$100 balance and pay a $10 a month 'maintenance' fee, our Royal Megabuck account, where we waive the fee provided you keep a balance of $5,000, or our Super-Duper Interest Checking that helps your money grow?"

Then came the emotional closer: "Do you prefer the blue checks with the whale art in the background, or the green ones with the daffodils and philodendrons?" Whereupon, he or she gave you a set of "starter" checks and a "Fee Disclosure" document on the bank's fees and charges (required by law) in small type. You probably didn't bother to read all that tiny mumbo-jumbo. That was mistake number one.

The Money Line

You're apt to see free checking accounts pop up when one big bank acquires another major institution in a different state, such as when Washington Mutual, Seattle, bought up Great Western Bank. To make quick points with South Florida consumers and steal away business, it offered an account that had no minimum balance or monthly service fee, returned all cancelled checks, didn't charge for live-teller access or telephone service, and didn't require direct-deposit payroll or Social Security checks.

The account rep may not have reviewed with you your month-by-month checking behavior so that you could match it against the different kinds of fees on the types of accounts the bank has available. And dollars-to-donuts, you weren't told the pluses and minuses of interest-checking versus non-interest checking. That was mistake number two. It would have helped you trim your checking costs.

The Different Types of Checking Accounts

It's enough to blow your mind. Some banks offer as many as five to seven different checking accounts, all with weird names like "Master Checking," "Super Value Checking," "Special Checking" and "Regular Checking". And you're supposed to decide on one, with no road map to guide you. Even worse, some banks try to palm off slightly higher-interest Money Market Accounts (MMAs) as checking accounts by giving them a weasel-worded name like "Money Market Checking" or "Money Fund Checking."

Here's the easy way to cut through the confusion. Just remember that most checking accounts generally fall into one of three broad categories:

➤ An account that charges lower fees but pays you no interest.

➤ An account that pays you a piddling interest rate, but charges higher fees and requires a higher opening deposit and a higher monthly balance.

➤ A "basic checking" account for people with low income. These accounts don't pay any interest, but they have low minimum balance requirements and low fees.

What does that translate into, dollar-wise, on the different accounts? According to Bank Rate Monitor, on the average non-interest checking, you'll need $80 to open the account, versus $319 for an interest-bearing account. The minimum-balance threshold will be $346 to avoid fees with non-interest checking, compared with $1,647 if the account pays interest.

How Low Can Rates Get?

Once upon a time, banks paid yields as high as six percent on interest checking. But when all interest rates plunged in the early 1990s, checking rates hit the basement and never came back up, even though CD rates did slightly.

Instead, checking rates bottomed out at a disgusting 1.5 percent average and stayed there for years. So on checking accounts with an average balance of $1,000, the typical customer has been earning only $15 in interest per year. If that customer pays a monthly maintenance fee of $12 just to have the account, he's already $129 in the hole. And that's not counting other checking fees, either!

Table 10.1   What Checking Interest Pays (Average Yield)

City	Rate
New York	1.07%
Los Angeles	0.99%
Chicago	1.26%
San Francisco	0.99%
Philadelphia	1.05%
Detroit	1.37%
Boston	0.96%
Houston	1.03%
Dallas	1.07%
Washington	1.53%

Source: Bank Rate Monitor

➤ Instead of keeping all your money in a checking account that earns only 1 percent interest, put most of your loose funds in a higher-paying Money Market

118

Account. Some out-of-state MMAs pay 5.5 percent and higher. Locally, with a $20,000 deposit or more, a bank may pay you the same amount. With an MMA, you're permitted to write up to three checks a month to parties other than yourself. Once a month, move enough money from your MMA to your local checking account to pay bills. You won't pay a penalty to transfer the funds, but be sure to allow at least five days for your check to clear.

➤ Get your checking account through a credit union (CU) instead of at a bank or thrift. In late 1994, CUs offered an average of 2.28 percent, while banks and thrifts paid an average of 1.50 percent. But at CUs they don't call them "checks," they call them *share drafts*, which operate just like checks. Note: Credit unions also pay higher rates on CDs, as you'll discover by reading Chapter 14.

Asset Advisory

Not all checking accounts pay interest, but on those that do, consumers earn an average interest rate of only 1.5 percent or less.

Those Frightening Fees

According to a study of big banks by the Federal Reserve, the banks' internal cost of maintaining a checking account fell from $7.38 a month in 1992, to $6.82 a month in 1993. By earning money on your money through lending, they reduce their cost to only $4 a month. Your costs, meanwhile, have been steadily inching up to where some of your one-time fees can range as high as $30. In other words, you're riding a down escalator, while the bank's is going up. This is why you need a defensive plan to keep more of your cash.

Some interesting bank fee facts:

➤ Banks owe a big chunk of their good fortune to higher fee income, according to *USA Today*.

➤ Fees accounted for 25 percent of banks' gross operating income in 1993, up from 14 percent in 1989, says the Federal Deposit Insurance Corporation, the regulatory agency that monitors the banks.

➤ Banks have been raising fees at a much faster rate than inflation. For example, the typical monthly maintenance fee has jumped by 15 percent in the past two years, while inflation has averaged 2.7 percent a year.

➤ According to the newsletter *Fee Income Report*, in 1993, banks charged 225 fees of all types, up from 95 in 1989.

Among the fee-disclosure documents that banks hand out to new customers, we've seen one that listed *64 separate fees of all types!* That's enough to throw an accounting major for a loop, much less the average Joe or Jane from Dubuque. To help you focus on fees, here's a list of the most common that banks charge you:

Monthly maintenance

Per-check fee

Exceeding number of monthly transactions

Dropping below the minimum balance

Using your bank's ATM

Using another bank's ATM

Higher fees if account pays interest

Bouncing a check

Depositing someone else's bad check

Stopping payment on a check

Copies of stored checks

Certified check

Cashier's check

Money order

Overdraft protection

Wire transfer

Traveler's checks

How much money do you usually keep in your account? The less you keep, the more you're charged. Banks will often waive fees for higher-balance customers. It's when you drop below the "threshold" (a certain balance level) that you get whacked. Banks also may waive fees if you maintain several different accounts in one "relationship package," or if they're trying to keep old customers or lure new ones. That happens, for example, right after a bank merger, when the surviving institution is afraid that customers of the acquired bank may flee out the back door.

The key to what banks charge for banking is this: They classify you as to whether you are a "low-balance," "medium-balance," or "high-balance" customer, and their fees favor—you guessed it—the high-balance crowd. For example:

➤ Mrs. Gottrocks is high-balance. Because she keeps $5,000 or $10,000 in her account, she's given a better break, such as having many of her fees waived, including her monthly balance charge.

➤ Susie Smith, with $1,000, is considered a medium-balance customer. She doesn't go below her required balance during the month, so she's charged normal fees, such as "monthly maintenance."

➤ Joe Doaks, with a $400 balance, is a low-balance guy, so the bank discourages him from making too many transactions that cost the bank money. How? They hit him with charges on a slew of services. His monthly maintenance charge may be a few bucks higher than what Susie Smith pays.

It doesn't seem fair, the rich getting richer and the poor getting poorer, but that's the way banks play the game. Your job is to beat the system by making decisions that will tilt things your way.

The Clearing Game

Just because you deposited the $100 check from Uncle Louie in your bank one hour ago, doesn't mean you can draw on any of the funds today. The process can take up to five days until the check clears through the national banking system. The reason it takes so long is that Uncle Louie's bank needs time to get the check back and reduce his account balance by the amount of the check. The same thing applies to the $500 check from Aunt Nellie, but in this case, many banks let you draw against the first $100 on the next business day, and hold the other $400 until the check clears her bank. (Regulations may *require* local checks to clear in one day. It all depends on location.)

If you deposit a $1,000 check in your account, here's how much you can withdraw against the check, depending upon what kind of check it is:

➤ One day later, you can usually withdraw all $1,000 if it's a federal, state, or local government check; a bank check, certified check, or traveler's check; a check written on your bank by someone else; or an electronic funds transfer.

➤ If the check was written on a local bank, you should be able to withdraw $100 of the $1,000 one day later, $400 on the second day, and the remaining $500 on the third day.

➤ On an out-of-town check, you can withdraw $100 one day later and the other $900 five days later.

Remember that if you write checks against somebody else's check that you deposited to your account, that person's check may not clear in time for your check to be honored. If this happens, it may overdraw your account and you'll wind up paying a bounced-check charge.

There are exceptions. If you keep beaucoups bucks in your accounts and know the branch manager by name, the bank may stroke you by letting you draw immediately on any type of check you deposit.

Balancing Act

Finding out how banks calculate your balance sounds like an exercise for Einstein, but it's not. You simply need to know which method a bank uses, because it will tell you when a fee will kick in on your account. The institution calculates one of two ways:

➤ Your *low-minimum balance*, which activates a fee if the balance falls below a certain level at any time during the month.

➤ Your *average-daily balance*, where the fee kicks in if the monthly average of each day's balance drops below a certain amount.

The average-daily balance method is better because it protects you if your balance takes a sudden, temporary dive during the month. By contrast, if you choose an account using the low-minimum method, and your balance sinks to $10 one day, but is $1,000 on all the other days of the month, you will still get hit with a penalty. The dollar difference between the two kinds of accounts can be substantial, as shown in the following example.

Mary and Thelma, who have checking accounts at two different banks, normally keep about $600 each in their accounts, give or take a few hundred dollars either way. Mary's bank uses the low-minimum balance method, and charges her a $10 fee if her balance falls below $300 any day of the month. Mary deposited her paycheck the first week of the month and her account balance went up to $950. Ten days later, after she paid her rent and other bills, Mary's balance sank to $285 for one day. But the next day she deposited another paycheck that pushed the balance up to $700. Mary's average balance for the whole month was $600, but the bank still whacked her with the $10 charge because it uses the low-minimum-balance method. Multiply that situation times 12 months a year, and you'll begin to understand why it pays to shop banks and ask the right questions.

Let's pretend Thelma's numbers were the same as Mary's—same pay, same rent, same bills, same everything. Thelma's balance dropped to $285 for just one day, just like Mary's. Even her average monthly balance was the same, $600. But she wasn't charged any fee because her bank uses the average-daily balance method. The $600 figure was all that mattered.

What Kind of Checking Creature Are You?

No one wants to go through the nuisance of analyzing his or her personal behavior, especially on something as small and common as a checking account. When people need to write a check, they write one, period, and once a month they balance their statement and pray they have enough in the account to get through next week.

When you dashed over to the ATM last Sunday to get some emergency cash, you may not have thought about how many similar trips you made in the past month. Or about whose automatic teller you were using, your bank's, or a different outfit's machine across the street. But those kinds of individual actions form a pattern of your personal checking behavior. The account that's just right for you probably won't be the one that's right for your child in college or for your neighbor. They're going to need one that fits their financial lifestyles.

The Money Line

Eighty-three percent of consumers believe checking is the most convenient way to pay bills, according to the Gallup organization. Cash comes in second at eight percent, followed by electronic banking at four percent. On average, people use checks to pay for their retail purchases almost half the time. One in 10 uses checks 100 percent of the time. Women (53 percent) use checks more often than men (42 percent) do.

Take stock of how you do things. Ask yourself:

➤ How do you usually buy merchandise and pay your bills? By check, credit card, debit card, online, PC home banking or a combination of those methods?

➤ What's the average amount of money you keep in checking every month?

➤ How likely are you to let your balance slip below that level?

➤ How many checks a month do you write?

➤ How often do you use an ATM?

➤ Which bank's ATM do you use? Your own bank's? Another bank's machine in the same town? An out-of-town ATM? How much do you usually withdraw each time?

➤ Where do you buy your check reorders?

➤ Do you bounce checks or issue stop-payment orders?

➤ Do you ever ask the bank for back copies of your statement or copies of old checks?

Next, haul out your last three or four monthly checking statements and add up all the various fees, including ATM deposits and withdrawals,

Asset Advisory

The number of U.S. families using checks rose from 85.1 percent in 1989 to 87.5 percent in 1992, the last year for which figures are available, reports the Federal Reserve. In 1992, 12 percent of those who didn't use checks said service charges were too high, up from 7.4 percent in 1989.

check reorders—the works. Then estimate what your checking is costing you per month and per year, because those are the bottom-line costs you want to cut to ribbons. Tape that information on your refrigerator door (or put it on your desk) and get ready to play hardball with the banks. Believe it or not, you're on your way to putting extra money in your pocketbook.

Finally, don't make the same mistake that many other consumers make by being too lazy to balance your checkbook or close out a costly account. Get ready to switch banks by keeping a record of how many checks are outstanding and how much money you'll need to cover them. Then you won't sweat the transition.

If you don't prepare, you can wind up costing yourself some money. For example, a fellow we know wrote his ex-wife a check that she didn't cash for two months. After he closed out his account—forgetting about the check—the ex deposited the check and it came back marked NSF (non-sufficient funds), whereupon she nailed him for issuing a bounced check.

Banks were making $2.2 billion a year in profits before they started adding "surcharges" to ATM transactions (now ATMs where you don't bank charge as much as $1.75 per transaction). When surcharging came along, that increased the banks' profits by $2.7 billion, according to the Center for the Study of Responsive Law.

You'd Better Shop Around

Outside of mortgages, a checking account—yes, little old checking—is one of the trickiest accounts to shop. "How can that be?" you ask. "What else are there besides a few fees, and maybe an interest rate?"

Plenty. Instead of just "a few" fees, you're going to come across dozens and dozens of different ones. Rarely will you see even two banks whose fees are exactly alike, or whose account requirements are absolutely identical. The trick is to ignore all the gimmicks and focus on these two key points:

1. The account you're looking for is the one whose low-cost features match your personal checking behavior. Nothing else.

2. Pretend you're shopping for a computer or a television set, not a checking account. You wouldn't buy a TV if it cost you a buck every time you turned it on, would you? Use the same demanding buying principles when you open a checking account.

You'll never be a checking idiot if you follow these two simple rules.

Basic Shopping Tips

When you shop, don't try to compare every single, cotton-picking fee charged by every institution. Otherwise, you'll go berserk and wind up in a straitjacket. There are simply too many different fees to cope with. So what do you do? You limit your comparisons to only the most common fees and charges that are apt to affect you, such as monthly maintenance, and so on.

Do this: Instead of scribbling notes on the backs of fee schedules the banks give you, organize the information on a piece of paper with headings for each fee type, *bank by bank*. Jot down each outfit's information under the appropriate heading, but remember to base each fee on the average monthly balance you carry in your account.

Match the fees on your shopping chart with your checking behavior that you determined earlier. Based on what you usually do with your account, what would Bank "A" cost you per month? What about Banks "B," "C," and the others? Also, ask yourself if your financial condition will likely change in any way that might affect your decision on where to take your business. Can you change any of your old checking habits, such as reducing the number of ATM transactions or checks you write, to cut costs even further?

The more banks you shop, the better your chances of cutting your checking costs. Keep your pencil sharp and your eye on the bottom line. One of those outfits is going to wind up being the cheapest place to do your checking, and it probably won't be your old bank!

Before You Sign on the Dotted Line

Banks have been adding so many new fees—and increasing their old ones—that almost everything you do with checks today is going to cost you. It's critical to ask the right questions up front, before you sign on the dotted line. These are the most important ones.

➤ What is the minimum deposit to open the account?

➤ Does the account pay interest? If not, what are the differences in fees between this account and an account that does pay interest?

➤ Is the account tiered? If so, what interest rate does each tier pay?

➤ What minimum balance must I maintain to avoid paying a fee?

➤ Under what conditions would you waive my fee?

➤ What is the cost per check?

➤ How much do check reorders cost?

➤ What are the ATM costs if I use this bank's machine or another bank's machine?

➤ How much is the bounced-check fee?

➤ Do you return my cancelled checks with each monthly statement? If not, how much extra would it cost?

Avoid the Traps: There's No Such Thing as a Free Checking Account

In a bid to get your business, many institutions offer "free" checking with "package accounts" that combine several of your accounts, such as savings and CDs, on one monthly statement (see Chapter 9). Even though the free checking part of the package many seem to be a good deal, the rest of the package may not be.

You'd probably be better off splitting your accounts among several outfits.

Free Checking, My Foot!

Banking associations claim that today you can find a so-called free, "no-frills" checking account at eight out of 10 outfits. Oh, yeah? Let's say you just saw an ad for "free checking." Better read the fine print. Even though a Truth in Savings law (which was supposed to reduce the number of tricks that banks can pull when they advertise the word "free") went into effect in 1993, it's still fairly easy for banks to mislead you. For one thing, although they can't say an account is free if they sock you with a fee for allowing your account balance to fall below a certain minimum (or if they require you to open another account to get free checking), they can peddle the account as being "free" if there are ATM or debit card charges associated with checking. Also, if you bounce a check with a no-frills account, your fee penalty could be double that of a regular checking account.

Here are some examples of when a free checking account isn't so free:

➤ You get an ATM card with your checking, but when you sign up, the small print in the agreement says that you'll pay a fee for using another bank's automatic teller. If your balance slides below the minimum, you'll also pay a fee when you use your bank's machine.

➤ The bank promotes free checking even though you pay an annual fee on a debit card (which electronically withdraws funds from your checking when you buy something).

➤ If you do your banking electronically from your computer and are charged a fee for the service, the bank can still claim the checking account is free.

How come banks can circumvent the rules? Because the Truth in Savings law says that if the transaction is electronic, it's not really part of the checking account. Rather crafty, don't you think?

Using Your Checking Account Wisely

The biggest mistake consumers make, over and over again, is that they don't understand that there's a cost almost every time they engage in checking activity. For example, Joe Doaks thinks he's exercising discipline by taking out only $10 whenever he withdraws checking funds from an ATM. Say he takes out 10 bucks a day for five days in a row. He forgets that each time he does this, the bank is charging him $1.50. That's $7.50 in fees altogether. Had he withdrawn the $50 all at once, he would have been nicked only $1.50.

It could even get worse. If Joe uses an ATM other than his own bank's, the foreign bank will also rap him with a $1.50 "surcharge," raising his total cost per transaction to $3. Now the five withdrawals cost him a total of $15, or the equivalent of 30 percent interest on the 50 bucks he withdrew. This section tells you how to avoid such costly mistakes and provides additional money-saving tips.

Using ATMs

A machine's a machine, but whose ATM you use will make a difference in the fees you're charged. Here's the lingo banks use in their literature:

Asset Advisory

Here's why having your checks, especially Social Security and payroll checks, deposited directly into your bank accounts is important. In 1992, when Hurricane Andrew hit Homestead, Florida, although everything was being destroyed by the storm, receipt of direct-deposit payments was not interrupted. The National Automated Clearing House Association reports that 48 percent of household payroll and more than half of Social Security beneficiaries are paid through direct deposit.

➤ Proprietary ATM: It means your bank owns the machine. Nine out of 10 banks don't charge customers for using their ATMs, but of those that do, most charge between 75 cents and $1.

➤ Non-Proprietary ATM: The machine belongs to another outfit. Expect to pay $1 to $1.50 per transaction charged by your own bank. Plus, the new costly wrinkle is a $1 to $1.50 "surcharge" by the bank whose machine you're using—that's *on top of* what your bank charges for you using a foreign ATM. Eight of every 10 outfits now surcharge.

➤ National ATM: The bank's machine is hooked up to a national or regional network such as Cirrus, Plus, or Mastercard. You'll see their emblems on the machine. When you make an out-of-town transaction on these ATMs, the fee rises to $1.50 or $2.50.

➤ "Foreign" ATMs: Another way of saying "non-proprietary."

Even retailers are cashing in on ATM profits. Grocery stores, convenience outlets, gas stations and even hotels want a piece of the high-profit ATM action. They're acting like banks by putting thousands of machines everywhere, just so you can get some fast cash when you need it. If you fall for this convenience, expect to get nailed a total of $2.50 to $3 every time you withdraw money. At gambling casinos, the robbery will be higher, like $5 or more. Who benefits? They do. Who loses money? You do.

The Money Line

When ATMs first appeared nearly 20 years ago, banks enticed consumers to try the new-fangled machines by offering free hamburger coupons, cotton candy, and balloons for the kids. It was sort of a try-it-you'll-like-it campaign to get us addicted—and all the ATM transactions were free.

You can reduce your ATM charges if you:

➤ Keep your checking account at a bank that doesn't charge you for using its machines.

➤ Don't use an ATM belonging to an institution where you don't bank.

➤ Withdraw all the cash you'll need for the next few weeks, instead of making several small transactions that run up your total ATM fees.

One final thing to keep in mind: using ATMs can be dangerous as well as expensive. To protect your money, follow these rules:

➤ Memorize your Personal Identification Number (PIN) and keep it to yourself. Don't keep it in your wallet.

➤ Keep your ATM card in a safe place. It's as valuable to you as your credit card. If the ATM card is lost or stolen, report it to your bank immediately.

➤ Keep extra deposit envelopes in your car, so you can fill them out before approaching the ATM.

➤ Have your paperwork and your ATM card ready when you reach the ATM so you won't have to reach into your purse or wallet.

➤ Stand between the ATM and people waiting in line so no one can see your PIN number or your transaction.

➤ Don't accept help from strangers while you're using the ATM. If you have a problem, contact the bank.

➤ Take your ATM receipt. Put away your cash, ATM card, and receipt *before* you leave the ATM.

➤ Report all crimes to the ATM owner and local law enforcement officers immediately.

Cost-Cutting Tips

As big as the world of check fees is getting, there are still a few ways to get around those little buggers. Especially now, as the merger pace quickens and banks try to romance you to do business at their place instead of someone else's.

For example, many banks will waive certain checking fees if you:

➤ Keep a big balance in your account.

➤ Agree to forego getting your cancelled checks back with your monthly statement.

➤ Are older than 50 or 55 years, depending on the bank's senior checking requirements.

➤ Open a package account that combines several of your accounts, such as CDs and passbooks, under one statement.

➤ Limit the number of checks you write per month to the maximum allowed without a fee.

➤ Don't exceed a certain number of ATM transactions per month.

The Ugliest Fee of Them All

The one fee you should absolutely try to avoid is the bounced-check charge. The banks call these checks "NSFs" (non-sufficent funds). The latest figures show that banks are raking in an astounding $6.2 billion in profits from rubber checks that people write, and fees collected from people who deposit them. In fact, consumer watchdogs say that banks have set "traps" so that checks are more apt to bounce, such as paying the biggest items first so there won't be enough money left to pay off the smaller items.

Though industry studies show it costs a bank less than $2 to handle a bounced check, the average NSF costs more than $20. In some cities such as Philadelphia, banks charge as high as $32. And across America, the bigger the bank, the higher the NSF charge.

Table 10.2   The Average Cost of Bouncing a Check

City	Bounced-Check Fee
New York	$18.00
Los Angeles	$14.74
Chicago	$22.00
San Francisco	$15.40
Philadelphia	$29.40
Detroit	$22.42
Boston	$19.79
Houston	$23.89

continues

Table 10.2   Continued

City	Bounced-Check Fee
Dallas	$23.89
Washington	$26.94

Source: Bank Rate Monitor

If a bank decides to honor the check instead of letting it bounce, it will cost you an average of $20.33 in addition to the amount of the check. If it pays the check against your funds that haven't yet cleared, the charge is $13.05.

An outrage? You ain't heard nothin' yet. More outfits have begun to hit consumers with an NSF charge if they deposit someone else's rubber check to their account, regardless of their own balance. That cost averages $5.24. One Chicago outfit charges a $20 fee.

Remember that if you don't have enough funds in your account, every check you write beyond your balance will bounce. If, say, your balance is $15 and you write three checks for $25 each, the bank will charge you a fee for each one. The fee will be between $10 and $30, so you could wind up with the bad checks costing a total of as much as $90!

Bounced-check charges are so out of control that it's possible for this to happen: A person writes a bad check for $10. The check is presented to his or her bank not once, but twice, and the customer gets nicked $20 each time. Plus, the person whose name is on the check gets charged five bucks. The fees add up to 45 bucks in all—just for a $10 check. Consider yourself warned!

Banks argue that they need those charges to dissuade people from writing bad checks, but that's a lot of hooey. An independent study showed that only 5 percent of institutions reported a decline in NSFs after they raised their fees. Meanwhile, other studies show that the average bounced-check charge is 84 percent more than the bank's cost of handling the check!

Stop-Payments

You just issued a check to Big Bubba's garage for a new transmission in old Betsy. On your way home, the transmission sounds likes a blender full of rocks, and you don't want Bubba to pocket the money until he makes good on the deal. What do you do? Immediately inform the bank to stop payment on the check. Tell them your account number, the check number, the exact amount (in dollars and cents), date of the check, and the name of the person or company you wrote it to.

The problem with stop-payments is that they don't come cheap. They'll cost you around $20, and fees have been going up. You will have to decide whether the action is worth it, by considering who you're doing business with on the other end, and how important it is that the other party not cash the check.

A Savings Tip That Might Not Save You Anything

Earlier we told you that you could reduce your account fees by not getting your cancelled checks back every month. The banks call this "truncation" or "check storage." It works like this: You receive only your statement, and they keep your checks in their warehouse. That will shave a few bucks off your checking fees, but if you suddenly need a copy of one of the checks—zing!—you may be charged about $3 to $5 per copy. And the process will take a few days.

Then there's something called *check imaging* where you get back miniature photos of the fronts of the checks you issued last month, printed out on a large sheet. The banks still keep the real checks.

Before you grab the bank's bait, ask yourself: Wouldn't the cancelled checks come in handy when you prepare your taxes or if you ever get entangled in a lawsuit?

How to Protect Yourself Against Forgery

The first step toward preventing check forgery is to keep your checks in a locked drawer or safe deposit box. The institution should try to protect you by comparing the signature on the checks it receives with the signature card you filled out when you opened your account. You should have a copy of that card. It's also your proof of your legal signature.

Once a forgery is committed and it gets by the institution, there's no automatic protection. Almost all states have adopted a uniform code on forgeries, but the interpretation and execution varies by state.

As soon as possible, notify the bank if a check is forged. You'll likely discover it when reviewing your statement. Your obligation to notify the institution may be spelled out on the back of the statement. In some states, it's as short as 14 days. You can call the outfit, but your rights are protected only if you put the claim in writing.

The institution may investigate, or it may not respond. If it doesn't respond, make follow-up phone calls and write more letters. The bank may claim that you failed to notify it on time or that you were negligent by letting other people use your checkbook.

In that case, you may be forced to sue the bank. That will be a headache if a small sum is involved. You may be able to raise enough ruckus with your letters to get some action.

131

The Least You Need to Know

➤ Most checking accounts are characterized by high fees and little or no interest.

➤ Interest checking often costs more money than non-interest checking because the fees are higher, and the minimum deposit and average monthly balance requirement are greater.

➤ You can get zinged for up to $3 every time you use an ATM, because rival banks now tack on a surcharge in addition to what your bank charges you.

➤ If you match your personal checking habits against what five or six banks charge in fees, you'll quickly see which outfit will save you the most money. Limit your comparisons to only the most common fees and charges that are likely to affect you. Also, remember to read all the small type before you sign on the dotted line.

➤ Be wary of offers of "super-high interest rates" and "free checking." The offer may be only temporary, or there might be extra fees involved that aren't immediately obvious. Again, read the small type.

➤ Getting your checking account through a credit union, or putting some of your money in a Money Market Account can boost your interest rate.

➤ Remember that there's a cost almost every time you engage in checking activity. To avoid unnecessary fees, get a copy of the bank's fee-disclosure schedule, know your bank's rules regarding ATM usage, and avoid bouncing checks and issuing unnecessary stop-payment orders.

➤ You can probably save $200 to $300 a year by switching your checking account to a different bank, and watching your checking habits more closely.

Chapter 11

Savings and CD Accounts: Beating the Averages

In This Chapter

➤ Knowing the pluses and minuses of savings accounts versus CDs.

➤ The secrets of shopping for highest-paying FDIC-insured accounts—locally and out-of-state.

➤ Key questions to ask before you open any type of account

➤ How to avoid paying fees and penalties that sap your hard-earned cash.

Not everybody wants to play the Wall Street game with uninsured investments. Many folks prefer the safety of FDIC-insured accounts, where their money is protected up to $100,000. But most of these bank accounts only pay a measly 2 percent yield on passbook accounts, and not much more than 5 percent on CDs. The trick is knowing how and where to shop the highest-paying institutions—and the right questions to ask!

Banks, meanwhile, are getting away with murder because millions of Americans are willing to settle for low yields. They're ignorant of where to go to earn more, and still have the benefit of FDIC insurance. Many are unwilling to go through the hassle of changing banks even if it would help their pocketbook. Millions of people, especially senior citizens, are still clinging to the old-fashioned savings habits they learned as children—plopping money into passbook accounts to "save for a rainy day" without worrying about low rates. The sad result is that today there's more money deposited in 2 percent savings accounts than in 5 percent and 6 percent CDs!

This chapter shows you how to turn those piddling-interest instruments into cash cows by doing business with the safest, top-paying banks. First, it explains how to earn more with the three basic types of *savings accounts*—then it tells the steps you should take to get the highest yields with *CDs.* You learn the key questions to ask before you hand the bank a penny of your money.

Savings Account Basics

Should you get a passbook, Money Market Account or a CD? The answer is simple. The first two accounts are *liquid,* which means you can add to your savings or withdraw funds at any time without getting socked with a penalty. Savings accounts also can act as temporary "garages," where you can park your funds while you're scouting around for a high-paying CD or other investment.

With a CD, you lock up your money for a specific period of time, usually anywhere from three months to five years. But if you withdraw funds early, you get hit with a penalty.

Savings accounts come in three flavors:

Passbooks   The same old account that Ma and Pa lectured about when you were a youngster. You deposit your money, and the bank gives you a little book to record your transactions. The accounts by law paid 5 percent interest until 1986, but after that the average rate dropped steadily to just a tad above 2 percent.

Statement savings   Walks, talks and quacks exactly like a passbook, except there's no little book involved. Instead, the bank sends you a monthly statement that shows all your transactions. This, of course, reduces the time you spend bothering a teller, which is precisely what the bank wants.

Money Market Accounts (MMA)   These pay only a tiny bit more than the other two accounts, and you're permitted to write a maximum of three checks a month (to parties other than yourself) on the account. That makes it handy for you to transfer enough money, once a month, from your MMA to your checking account to pay bills, as discussed in Chapter 10.

Which Type of Account Pays More?

CD yields have been beating the average Money Market Account by as much as three to four full percentage points. The longer the CD term, the higher the yield and the more it tops what you can earn on an MMA. Here's what the two accounts typically paid over a several-year period, using a one-year CD as an example:

Table 11.1   A Comparison of CD and Money Market Account Yields

| | Yearly Averages (yields) | |
	1-year CD	MMA
1994	2.44%	4.01%
1995	2.86%	5.39%
1996	2.70%	4.95%
1997	2.64%	5.15%
1998*	2.53%	4.92%

* Through third quarter, 1998
Source: Bank Rate Monitor

Tiered MMAs Pay More for Larger Deposits

If you're lucky enough to have $25,000, $50,000 or $75,000 to deposit into a Money Market Account, many banks will pay you between 5.5 percent and 6 percent for what they call a "tiered" account. The more you deposit, the higher the yield. The rub is that generally you must open the account with at least $10,000, and if your account balance ever sinks as low as $1,000, your yield will plummet to only 1 percent or 2 percent.

Beware of Fees, Right and Left

Nothing in life is free, especially not savings accounts. All three kinds hit you with tariffs, as fees have been on an upswing throughout the entire banking industry (see Chapter 12). The following types of fees are common:

➤ A monthly or quarterly "maintenance fee," just for keeping your money in the bank. It will probably be between $4 and $12.

➤ A special fee if your account balance falls below a certain minimum during the month. Figure about $10 or higher.

➤ An ATM fee every time you use an automatic teller that doesn't belong to your bank. Now there's also a "double-whammy" charge, because the other outfit whose ATM you use, slaps you with a fee, as well.

➤ On an MMA, you'll probably get charged $10 to $15 if you write more than three checks a month. Plus, some banks will charge a $15 to $25 penalty if you close your MMA account within, say, six months after opening it.

Shopping for Savings Accounts

Banks are not dopes. The biggest reason they covet your basic savings and checking business is because those are their bread-and-butter, "core" accounts. Once you become a customer, you're also a prospect for buying CDs, bank mutual funds, personal loans, and mortgages. To bait the hook, the bank may offer you a "relationship package" deal that offers a slightly higher yield on your CD, plus maybe a no-fee credit card, if you maintain a combined balance of $20,000 or more for your accounts. The downside is that you'd probably do better by splitting the accounts among several different outfits.

The fact is, not enough consumers do a thorough job of shopping banks before they sign on the dotted line. They just stay at the same old place where they've been keeping their checking or savings. They don't check out what other outfits are offering, and they fail to compare the fees as well as the rates—preferably at a half-dozen institutions. In short, they're trading "comfort and convenience" for getting mugged by costly banks.

Here are the two big secrets for earning more on your savings and CDs:

➤ In the same city, on the same day, the odds are 10-to-1 that you can find another bank that will beat your bank's MMA yield by one-half percent to a full percent or more. All you have to do is get on the phone and call around.

➤ Don't just shop local banks. Contact the top-paying FDIC-insured banks in other states that will offer double what your hometown institutions pay on Money Market Accounts. There's a free list of these banks on the Internet at www.bankrate.com, with their toll-free phone numbers. These FDIC banks are super-safe, and just as convenient to do business with as the bank down the street.

Key Questions to Ask Locally

Even though banks use confusing account names, such as "Master Passbook Account" and "Money Market Passbook," you can cut through the confusion by asking these questions:

➤ What are the rate (before compounding) and yield (after compounding)? Compounding is explained in Chapter 9.

➤ Is the account tiered? That is, does it pay higher yields on larger balances? (This has become a big deal with Money Market Accounts.)

➤ What is the monthly maintenance fee?

➤ Is there an additional fee if I don't keep a certain minimum balance?

➤ Is there a fee if I close my account early?

➤ Is there a per-check fee on my MMA (three third-party checks are permitted per month)? Is there an additional charge if I *exceed* three checks a month?

➤ Is there more than one version of this account?

➤ Is the account federally insured?

Higher-Paying Out-of-State Banks Are Just as Safe (or Safer)

If you don't check out higher-paying banks in other states, you're making a big mistake and losing money. Just because an institution is 1,000 or 2,000 miles away doesn't mean it's not 100 percent safe. The banks are not only FDIC-insured, they're also rated among the strongest in the nation. Most of them boast a top three-star safety rating by the respected independent research firm of Veribanc, Inc., in Wakefield, Mass. Veribanc uses FDIC data to verify each institution's financial health.

These institutions will pay you up to twice as much on a Money Market Account than your local bank, and 1 percent to 2 percent more on your CD. No one has ever lost a dime in an FDIC-insured bank, thrift or credit union, up to the $100,000 limit, regardless of where it is based.

Of course, the whole idea of going out of state to make more money will go over like a lead balloon with your local banker. He'll tell you it's not patriotic to pull money out of your community and hand it to some faraway outfit. But, hey, aren't big banks gobbling up little banks in other states? And don't giant outfits like Citibank and Bank of America peddle credit cards across state lines? What's good for the goose ought to be okay for the gander, right?

Here's How You Do It for MMAs:

These are the basic steps for investing in a high-yielding, federally insured Money Market Account out of state:

1. Contact the institution by mail or by phone, to the attention of the person in charge of consumer deposit accounts. Some banks have a "national money desk," which handles inquiries from individuals outside the institution's local area.

2. Is the account federally insured? Explain how much you want to invest and for how long.

3. Ask for the latest rate and yield on the account you are interested in, and how long the rate is good for. Some may be "introductory" deals where the rate plunges after a few weeks or months. Banks are apt to change their rates on a weekly basis or more frequently. Many change their rates on Wednesdays.

4. Is the account "tiered"? That is, are there higher yields for larger deposits?

5. What are all the fees, and how can you avoid them?

6. Ask when your deposit will begin earning interest, and how many days after opening an MMA account you can withdraw funds.

137

7. Ask for an account-opening form and a preassigned account number.

8. Get the correct mailing address of the bank branch you are dealing with. The bank may have several locations.

9. If you open the account by mail, make your check payable to the institution, not to an individual. Write "For deposit only" on the back of the check. For maximum protection, include your Social Security number.

10. If the institution doesn't provide a deposit form, attach a letter specifying how much you are depositing, the type of account, the preassigned account number, the check number, and the amount. Include your name, address, phone number, and Social Security number. Keep a copy of the letter.

11. Mail your letter and check to the correct bank branch.

More Savings Shopping Secrets

Before you agree to open an account, check out the following tips:

➤ The time for you to wheel and deal is *before* you sign. You may not know it, but banks now are willing to negotiate with customers a lot more than in the past. You can try wheeling and dealing on everything from having certain fees waived, to asking for a cheaper credit card rate. Don't be bashful. Stand up and bark, and tell the bank what you want in exchange for your business. But don't tell it to an account representative or teller. Tell it to the branch manager or an officer.

➤ This is critical. Bank fees today are hammering every consumer to death. When you shop your half-dozen banks, get a copy of each outfit's "fee disclosure" document. Compare each fee—every one—with your own personal banking behavior. How many checks do you usually write per month? What average balance do you typically maintain? How often do you use an ATM? Then ask the banker, "Are you sure you've told me about all ways I can earn more interest, avoid fees, and save on my loans?" You're not being a pest; it's simply good business. The squeaky wheel always gets the grease.

➤ Read your contract *before* you sign anything. Also check the flyspeck footnotes at the very bottom of bank ads. This is *your* money we're talking about, not the bank's!

Where the Money Is—in a 2 Percent Rut

Shockingly, Americans not only keep $1.3 trillion in low-paying savings accounts, but whenever Wall Street shudders a little bit, more of them run like lemmings to deposit even more of their funds in those 2 percent investments.

The result is that today there's 50 percent more money in the three basic types of savings—passbooks, statement savings, and Money Market Accounts—than in small-denomination CDs.

At the end of 1989, consumers put 56 cents of every savings dollar into small-denomination CDs and 44 cents into basic savings accounts such as MMAs and passbooks. But nearly 10 years later, 62 cents of that dollar went to lower-paying savings accounts and only 38 cents to CDs. Table 11.2 spotlights this trend.

Table 11.2   Where the Money Is—Annual Figures (in Billions of Dollars)

Date	CDs	Money Market Accounts and Passbooks
1989	$1,148.1	$893.7
1990	$1,171.0	$923.8
1991	$1,106.3	$1,045.2
1992	$866.2	$1,187.4
1993	$780.2	$1,219.4
1994	$814.6	$1,149.9
1995	$929.8	$1,134.7
1996	$946.0	$1,271.7
1997	$967.1	$1,397.5
1998	$960.0	$1,536.7

How much are American savers losing by keeping so much money in low-paying savings accounts? Plenty. Suppose that 1,000 people each keep $1,000 in a Money Market Account paying two percent interest. That comes to a grand total of $200,000 in interest per year. Now let's assume those same 1,000 customers move their MMA accounts to other banks that offer five percent—something they could easily do. The interest increases to $500,000. If the customers decide instead to put their money into CD accounts paying seven percent, the interest jumps to $700,000.

As you can see, CDs are definitely worth looking into. However, keeping a lot of money in a savings account might be the better strategy if any of the following apply:

➤ You might have to access the money suddenly for some reason, such as putting a new roof on the house or getting Junior a set of braces. There's no penalty for withdrawing funds from an MMA, as there is with a CD.

➤ The high-tier rate on an MMA is paying more than CDs are paying. That can happen if you have $20,000 or more to open an account. But on longer-term CDs such as five years, the CD yield could top the tiered-MMA yield.

The Least You Need to Know

➤ The three basic types of savings accounts are passbooks, statement savings, and Money Market Accounts.

➤ Basic savings accounts almost *always* pay less than CDs.

➤ Comparison shopping for the best savings account deal can really pay off. Banks vary widely in their fees and interest rates.

➤ Some out-of-state, FDIC-insured institutions will pay you 1 percent to 2 percent more on CDs than your local bank. All the highest-yielders are listed on the free website www.bankrate.com.

Chapter 12

Ugly Bank Fees and How to Avoid Them

In This Chapter

➤ How banks justify increasing their fees

➤ The importance of shopping around for the lowest fees available

➤ Spotting outrageous fees in the fine print

➤ Avoiding the worst fees, minimizing the rest

It's disgusting. You work hard for your money, and hope to make it grow by entrusting it to a financial institution that smothers you with promises about what a great outfit it will be for you. In the first place, you're doing *them* a favor by letting them borrow your money. And what do *they* do? They invent a slew of new fees, increase the old ones and make it virtually impossible to conduct your banking without getting slapped silly by one charge after the other. Not only that, but the little guy who can least afford the fees is getting hit hardest of all, while Mrs. Gottrocks and her six-figure balances escape scot-free.

Banks argue that they need to raise fees to cover their costs of "expanding" their services, such as later hours, online banking, more ATMs, and branches in supermarkets. But that's a lot of hooey and you know it. The fact is, banks have added billions of dollars in new profits by hiking the bank's fees. If you bounce a check, for example, you're charged between 11 and 32 times their cost of processing it. And the bigger the institution, the higher the fees. This chapter takes you behind the scenes and explains the real reason why bank fees are soaring, which ones are the scariest, and how you can avoid such ridiculous highway robbery and keep more money in your wallet.

How the Fee Robbery Started

Back in the late 1980s, banks took their lumps when interest rates skyrocketed. There they were, sitting with tons of mortgage loans on which they were collecting 6 percent in interest, but having to pay 10 percent and 12 percent to people buying CDs. You don't need a Harvard degree to guess what happened. Thousands of banks and savings and loans folded.

The Money Line

Way back in the late 1980s, the word "thrift" was a nasty word because so many savings and loans were failing because of making bad loans and because of mismanagement. The number of thrifts that went down the tubes was in the thousands. Many banks failed, too, but not to the degree that thrifts did. By the mid-1990s, however, both banks and thrifts executed remarkable turnarounds. They began reporting record profits because of wider "spreads" between loan rates and savings rates, and from tacking new fees on customer accounts.

At the same time, institutions were becoming savvier in the use of computers. They began using electronic programs to identify which customers were most profitable, versus those who were costing them money. A customer who maintained high-balance accounts, but made only minimum use of live tellers was a lot more profitable than Joe Six-Pack, who kept a couple hundred bucks in his account, but pestered live tellers with a slew of labor-intensive requests. Banks started penalizing people who took up their employees' time with human, time-consuming transactions, and thus began the onrush of new and bigger fees. Their strategy has made them so much money that they're inventing new ways to clobber you with fees every day.

How Banks Baited the Trap

To keep the "cattle" out of their lobbies, banks said that one way to avoid fees was to conduct most of your banking by ATM, by phone or by computer. At first that sounded okay—on the surface—but it's become a lose-lose situation for the consumer. Here's why: When ATMs were first introduced in the late 1970s, banks offered all kinds of incentives, such as cotton candy, clowns, balloons and free hamburger coupons, to get you to try an ATM. Then a few years later, after you were hooked on the electronic marvel, institutions began charging a fee if you used another bank's automatic teller.

Most recently, that other bank added a surcharge—a double-whammy effect—that increased your total ATM cost to $3 per transaction, even if you only withdrew 20 bucks.

A Buck Here, a Buck There...but Wow, It Adds Up!

One study showed that today the typical bank, on average, charges 235 different fees. Even that figure may be low, when you check out the lists of fees on some mortgage loans. They're as long as your arm. It's not uncommon for the unsuspecting checking customer—who foolishly doesn't shop around town for a cheaper account—to pay $200 to $300 a year in fees they could easily avoid. And therein lies the rub: Research by behavioral psychologists show, time and time again, that consumers are insensitive to bank fees, when they really should be yelling and screaming about them.

Why are people so complacent and gullible? Several reasons: The amounts are small, a buck here, a buck there. Hardly noticeable. When they need cash, no one gripes about paying $1.50 or $3 to get emergency money out of an ATM in the middle of the night. The person with a bad credit record who gets a secured credit card for him or herself doesn't complain about paying a sky-high annual fee. Few people ever sit down and study their outfit's "fee disclosure" document which, by law, must explain each and every fee on accounts. And few notice the sneaky way that banks sprinkle their little debit items on your monthly statement. The list goes on, yet all these charges add up...*way* up! You, my friend, are being quietly and consistently ripped off.

Watch Your Wallet

Remember: Banks want your money, not you—your visits cost them time and money, so many of them will try to get it back in fees when you take up time at the teller's window. If your bank does this, keep your visits to a minimum—or better still, change banks!

Step 1: Beware of the Danger Zones

No one is going to tie a string around your finger with a sign on it saying, "Here's exactly how to avoid paying that next fee." You simply need to remember several things. First, be aware of the trouble areas where you're likely to encounter bank fees. They usually pop up if:

➤ There are a lot of human transactions involved, such as making any—or too many—trips to a live teller during one month.

➤ You're a very-low-balance customer and make a lot of time-consuming transactions, or don't keep several accounts at the same bank.

➤ You have a bad habit of always using another bank's ATMs.

➤ You're so much as one day late with your payment, or exceed your credit limit.

➤ You take advantage of a checking account that pays interest. Not only must your opening deposit be higher, but so must your required average monthly minimum balance.

➤ You close out your Money Market Account or passbook account only a few months after opening it, or withdraw any of your CD money before the account's maturity date.

The newest and ugliest fee of all? A special charge if you don't use your credit card at all for six months, always pay your card balance off on time, or fail to borrow any money from your home equity credit line over one year. You mean you pay a fee for being a Goody-Two-Shoes customer? That's right. You're penalized for *behaving yourself* or doing *nothing*, instead of doing *something*. Banks can't make a dime off you under those circumstances.

Step 2: Absolutely, Positively Shop Other Outfits

Here's the biggest mistake consumers make: For whatever reason—apathy, laziness, or because they say they don't have the time—they simply roll over and play dead instead of shopping other banks beyond their present one. It makes no difference how convenient your bank is, how much you like the folks who work there, or how stubbornly loyal you've been to the bank all these years. Odds are there's an institution out there whose fees are lower than what you've been paying. Ask yourself: Why would you *not* shop if you knew you could save money? It's *your* cash we're talking about, not the bank's!

Fiscal Facts

A bank's **Fee Disclosure Statement** is a document that lists all fees and the reasons why they're imposed. It's required by law, and your bank must make a copy available to you on request.

Instead of being hung up only on interest rates, as most people are, tell yourself now that you're going to start looking at the rest of your banking picture—the one that's costing you more money every year—those outrageous fees and charges. In Chapter 10, we describe the key to your hunt: Asking your bank—and about four or five other institutions—for a copy of their Fee Disclosure document. They must offer it to you, by law. The document will be fairly short and look like a bunch of gobbledygook, but it breaks down all the fees, one by one, for each type of account such as checking, savings and credit cards.

Step 3: Match Your Behavior Against the Fees

Next—this is critical—outline on paper *how you personally bank*. For instance, how many checks a month do you write? What's your average monthly balance? How often do you slip below that figure? How often do you reorder checks? What about late payments? How often do you visit a live teller? Make ATM transactions at another bank or your bank? How many times do you go over your credit limit? Or get a cash

144

advance on your credit card? *Et cetera*. (Whatever you do, don't feel embarrassed. You're just going to bite the bullet this one time so you can slash your banking costs. And it won't change the rest of your life one iota.)

Next, match your personal banking behavior against each bank's fee disclosure document. Add up the costs, bank by bank, based on that behavior. You'll be amazed by two things: The differences in all the banks' fees, and how much money you can save per year. It's a sure-fire method to cut your banking costs, but to really save the most, you must also discipline yourself a little bit by, for example, never using any ATMs except those owned by your bank. The bottom line here is, we're potentially talking savings of hundreds of dollars annually, not just nickels and dimes!

Asset Advisory

Keep track of how often you visit your local ATM. It's false economy to make lots of tiny individual withdrawals—you know you'll just have to go back again later to take out more. Avoid getting hit with fees twice (or more) by making a single withdrawal of enough money to get you through the day.

Step 4: Know How to Spot the Latest Tricks of the Trade

Banks are pounding you with new fees, or boosting old ones, every time you turn around. Today there is virtually no aspect of banking that is fee-free that doesn't reach into your wallet whenever you cough or sneeze. It would take several books the size of this one to list all the idiotic charges U.S. banks have invented in the past few years, but here are some of the most infamous ones we've come across:

➤ MBNA America and scores of other outfits raised their credit card late-payment fee from $20 to $25, and also posted higher over-the-limit fees—even if the customer only exceeded the limit by $1. Amalgamated Bank, Chicago, increased its late-payment fee to $35.

➤ At many banks, even if your payment arrives after 2 p.m. on the day the payment is due, the institution will post it the next day and sock you with a late fee.

➤ Most annual fees on credit cards are $25 to $40, but Sterling Bank & Trust in Michigan charged secured-credit-card customers $75.

➤ Several card issuers, including AT&T, eliminated their grace periods, meaning the interest rate meter started clicking the moment a purchase was made or the day their bills went out. Others reduced their grace periods from 30 to 25 days.

➤ General Electric Capital Corporation's GE Rewards program began charging a $25 maintenance fee to cardholders who didn't incur at least $25 in finance charges during one year.

➤ It cost $10 to replace a lost credit card at Franklin Savings & Loan, Cincinnati.

➤ To obtain a counter check, First Union Bank charged 50 cents and Signet Bank charged $1. First Union also charged an $8 "teller assistance" fee on its Express Checking in Philadelphia, Washington, and Miami. On the other hand, Nations Bank and others discounted their fees if the customer used direct deposit and didn't make any live-teller deposits or withdrawals, or by-mail deposits.

➤ Thousands of banks and S & Ls charged higher fees on checking accounts if the customer insisted on having their canceled checks returned with their monthly statements. When checks aren't returned, that's called a "truncated" account. In that case, it costs money to retrieve an actual paid check.

Watch Your Wallet

Beware: Banks choose the order in which they process the day's deposits and checks on your account. Even when you know that you've gotten a deposit in on the right day to cover your outstanding checks, if it's processed after the checks are, you STILL get hit with a bounced-check fee.

➤ ATM surcharges ran as high as $3 at Colonial Bank, Atlanta—that's *in addition to* the ATM charge by your own bank for using another outfit's machine. There's also been a dramatic increase in annual ATM system charges when you use an automatic teller that's part of a certain electronic network. The fee ran as high as $15 a year at Norwest Bank, Boulder, and $7 at First Bank, both in Boulder, Colorado.

➤ Unlike with CDs, which charge a penalty for early withdrawal of funds, banks make a big deal of advertising Money Market Accounts as "flexible, liquid" accounts where you can add to the account or take money out with no penalty. But they make up for this by hitting you with a fee of $15 to $20 if you close the account several months after opening it.

How Check-Cashing Outfits Rob You Blind

What's even worse than a bank? The neighborhood check-cashing store that says it will cash any check for you, no matter what. These guys say they're providing a necessary service, especially in poor neighborhoods, and that there are 12 million Americans without a checking account. So what do those people do? They're forced to pay their bills by buying expensive money orders at the check-cashing company.

Let's say somebody needs cash to tide him over until he gets paid by his company 10 days from now. He runs to the check-cashing outfit and writes a post-dated check for $220. The check-casher gives him $200. On an annualized basis, the interest rate on these transactions can range from 300 percent to an astronomical 1,800 percent!

In some parts of the country, those same check-cashers are ripping off seniors who cash their Social Security checks. One expert estimated that it cost a retiree trying to live on $8,000 a year almost $200 a year to get his cash that way.

The Bigger They Are, the Worse It Gets

Surprise, surprise. Nationwide, it costs you nearly $30 more in fees per year, on average, to maintain a checking account at a big bank than at a small one. "Small banks and credit unions are usually the places to get better deals," says the U.S. Public Interest Research Group, known as PIRG. In 1997, consumers paid 15 percent more, or $27.95, at a big outfit—and that gap had increased by 57 percent from only two years before, in 1995.

The Money Line

Smaller is better. It's true. Smaller community banks and credit unions tend to be friendlier and give you more personalized service than mega-institutions. For one thing, small outfits don't have the same big overhead that big banks do. For another, they depend more on serving the little guy than making nine-figure loans to big corporations. Credit unions, meanwhile, are non-profit, pay higher rates on deposits and charge lower rates on loans.

By contrast, in 1997 the big bank customer paid an average of $218 in checking fees compared with a small bank figure of $190, and only $108 at a credit union.

Free checking? Don't hold your breath. PIRG's survey showed that only 15 out of every 100 banks offered it, while 41 out of 100 gave free checking with direct deposit of payroll, pension or government checks.

Whatever happened to the big banks' promises that, by merging with another large outfit, they'd become more efficient and pass along the savings to you? Those were pipe-dreams, friend. You're talking out-and-out greed, and bankers' efforts to satisfy their shareholders, that's what.

How Bad Can It Get? Real Bad!

One poor soul had this happen to him: He inadvertently overdrew his checking account by $4.50 without knowing it, but needed cash. Over a two-day period he used his own bank's ATM three times (to avoid paying a surcharge). He withdrew $20, $20, and $40, for a total of $80. Nothing on the ATM screen warned him he was overdrawing his account each time.

The bank nailed him with a $28.50 charge for each overdraw, or $85.50 altogether—the equivalent of paying an 85.5 percent interest rate on his money.

In another situation, a father asked a bank why it charged his nine-year-old daughter a $5 per month maintenance fee on her $75 savings account. Answer: She had to make a deposit every month to avoid the fee.

If you want to avoid this kind of banditry, run, do not walk, to the closest credit union that will permit you to sign up as a member. Because if you don't, sooner or later your bank is going to get you, too!

The cost of bouncing a check depends on where you live. The average is about $21 nationwide, but in Philadelphia it's about $30, while California is lowest at around $11. One way banks really slap it to customers is by paying the largest check first when several of your checks come in for payment at the same time. This increases the odds that one or more of your other checks will bounce. And each time one bounces, you get nicked with a fee. By the way, guess how much profit banks make off bounced checks? Would you believe $5.2 billion a year from people who wrote the rubber checks and another $900 million off the people who tried to cash them?

The Least You Need to Know

➤ All bank fees are going up, and banks keep investing new ones.

➤ Some of the banks charge new fees for doing nothing—that is, having an inactive account, as opposed to doing something bad.

➤ You need to be aware of which banking areas are liable to hit you with a fee. For example: The less you bother the bank's employees, and the more you conduct all your banking electronically, the lower your fees will be.

➤ If you shop five or six banks and match their fees against your personal banking behavior, you can switch institutions and easily save a couple hundred dollars a year.

➤ Big banks charge higher fees than small institutions. You're best off at a credit union where the fees are lowest.

Chapter 13

When It's Time to Kiss Your Banker Goodbye

In This Chapter

➤ What to do when you've had it up-to-here

➤ The big tip-offs on when to make the move

➤ Why you shouldn't feel embarrassed or guilty

➤ Critical steps to cover yourself during the change

Forget the loyalty. Especially when you've had-it-up-to-here with your bank because you've become nothing more than a "number" following a merger. Or because you don't know any of its people any more, and they don't know you. Or because they're trying to throw you out of their lobby and onto their ATM machines, and charge you a few bucks in fees every time you turn around. If that's the case, you're a prime candidate to find a new life at a different bank.

Sure, parting is such sweet sorrow, but there's nothing wrong with saying "sayonara" when you're being ripped off by a bank's lopsided savings and loan rates, or when you need the special pampering you're not getting. Most people dread the inconvenience of switching banks, even though it takes very little time and energy. The result is more than worth it, because it's your *money* that's on the line, not how close the institution is to your home or office.

This chapter examines the important issue of whether you should change banks or stay with your current outfit. If you do move, it tells you the step-by-step procedures you should follow to avoid fees or a bad credit record that will haunt you forever.

Should You Switch?

Okay, let's say you're hopping mad. You're almost at the boiling point because your bank just screwed up on one of your accounts. Is it time to kiss those guys goodbye? It is if you keep you keep running into these kinds of problems:

➤ **Other banks pay more than your bank on savings and checking accounts.** If you haven't checked your bank's rates lately, do it. Rates have been flipping and flopping all over the place, and just because your outfit offered the highest rates in town a few months ago doesn't mean that's the case today. Compare all their rates, not just a few of them.

➤ **The bank's loan rates are moving up faster than its savings rates.** Do you know what that means? The bank is fattening its profits at your expense. Before you yank your accounts, try negotiating by asking the bank to lower your loan rates. Don't be surprised if they say yes. If they say no, you have another reason to switch.

➤ **The bank's fees have increased.** Believe us, they have at most banks. Study the fine print in your monthly statement. Compare your latest statement with one from a year ago. Ask the bank point blank to tell you which fees have gone up in the past year—on your accounts, on your ATM use, on your credit cards, everything. Notice any difference in those nickel-and-dime fees? We thought so.

➤ **They don't bend over backwards for you.** Is the bank ever liberal and kind when you need a special favor or make an innocent mistake? You may not know it, but some customers probably get sweeter treatment than you get. Here's an example: If you don't have the funds in your account to cover a check that comes through, will the bank courteously phone you first thing that morning and let you race over to cover the check before it bounces?

➤ **The old personal service is missing.** Banks are like any personal service business. You're happy when they are pleasant and courteous, cater to you when you need it, and go that extra mile when you have a special problem. But we all know that as banks have expanded by buying up other institutions, their turnover in personnel has been humongous. You're no longer a human customer; you're a number in a computer. Plus, as they push you toward ATMs, banking-by-phone and electronic PC banking from home, the old "personal touch" has gone out the window. At big outfits in particular, you've become a robot more than a person. If any of these things bother you, start the process toward switching to a small community institution or a credit union.

➤ **The teller lines always go around the block.** Sure, automatic tellers have cut your banking time down considerably, and many institutions have extended their weekday hours and are open on Saturday mornings. But suppose you've got a question, and the only time you can make it into the bank is late Friday afternoon—when everybody and his brother, sister, and cousin are depositing their paychecks, and they're all ahead of you? Time is money; you shouldn't spend it cooling your heels in a line.

➤ **They just closed the branch in your neighborhood.** It's happening more and more. Megabuck Bank buys up little old Friendly Federal, whose name disappears along with the Friendly branch where you've been doing business for years. To keep your business at a Megabuck branch that's farther from your home (and where nobody knows you), you'll probably have to spend more on gas than you'll earn on your meager savings account. That's another big reason to split.

➤ **They still apply the old, tough credit standards.** After applying very strict criteria to those who qualified—or didn't qualify—for loans in the early 1990s, most banks today have relaxed their lending rules. They are making personal and mortgage loans—and issuing credit cards—to folks who couldn't get to first base before. If your outfit hasn't yet hopped on the easier-credit bandwagon, this alone is a big reason to change banks pronto! But check the higher rates they're charging to people with not-so-perfect credit!

Asset Advisory

Banks today are extremely competitive. Even if you're fairly happy with your current bank, it may still be worth it to switch to a new one because of the special deals they offer to new customers.

➤ **The bank doesn't offer any special rate breaks.** Do you get special rate breaks if you maintain a big balance? Many outfits will pay higher interest on CDs or knock a half-percent off your loan rate if you keep beaucoup bucks on deposit, such as in a relationship package account, have your payroll or Social Security checks direct-deposited, or have your monthly payments automatically deducted from your checking or savings.

➤ **The bank doesn't offer good information.** What are the brochures in the lobby like? Are they complete, easy-to-understand dollars-and-cents information that you can use to make your money grow? Do they give you good answers to your toughest financial problems in plain English? Or is the literature blue-sky propaganda that only hustles your business and leaves you hanging? When was

Asset Advisory

An excellent way for you to check out the financial soundness of any bank is to phone Veribanc, in Wakefield, Massachusetts, at (781) 245-1226. For a very small fee, this independent and respected research company will provide you with a report on the institution, including its safety rating.

the last time your bank explained all its costly fees, where mortgage rates are probably heading, how to reduce your credit card costs, or the smartest way to manage your payments on a loan? Not recently? We thought so.

➤ **Your bank hasn't been making a profit recently.** Your bank's probably more financially sound than you think, but there's no harm in checking. The average person would need a Ph.D. in math to understand all the numerical gobbledygook that banks put into their annual and quarterly financial reports to federal agencies. You want to know how safe the institution is—in simple language. Stick with a bank that has made a profit at least five quarters in a row. If it hasn't, simply say, "See ya!"

Dealing With the Guilt

You've looked at the facts and decided that your current banking relationship is no longer working for you. Don't worry about how the bank will view your decision. You're not out to win a popularity contest. There's nothing awkward or embarrassing about changing banks, nothing whatsoever. After all, the bank employees may be very nice people, but remember, the bank has been making money on you all along. It's your hard-earned cash that you care about. And the day you leave, they'll probably pick up other new customers and probably won't miss your business one iota.

Okay, You've Decided to Switch. Now What?

Take a tip from how the apes and monkeys swing through the trees in a jungle. They never let go of one branch until they have a firm grip on another one. The same goes for changing banks. Don't let go of the last one until you've shopped and found a better one.

Don't decide on a new institution until you've read its literature and, very important, gotten a copy of its fee disclosure document.

Once you've decided on the new bank (or credit union), some housekeeping chores are necessary to protect you and your money:

➤ Make certain all your checks have cleared your checking account, otherwise you could wind up being liable for high bounced-check charges.

➤ Write the bank a dated letter—be sure to keep a copy—informing them that you are closing out your account(s) effective immediately. List each account number and the name(s) on the account(s). Otherwise, you could run into a problem. For example, if you have a checking account and haven't formally closed it, you could get zapped with an "inactivity" or "dormant" fee after as little as six months. That could run as much as $5 to $10 a month, and even cause an overdrawn-account charge of $30 at some outfits. Watch it!

➤ You have to be careful if you have a relationship package account, which combines several accounts on one statement. Close out all your accounts at once or you'll risk getting hit with fees on the remaining ones.

➤ Review your old bank's account-closing fees. Increasingly, outfits will slap you with a $10 to $25 charge if you close out a Money Market Account within 90 days to six months after opening it. That's particularly common in tourist areas. Second, if you withdraw any of your CD funds before the account matures, you'll get socked with a penalty of as much as six-months' worth of interest. Inform the old bank in writing that they are to give you all the funds when the CD matures, and not roll the account over into a new CD. In other words, keep your CDs at the old outfit until they expire.

➤ Hold onto your old checks when you leave. If you open a new account, many institutions, hungry for new checking business, will offer to pay you a few bucks for your old checks.

➤ If you don't turn in your unused checks at your old bank, or use them as an incentive at the new bank (see above), be sure to destroy them along with any unused deposit slips *and* any credit cards from your old bank. This will prevent them from possibly falling into the hands of someone who could abuse your accounts.

➤ Don't forget to turn in your old safe deposit key! Otherwise, you could pay a fee. Most folks don't remember this.

➤ If you're leaving the area, don't forget to leave a forwarding address for your loan records. Just because you move doesn't mean your outstanding balances won't follow you on your credit record. Plus, if you misplace or don't receive a bill, it doesn't mean the interest will stop piling up.

➤ Don't burn your bridges behind you. You never know when you might need those guys again at the old bank!

Once you've made the switch, don't forget to change your records at all the other places where you do business, such as supermarkets and drug stores. It's something many consumers forget to do when they switch banks. The reason for doing this is that one day, for some reason, the store may try to contact your bank to verify that you have an account there. (Yes, it's a big hassle to have to go through this, but the inconvenience later could be even worse.) *Tell the store your new account number in person—never over a cordless phone.* As paranoid as it may sound, your conversation on that type of phone can be picked up by other people. Whenever it your money is concerned, better to be safe than sorry!

The Least You Need to Know

➤ Stay informed about what your bank is doing. Have they been raising fees? Hiking loan rates? Turning you into nothing but a "number" following a merger? If so, it's probably time to find another bank.

➤ Compare what other banks are paying and charging. Do they offer higher interest on savings? Lower loan rates? Cheaper fees? Better customer service? If so, it may be worth switching.

➤ Lack of personal attention and an unwillingness to be flexible when you have a personal financial problem are good reasons to switch banks.

➤ Have a heart-to-heart chat with the branch manager before you close your accounts. Is the bank willing to negotiate any of your interest rates or fees before you bid them adieu?

➤ Make sure all your checks have cleared, then close your accounts in writing to avoid any misunderstandings later on.

➤ Avoid fees related to closing accounts by making sure your checks have cleared before you close an account, leaving a forwarding address for your loan bills, and turning in your safe deposit key.

➤ Don't feel any guilt or embarrassment when you change banks. Your old bank won't, and some poor sap will come along and take your place.

➤ Get to know the manager at the new bank or credit union before you sign up.

Chapter 14

Parking Your Money: Broker or Credit Union?

In This Chapter

➤ How to buy and sell stocks online—the easy way

➤ Where you can open an account for less than $1,000

➤ Why credit unions are better deals than banks

➤ How your CU deposits are protected up to $100,000

➤ Five ways to quickly find a credit union that you can join

There are more profitable places to keep your hard-earned cash than a low-paying bank that pays zip in interest, charges horrendous fees, no longer knows you by name, and maybe costs $1 to talk to a live teller. One is with a broker, who increasingly can handle your investments via on-line trading. Another is by joining a credit union, where, unlike with a broker, your money is insured for up to $100,000, and your rates and fees beat what the bank offers. If you're a novice in the money world who's been wondering if either of these options is for you, this chapter will explain the basics and how to get started.

The name of the game is to make your money grow the best way you can, without being hassled or disappointed by your institution. A broker can guide you into big stock or mutual fund earnings when the market is roaring, or give your heart fits when the Dow Jones drops and the bears take over. With credit unions, the pluses can be as long as your arm—starting with friendly people who often are as hospitable as your next-door neighbor. The following are the upsides and downsides of doing business with either place to park your do-re-mi.

Banking Wins Online, but Where Does Trading Fit In?

Banking over the Internet is becoming almost as common as using an ATM machine, but trading online has yet to win wide acceptance, especially among full-service brokerage firms.

Why is this? Call it the human touch, as many investors like to access account information online, most like the one-on-one service that a full-service broker provides.

Online trading is popular, however, as trading activity jumped nearly 50 percent in the last six months of 1997. Average daily trades grew to 200,000 by the end of 1997, 45 percent higher than the beginning of the year. And online discount brokers want those 'Net-savvy customers—so much that industry experts estimate that firms will spend more than $250 million in 1998 to get them. Maybe those lofty commissions have something to do with it. Online trading is expected to generate more than $700 million in commissions in 1998.

Where does Joe Consumer fit into all of this? Right smack dab in the middle of a price war.

Online discount brokerage firms such as Fidelity, Quick & Reilly, Suretrade, and Ameritrade, lowered their transaction fees. In the fall of 1997, Fidelity reduced its commissions 40 percent for investors placing 36 or more transactions per year, while Quick & Reilly took its fees down 44 percent. As of the summer of 1998, Suretrade boasted the least-expensive transaction fees—$7.95 per trade.

The bottom line is clear: Online brokerage firms want your business. So what can you do?

If you have already pinpointed your investment objectives, your level of investment risk and established your investment goals, and most of all, are comfortable trading on your own, then boot up and log on, baby. Take advantage of these low-cost transaction fees.

Getting Into Online Trading

Once you open up an online trading account with a brokerage firm such as Charles Schwab, E*Trade, Suretrade, or DLJ Direct, for example, you're ready to buy and sell online. If you don't already have an online trading account with one of the firms, you can find out more about the services offered and—with some brokers—even open up your account right online. All trades are carried out at the brokerage firm's site.

Many of the online brokerage firms offer investment research reports, so you can dig through their database to get financial data on the companies you're buying and selling. Almost all firms offer stock quotes, some of them real-time rather than

20-minute delays, as well as market snapshots to review how major indexes (the Dow Jones Industrial Averages and Standard & Poor's 500) are performing.

Here are a few brokerage firms that offer online trading with $1,000 or less to open up an account and offer less than $15 commission per trade:

> Suretrade (212) 566-2031
>
> Trading Direct (800) 925-8566
>
> Investex (800) 822-2050
>
> Web Street Securities (800) WEB-TRAD
>
> Trade Fast (888) 781-0283

Asset Advisory

Here's a tip: To make a quick comparison of commissions, services, and fees for online brokers, visit Microsoft's Money Insider's Discount Brokers page on its website at www.moneyinsider.msn.com. It is listed in the Features section under "Discount Brokers".

Hey, How About a Credit Union?

This might be the best deal of all—for your nerves as well as your pocketbook.

A credit union is a cooperative financial institution owned and controlled by people like yourself who use its services. That's "cooperative," as in "working together." These people are called "members" instead of "customers," and their members all have something in common, such as where they work, live or go to church. A credit union provides a safe, convenient place for the members to save money and get loans at cheaper rates.

Most people who join a credit union wish they'd done it years ago. Why? Because of the CUs' caring attitude toward their members, and the fact that their deals are better than a bank's. Credit unions' deposit rates are almost always higher, their loan rates are lower—as much as three to four percentage points below what a bank charges on credit cards. Plus, you won't run into the same blizzard of fees that you encounter at a bank.

Most important, CUs are not-for-profit. They're simply made up of people who want to pool their money and make loans to each other. The idea goes back to 19th Century Europe, and believe it or not—unlike at a bank—a credit union member's *character* and *desire to repay a loan* are more important than his income or credit record. Some difference, eh? Banks and thrifts, on the other hand, are in business to make a profit because they're owned by stockholders who expect to make a healthy buck on their investments. So if your friendly banker keeps sticking his hands in your pockets, you know why.

The Money Line

The first state to pass a credit union act was Massachusetts in 1909, but by 1935 there were 39 states with credit union laws, with 3,372 CUs serving 641,800 members. By the 1970s they grew to more than 43 million members, and today there are more than 72 million. Today, every state has a credit union league that coordinates the CUs in its state.

The banking industry hates credit unions with a passion. It has mounted intensive lobby efforts in recent years to get Congress to pass laws to make CU operations taxable, which they still are not as of this writing. But Congress, in 1997, voted the other way, making it even easier for credit unions to expand their membership bases—as bankers everywhere howled.

It's Easy to Join a CU

Credit unions are for everyone. If there's a credit union at XYX Manufacturing Company, for instance, any employee of XYZ is eligible to join. But there's a good chance that somewhere in your area there's a credit union that will welcome you as a member. There are many ways you can find one, says the Credit Union National Association (CUNA).

1. **Call a state credit union league**. CUNA will give you a list of all their phone numbers. Contact the association at (800) 358-5710.

2. **Ask your boss.** Your company may sponsor a credit union, or may be a select employee group (SEG) that has access to a credit union. Many employers offer direct deposit of your payroll to your credit union.

3. **Poll your family.** Your spouse's employer may have a credit union. Many CUs allow a member's entire family to also join, including cousins, uncles and aunts. But some may limit membership to just the immediate family.

4. **Ask the neighbors**. Some CUs have a "community" field of membership for folks living in a certain area.

5. **Read the Yellow Pages.** Credit unions rarely advertise, but a CU ad in the phone book may tell you its field of membership. Or, they can steer you to a credit union that you can join.

One more thing: When you join a credit union, you're a member for life.

Other than the membership requirement, you can do just about anything at a credit union that you can do at a bank. You can open a checking account—which CUs call a *share draft account*—or a savings account—which they call a *share account*—or a CD, just like at a bank. On the loan side, you can get a mortgage, a new- or used-car loan (where the CUs' low rates will beat the banks' pants off), a home equity loan or line of credit, or a credit card. And credit unions have ATMs just like those other guys.

Because credit unions are genuinely interested in their members' welfare, many of them do a better job of educating you about money than banks do. Because of their cooperative nature, they tend to have strong ties to their communities. Most CUs, for example, issue their own newsletter to members.

Fiscal Facts

The terminology is different, but the services are similar: credit unions call a savings account a **share account**, while the term for a checking account is a **share draft account.**

How CUs Beat the Banks' Rates

Here is what credit unions were paying and charging, on average, compared with banks and thrifts in a recent nationwide survey by *Bank Rate Monitor*. Except for mortgages, credit unions offer a big edge for your pocketbook.

Table 14.1   Comparison of Loan and Interest Rates

	30 year fixed-rate mortgage	New Car	Credit Card	Money Market Account	One Year CD
Banks	6.89%	9.04%	16.65%	2.28%	4.79%
Thrifts	6.88%	9.07%	13.47%	2.79%	5.07%
Credit unions	6.97%	7.76%	13.11%	3.58%	5.49%

Source: Bank Rate Monitor

Credit Unions Also Offer $100,000 Insurance Protection

Is your money safe at a credit union? Oh, yes. Your deposits are insured up to $100,000 per person by the National Credit Union Administration, an agency of the federal government, which insures the deposits of CU members at more than 12,000 federal and state-chartered credit unions nationwide. The $100,000 protection is similar to the $100,000-per-person coverage of bank deposits by the Federal Deposit Insurance Corporation.

Friendship, Not Confrontation

Any downsides to a credit union? We can only think of one: Because CUs are smaller, you won't find as many of their branches or ATMs in your local area. But their benefits far outweigh that relatively slight inconvenience. In fact, lots of CU members we know swear they'd never do business anywhere else. Said one, "The difference is this. When I did business with a bank, and tried to borrow some money, some squinty-eyed loan officer sat across the desk from me, shaking his head and saying 'No.' Now, when I visit my credit union for the same reason, there's a person just like myself sitting at the same side of a table with me, helping to figure out how I can get the money I need at the cheapest possible cost. It's friendship, not a confrontation!"

Many CUs Are also Online

Banks, brokers, insurance and finance companies aren't the only outfits that offer helpful advice for your money online. Many credit unions also have a presence. Just click on the keywords "credit union" and start from there. In fact, one of the best electronic calculators we've found to help you compare the cost of leasing versus buying a new car, is at www.forestparkfcu.org/alvb.html.

The Least You Need to Know

➤ Trading online has become as easy as using an ATM, but not every broker is excited about it yet.

➤ There's a big price war on online commissions and transactions among brokers, which you may be able to take advantage of.

➤ Credit unions are non-profit, cooperative organizations that pay higher savings rates and charge lower loan rates than banks.

➤ CUs call their customers "members" and have a membership requirement, such as belonging to a certain organization or living in a particular geographic area, but you can easily find one that you're eligible to join.

➤ Credit unions have the same $100,000 federally insured deposit protection as FDIC-insured banks, so your money is safe.

➤ You'll probably find friendlier service at a credit union, because you'll be served by people who have the same interests at heart.

Booting Up and Banking On It

Did you know that personal computers are outselling televisions? Well, if you're one of the millions of consumers who have purchased a computer, you now have the latest tool that will take you out of the bank lobby and directly into your checking account—all from the ease of your armchair.

If you're still doing your banking and bill-paying the old-fashioned way, forget it. Those sheafs of envelopes and books of stamps may soon become collector's items as more banks and businesses become wired to help you balance your checkbook, pay bills—even directly deposit your Social Security checks.

This chapter will explain the basics to booting up and banking online, explain online security issues and key questions to ask your banker about doing your banking through cyberspace.

Even a Kid Can Do It

Just when you thought all the kids have gone to sleep, you hear cries of "I've got it!" and "That was so-o-o easy!" coming from the den. Your 10-year-old is still up, playing on the family computer. You know, the 300MHZ-pentium with the 3.2 gig hard drive and 32 megs of RAM the children begged and squealed for during the 10 weeks before Christmas.

You're hip—you know that "edu-tainment" is in. So you ask your child if he's having fun with the Megablaster Tri-color-rama battlefield game on the CD-ROM. Your child gives you one of those "get real" stares, and says, "Nope. I just balanced your checkbook, paid off your credit line at the bank, and reconciled your VISA account. Wanna update your stock portfolio?" he queries. "I got the 56K modem all set up on COM port 2."

"Geez," you say, as all the pride of learning the difference between the floppy drive and hard drive flushed right out of your toes. Welcome to managing your money in the 21st century.

Here's why you shouldn't feel like a speed bump on this information superhighway to online banking.

➤ Your checkbook is always balanced. By calling up your bank's web page and simply typing in a password, all you have to do is click on a button labeled "account history" to see your balance without having to wait for your statement in the mail.

➤ Your bank is a 24/7 shop. Online banking enables you to transact your banking business whenever you want—you are not at the mercy of lobby hours.

➤ Some online savings accounts pay more interest than regular savings accounts. For example, Atlanta Internet Bank offers higher yields on money market accounts if you open up a bank account online. And depending on your balance, you can earn almost *double the yield*!

➤ Save time on bill paying. Rather than writing out checks and using stamps and envelopes, all your bills can be paid in less time with just a few keyboard strokes.

Past, Present and Future

In 1998, a ground swell of banks offered online banking as a predominant feature to customers, allowing them to get bank balances, pay bills and transfer funds between accounts.

And, while home banking has been discussed for dozens of years, it really wasn't until the mid 1990s when many banks made all those predictions happen. By the middle of 1996, 38 percent of the top 150 banks in the U.S. offered PC-based home banking services and most of the remainder plan to offer services by the new Millennium. And virtually all have some sort of telephone-based banking service already.

For example, Citibank in New York is believed to have signed on 250,000 consumers for its online banking program, and at least 75 percent of those have signed on since 1995.

Another reason for diving into cyberspace? The average time spent setting up new accounts at a traditional bank branch is more than five hours, while online accounts can be set up in a little over an hour. With customers demanding flexibility and responsive services, it's no wonder that millions of consumers are choosing to save time by banking online.

Shipping Your Money Inside a Steel Safe

Computer hackers are everywhere, and that's probably why online security is the number one concern for consumers in banking online. Banks take online security very seriously, especially when even the slightest flaw could severely damage customer confidence. Bank of America, for example, explains all the security problems that occur on the Internet and countermeasures that are taken, to its customers.

Even so, security, of course, is always a major concern for customers. When you're sending credit card numbers, passwords, electronic cash and personal information over the Internet, it makes you wonder if this information can be intercepted by others.

Banks and solution providers are stacking up firewalls, encryption, pin codes and passwords against hackers, like sandbags against the flood. Tip: Change your password often as a measure of protection (just don't forget it!).

Typical online banking services available are protected with a PIN number, meaning a personal identification number that you choose, that will verify and confirm each banking transaction that you perform.

You should look for a bank that features key encryption measures, meaning, security "codes" they have implemented so that only you and your bank see your account information.

For example, on America Online, an online service, its Banking Center features a product called BankNOW that is used along with several of AOL's banking partners to transfer funds between accounts, get balances, and pay bills. This BankNOW software, created by Intuit, the makers of Quicken, uses a 128-bit encryption method and states that it is virtually impossible for anyone using current technology to steal information. Simply put, it is like sending your money inside of a steel safe. Restrictions do apply, as the 128-bit standard is so powerful that the U.S. government has made its sale overseas illegal. Federal regulations only allow U.S. and Canadian customers to download the 128-bit encrypted software.

Q&A with Your Banker

Some banks offer both Internet and dial-up access. And their fees for account transactions and investments vary between banks as much as the services they offer. For example, most banks with an online website will let you view account balances and transfer funds between accounts for free, but paying bills can generate another monthly charge.

If you are considering banking online, here is a list of questions you should ask the customer service rep at your bank.

➤ Does your bank offer, or plan to offer, its own online banking service, either through their own website or a software application with online access to its central computers? You will want to find out all the charges and fees involved and what types of transactions you can and cannot do online.

➤ How long does it take for each transaction to be executed? Does a funds transfer take place immediately? If you pay your mortgage on a Monday, when will the payment be debited from your account and credited to the recipient?

Here's why: Let's say you pay your mortgage via cyberspace on Tuesday. However, once your financial institution's processing department receives your "electronic request," many financial institutions may still have to print out a check and mail the payment to the electric company. The result? Your electronic bill payment might not get paid until five business days later. Find out the details from your financial institution. Some banks debit your account the day the check clears.

➤ What type of security does your bank offer with its online banking services? Typically, the types of encryption used in online banking allow only you and the bank to see your account information. Ask your banker to explain how it works in laymen's terms.

➤ What happens if an error occurs? Sure, online banking may have been around a decade or so, but mistakes can happen. What can you do if there is a technical glitch resulting in a duplicated transaction? Ask your banker what steps you will need to take to rectify any situation—be it your error or not. If you inadvertently duplicate a transaction or send money to the wrong creditor, you need to know how to correct the error and not pay substantial bank fees in the process.

➤ What is the process to close an online bank account and what types of charges are involved? It may be easy to open an online banking account, but how difficult is it to close it? Your banker should tell you what is involved from a financial, as well as technical, perspective.

If you sign up with one of the financial institutions on an online service or the Internet, make sure you understand all of the features and whether or not additional charges are assessed.

The Least You Need to Know

➤ With online banking, you can balance your checkbook and pay bills whenever it is convenient for you. You're not be at the mercy of lobby hours.

➤ By the mid- to late '90s, virtually all banks have some sort of telephone-based banking service, and more than a third of the top 150 banks in the U.S. offered PC-based home banking services.

➤ Look for a bank that offers 128-bit encryption method with its online banking features. This type of "security code" makes it virtually impossible for anyone using current technology to steal information.

➤ Just because you don't need to go into a bank branch doesn't mean there aren't charges associated with online banking. Find out from your banker how much it costs, as well as if there are fees associated with closing the account.

Part 4

Credit and Loans: Getting Money When You Need It

If you only want to make the best possible mortgage or auto deal for your pocketbook—or even if you're up against the wall with personal debts or credit problems—this section is for you!

Banks and finance companies are taking it out of borrowers' hides right and left. The whole country's on a plastic binge, using credit cards like there's no tomorrow and foolishly paying through the nose to do it. More people are slipping closer and closer to the financial edge—1.35 million of them filed personal bankruptcy in 1997 alone, yet banks keep offering them more "easy credit." Meanwhile, the average Joe and Jane don't realize how much intimate personal financial information the big credit bureaus have on them in their computers. And rarely do they bother to find out, even though their credit problems keep growing.

This section tells you how to strengthen your credit to get the loan you need and how to prevent a financial crisis even if it's at your front door. You'll learn how to beat the auto dealer salesman when you're in the market for a new set of wheels. How to shop for the cheapest new mortgage loan or refinance your old one with a lower monthly payment. Where to get a low-rate credit card that'll save you big bucks, and how to easily consolidate your debt at far less than you're paying now!

Don't borrow another dollar until you check out these tips to save on loans—not to mention saving your skin at the credit bureau!

Chapter 16

How Strong Is Your Credit Rating?

In This Chapter

➤ How much personal data about you the credit agencies already have

➤ Red flags that creditors look for on your credit report

➤ How to get a copy of your credit report

➤ How to improve your chances of getting credit and removing errors from your credit record

➤ How to handle disputes

Like it or not, the credit bureaus and the guys who figure your credit score have the goods on you. Plus, you're living in a nosy credit society where everyone wants to know your shirt size and blood type before they'll lend you a buck. Your ability to borrow money or get a new job swings almost entirely on the information contained in your personal credit file. Who has the data? Three giant companies that have personal credit information on just about every person in the U.S.

Nobody ever told you how to get around this super-snooper system, but there are ways. People with bad credit? They get stung with extra-high interest rates by banks and finance companies that are making a killing from those "sub-prime" loans. Even those with *good* credit can easily become victims of erroneous information that—one time out of three—winds up their report without their knowing it.

Yet shockingly, most consumers don't even bother to get a copy of their own credit report to look at and check for errors. They remain in the dark, never realizing how much negative stuff the credit agencies have dug up on them. The info can range from their date of birth to their income, payment habits, and the people they owe. Even worse, few people know the inside scoop on how credit reports work and what lenders look for.

This chapter goes inside the shadowy world of credit bureaus, explains how they "score" your credit history, and tells you what to avoid. You'll learn how to strengthen your credit file and greatly improve your chances of getting a loan.

Big Brother Is Watching You

You can forget about how "private" you think your personal financial life is. The odds are 450-million-to-1 that if you have a credit card, department store account, savings or checking account, auto loan, student loan or mortgage, there's a computer file on you. Everything is in it—your job, how much money you make, where you've lived, and how you've paid your bills.

A little scary? You bet. Big Brother is watching you like you wouldn't believe. Its computers sit in a company you've maybe never heard of, run by people you've never met. Make that *three* companies: Experian (formerly TRW), Equifax, and Trans Union. They're the three big guns of the credit-agency business, and all three probably have the same information on your life.

In the late 1980s, the three outfits got together with a company named Fair Isaac Co., in San Rafael, California, and worked out a system to predict the probability of individual consumers paying—or not paying—their bills based on the characteristics in their credit report. Using this as a model (called FICO, after Fair Isaac), each credit bureau came up with a credit "score" on each person. With a little weighting, juggling and tweaking, they're able to compare any bureau's score against the others. Sort of like working with three bathroom scales to get a comparable answer.

Watch Your Wallet

Be careful to protect your credit rating—it affects more than you know. Not just potential creditors, but prospective employers, landlords, just about any *business* can file for a copy of your report and, for a mere $10 fee, know everything there is to know about your credit history.

Nowadays, your credit score can be the number one thing that causes a credit company to say "yes" or "no" to your loan application. Cold and heartless? Yes. But getting accepted or turned down also can depend on whom you're doing business with. One typical minimum score to be approved for a loan is 620, based on the Fair Isaac model. But an auto dealer may finance your car if you score only 550, while a lender giving you an unsecured line of credit (you put up no collateral) may require something higher than 620. But you can bet the auto dealer will charge you a higher-than-average interest rate.

Smaller, regional credit bureaus supply personal credit data about you to any place you go for credit—from credit card companies and auto dealers to, yes, even the company that's considering you for a job. Whenever you apply for credit, those outfits feed your latest personal information into the Big Three's computers.

Money Line

The Big Three agencies aren't the ones who finally decide whether you'll get a loan or be hired. They only "compile the data," as they say, and provide it to organizations that determine whether they'll extend credit to you. It could be the car dealer, department store, bank, or credit card issuer. And to confuse the issue, all those guys might evaluate your credit history differently. Little wonder the Big Three are a mystery to the average consumer, who knows zip about how the credit system operates.

Despite the fact that credit agencies have 450 million consumer credit reports on file, in one recent year only 9 million Americans bothered to peer into their own files to see the often gory information on their credit records. Of those, one out of four discovered an error they eventually had corrected, according to the National Center for Financial Education, San Diego, California.

You Wouldn't Believe What They Know About You

Here's what you're up against. Those credit agencies look under every rock. They gather information on you from hundreds of thousands companies such as retailers, banks, finance companies, and credit card issuers. In turn, those companies feed monthly updates on consumers back to the Big Three. The information includes, for example: names, old and current addresses, Social Security numbers, birth dates, employment information, and how people pay their bills. They also gather information from public records in state and county courts. But this information is limited to tax liens, legal judgments, bankruptcies, and, in some states, child-support payments.

With a couple of little touches on a computer keyboard, an agency can pull up your credit's life story and send it immediately to Megabuck Bank or Bubba's Auto Emporium where you're sweating out a loan. In turn, the information you filled out on your credit application at Megabuck and Bubba's also winds up in the Big Three's computers for the *next* place you apply for a loan. They get you coming and going.

Asset Advisory

If you consolidate your student loans, make certain that you contact the credit reporting agencies—and follow up to make certain that the consolidation is recorded. Your new status should be reflected on your next credit report.

And now you know why banks and mortgage companies say they'll "get you an answer within an hour" after you submit your loan application. They use a Desktop Underwriter system. All they do is plug in the data on your application, and—bingo!—as fast as lightning, the computer spits out a score, whereupon the loan officer turns to you with a smile—or a frown.

But what if a loan clerk enters the wrong number on your personal-assets dollar figure into the computer? You could get rejected for the loan.

How "Predictable" Are You? The Big Three Think They Know

Credit agencies work with outside mathematical experts to develop what they call "predictive models"—computer programs that try to estimate your *future* credit behavior based on your *previous* behavior. Einstein would have trouble understanding these complicated computer whatchamacallits. They involve far-out terms such as "regression analysis" and "neural network"—concepts that are way above the heads of average people.

These programs can predict the probability of someone going bankrupt three, six, or nine months down the road, or they can determine the likelihood of a person stiffing his or her creditors by never paying bills over the next 24 months.

The Money Line

Ever wonder how big banks get their mailing lists for the 3 billion credit card solicitations they stuff in mailboxes every year? The bank makes a list of the kinds of new customers it's seeking, goes to a credit bureau, and asks, "Who has two credit cards and has never been 90 days late on a payment?" The bureau prints a list of millions of people who match those criteria. The bank then mails out offers of credit to everyone on the list. The approval rates on these applications are higher than if the bank were to simply mail to everybody in town.

The Biggest Mistake of All: Not Starting Early

If you ask lenders about the biggest mistake consumers make with credit reports, they all agree on one thing: People don't bother to get their report in shape *before* they try to take out a loan. Instead, they waltz into the lender's office, fill out an application, and look like they've been run over by a truck when the loan gets rejected.

A little advance homework and spending $8 for a copy of their credit report could have avoided that mess.

Credit experts say that:

➤ for a mortgage, you should check your credit three to six months before you apply.

➤ for a car loan, check your credit and get pre-approved by a bank or credit union before you step inside an auto dealer's showroom and get whisked into some loan guy's office.

➤ for credit cards, always review your credit report with a fine-tooth comb before you apply.

Look at it this way: If you don't do your homework and get turned down for a loan, that's one more black mark on your credit record!

Uncle Sam Protects Job Seekers—Sort Of

Under federal law, if you're turned down for a job on account of your credit report, the employer must notify you of your right to get a copy of your credit report for free from the credit agency. The credit agency must notify you automatically that the employer accessed your credit file if it contains any derogatory public information about you (such as bankruptcies, liens, and judgments).

In a few states (such as California and Minnesota), employers must notify you before they obtain your employment history in your credit report. The biggest users of employment reports? Companies in sensitive industries such as banking, defense, pharmaceuticals, and other medical fields.

The Bad Stuff Comes Off—Eventually

Fortunately, under the Fair Credit Reporting Act of 1971, negative information on your report can't hang around forever. By law, the agencies are *supposed to* wipe off any bankruptcy data 10 years after it was entered. They're also *supposed to* erase any tax liens, lawsuits, judgments, or accounts put up for collection after seven years.

But don't assume that will happen, or that everything on your report is accurate. The agencies, like every company, are working with the human factor. A data clerk can easily hit the wrong computer key

Asset Advisory

Lesson #1 in credit reports is, don't trust the information in your personal credit file, and don't expect anybody besides yourself to correct it.

when he or she enters your information. He may have misread something on your credit application back at Bubba's Auto Emporium.

Here's another unpleasant possibility. As has been charged by Congressional committees investigating how the credit reporting services operate, an agency could just plumb forget about eradicating your negative information when it's supposed to. It's happened thousands of times.

The Three C's—An Old-Fashioned Pipe Dream

There was a time when you could go into a bank, and the banker—who was your friend and neighbor—had known you since you were in pigtails or knickers. He'd okay your loan with no credit check or other hassle. You can kiss those days goodbye. Banking has become big business, and big business today doesn't want to take any risks. You and your habits are now impersonal numbers in a Big Three computer. Oh, sure, banks still insist that they lend money the old-fashioned way—on the basis of what they call the "Three C's":

➤ **Character** It may not have anything to do with what kind of person you really are. More than likely, admit the credit agencies, it means how long you've lived at the same address and worked at the same company.

➤ **Capacity** How much debt can you afford, based on your present income? The lender looks at your living expenses, current financial obligations and the payments that your new loan would require.

➤ **Credit** How long have you had credit accounts such as credit cards, mortgages, and personal loans? What is the credit limit you're allowed on each one? How close are you to those limits now? Have you made your payments on time?

Sometimes lenders use a different third "C"—collateral—meaning, "How much security can you put up, so in case you don't pay us back, we can grab your stocks and bonds or Aunt Agatha's jewels?"

Nobody's perfect, and lenders know that. But if you've had a car repossessed, or another lender has given up trying to collect on what you owe, the Three C's have probably gone down the tubes in your case.

Your Credit "Score" Is How You're Judged

Remember, it's not the credit agencies that decide aye or nay on your loan applications. It's the outfits where you apply for credit. They all put a different value on the information on your report.

One may look more closely at your income, job, number of years at the same address, and whether you own your own home or rent. Another may be more interested in examining your bank accounts and payment track record. There's no way you're going to find out how they do their thing. You must be prepared for any roll of the dice.

What most credit grantors have in common, though, is that they use a "scoring system" all their own to judge you as a credit risk. That's why, in their back rooms, they call it a "risk score" based on whatever criteria they use. Your total score is made up of up a bunch of little individual scores, one for each thing about you the lender is examining.

For instance, if you've lived at the same address for five years, the lender might score this item as "5." If you've resided at the same place for between two and five years, the score might be "3." And any period less than two years is scored as "0." In other words, it's possible that an axe murderer who's lived in his home longer than you've lived in yours could (technically) score higher on this item than you would.

Other items on your credit report you might be scored on include your current monthly debts versus your monthly income, number of credit accounts, late payments, unpaid accounts put up for collection, tax liens, and the number of inquiries on your credit report.

The lender adds up the scores for all the items and comes up with a *total* score. If it's high enough, you get the loan; if it isn't, then sorry, but so long. Numerically, the range between good and bad in a lender's scoring system can be all over the lot. For example, it could be from 0 to 1,000, or from 375 to 850, depending on the credit grantor. There might be one minimum score that Joe Doaks has to reach to borrow $1,000, and a different minimum for Mrs. Gottrocks, who wants to borrow $50,000.

Just try to get a bank or any other lender to confide its secret scoring formula to you. It won't—not yet, anyway. But one day it may have to, because the Federal Trade Commission has proposed making the secret scoring systems open to the public. That would include how a person's score stacks up against others, and how lenders use a score to approve or reject a credit application. All kinds of things are apt to bust loose when this heretofore-confidential system is made public.

As of this writing, scores do not appear on anyone's credit report. But a person's score can change over time. How bad can scoring get? One bank employee told us she's seen a huge pile of loan applications on a branch manager's desk on a Friday afternoon—all to be graded by one person arbitrarily, within a few minutes. One applicant, she said, was turned down because he happened to drive a truck instead of a car.

Watch Your Wallet

One mistake that many people make when they fill in their annual income on a credit application is forgetting to include the earnings of other people in the same household. If the other incomes were counted, it might raise their risk score and increase their chance of obtaining credit.

Are You Good, Bad, or Gray?

Lenders have a habit of lumping you into one of three ranges—"good," "bad" and "gray." Its computers make the first cut. The top scores are considered "good," and these customers are automatically approved for a loan. The "gray" scores are for people who score somewhere in the middle of the range. These are personally reviewed on an individual basis. The "bad" group might just as well have leprosy. But occasionally the lender may move a person into the "gray" group to give him or her "an extra chance."

Fiscal Facts

A *charge off* is any loan that a creditor has given up on collecting and wiped off its books. Avoid charge offs: the creditor may be leaving you alone, but the black mark stays on your credit report for years.

An example of a person who would immediately be lumped in the "bad" category is someone who has had "charge-offs" in the past. *Charge-offs* are loans that creditors eventually have to wipe off their books because they've never been paid. "If we see someone who has had charge-offs greater than $300 in the last four years, we just immediately decline it," explained one credit agency executive. "I don't want anyone in my office spending any more effort on that one."

If you've been habitually 30, 60, or 90 days late in making your payments, you could be hurting your credit record even more. All late payments are bad, but 90 days is worse than 30, as you might guess. Credit card companies are a little looser when you don't pay on time, because after all, those guys *want* you to go past the due date so they can charge you interest on your balance!

The "Sub-Prime" Revolution: Low Scores Get Loans

The biggest new trend in credit reports and the loan business are *sub-prime* loans, made to people with less-than-great credit, who pay higher rates to borrow. By using Fair Isaac's technology and massaging all the data that credit bureaus collect, sub-prime lenders believe they've figured out which low-score consumers are still likely to pay back their loans.

Instead of charging a sub-prime customer 8.5 percent to finance a new car, he might pay 10 percent to 13 percent. Ditto for mortgages. The home loan might be 9 percent to 11 percent instead of 7 percent. But the difference in total interest cost can be tens of thousands of dollars over the life of the loan!

No wonder banks and finance companies are falling over themselves to buy up sub-prime lending companies. One Florida thrift institution we know now engages in this business almost entirely, for mortgages. It has scores of credit representatives doing nothing all day but phoning all slow-paying accounts and goosing them to get their payments in ASAP. In the lending business, they call these institutions "bottom-feeders."

It's Thumbs Down in Most Cases

The most closely guarded secret of all? The lenders' *approval ratio*. It's the percentage of applicants who get approved or disapproved for their loans. Sources at the Big Three agencies give this picture:

➤ If a credit card issuer sends a mailing to consumers that says they have "pre-approved" status for credit, the odds are nine out of 10 they'll actually be approved. But if the card company somehow finds out that the person's credit has "deteriorated" lately, it may conclude, "Hey, this guy is not as good as we thought he was." Result? He'll get approved, all right, but the creditor may bust his credit limit down to $200–$500. He also may pay a higher rate of interest on the money he borrows.

➤ The person who just picks up a credit application at a store, then fills it out and mails it in, has a two out of 10 chance of getting approved.

➤ The person who applies for a Gold Credit Card (with a $5,000 credit line and other perks) has a four out of 10 chance of being okayed.

➤ New car loan applicants also have a four out of 10 possibility of approval.

For a plain-vanilla credit card, credit scorers used to look for someone with an annual income of at least $12,000. Now, some have dropped the requirement to as low as $8,000. To obtain a Gold Credit Card, a person needs an income of about $30,000.

Why are the minimums falling? Because of fierce competition for customers. The credit card pie is just *so* big, and more and more outfits want a piece of it. To cover their higher risks, creditors may charge a higher interest rate (plus special fees) and monitor these new customers once a month. Another reason for easier credit is that the percentage of delinquencies—people who fall behind in their payments—is decreasing.

How to Boost Your Chances of Getting Approved

It's not easy for a lot of people, but the sure way to increase the odds of obtaining credit is to follow these basic rules:

➤ Pay your bills on time.

➤ Pay down the debts you owe.

➤ Don't take on any more credit than you need and can afford.

➤ If, say, you have an auto loan and several credit cards, reduce the number of cards immediately.

➤ Don't apply for credit too frequently. Each application shows up on your credit report. Eventually, a creditor is going to see all those items on the report and wonder why you're trying to run up so much debt. Are you planning to disappear to Rio de Janeiro someday, maybe?

➤ Use the credit you have wisely. Don't live up to your credit limit.

➤ Ask the credit agencies for a copy of your report every year or two, so you'll know what kind of picture they have of you.

➤ Correct any errors on the report. Odds are, there are some.

How Credit Inquiries Can Haunt You

Let's say you've been pretty good about paying your bills on time. You earn a nice income, and you've lived at the same address for two years. You can't think of anything that could possibly prevent a lender from giving you credit. No tax liens, no bankruptcies, no nothing.

You carry one credit card, but in the past three months you've applied for two more, and are now in the process of also trying to borrow money to finance Junior's college education. You've also contacted a couple of companies about changing jobs.

That makes six new inquiries on your credit report in a very short time. What happens? The two credit card companies check you out at one of the Big Three credit agencies and count four inquiries besides their own. Alarm bells ring in their minds. They figure that all those inquiries mean you're about to plunge into big debt. They look like red flags to a bull. Whammo! You get turned down.

The Money Line

Certain inquiries don't show up on your credit report. Examples include inquiries made by you to monitor your report for accuracy or to obtain a copy for your records, or inquiries made by companies who want to send you an unsolicited credit offer through the mail.

How to Get a Copy of Your Credit Report

For all the reasons we mentioned, you need to get a copy of your report. You can do it easily in a couple of ways. If you're denied credit for any reason, within the next 30 days you can get a *free* copy by contacting any of the Big Three credit agencies. The outfit that denied you the credit must inform you, usually by mail, of the name and address of the credit agency or bureau that supplied the information. What's on your report at one of the Big Three agencies may also be on your reports at the other two credit agencies. But don't count on it. Contact all three. One of the agencies, Experian, has extended the free-report period to 60 days.

If you haven't been turned down for credit, you can buy a copy of your report for an average of $8, although the price may vary by state.

How do you do it? First, phone the agencies. When you phone an agency, don't expect to get a live person on the other end. And don't get exasperated. A robot voice will walk you through the instructions, such as, "Press number 1," "Press number 2," and so on. Stick with it; it's worth the aggravation. Then write a letter to all three credit agencies, send it by certified mail, and keep copies. When you write your letter, be sure to state:

➤ Your full name (don't forget the "Jr." or "III" after your name).

➤ Current and previous addresses, with ZIP codes.

➤ Your date of birth.

➤ Your spouse's first name, if you're married.

➤ Your Social Security number.

➤ Your phone number.

➤ The name(s) of your business, if you are a small business owner.

Here are the addresses and phone numbers of the Big Three credit agencies:

Experian (formerly TRW)
P.O. Box 2104
Allen, TX 75013-0949
(800) 682-7654
Website: www.experian.com

Equifax
P.O. Box 740241
Atlanta, GA 30374-0241
(800) 685-1111
Website: www.equifax.com

Trans Union Corporation
760 W. Sproul Road
Springfield, Pa. 19064-0390
(800) 888-4213
Website: www.tuc.com

Guard Against Mix-Ups

When Congress was considering the Credit Repair Reform Act of 1994, which unfortunately, died on the Senate floor, it found that one in four credit files contained errors. Then, a recent study by the respected, independent U.S. Public Interest Research Group found that 70 percent of the reports it checked contained errors of some kind. Twenty-nine percent of the errors were serious, such as false delinquencies or judgments that belonged to somebody else. Yet, said PIRG, consumers often can't reach the credit bureaus to request copies of their reports. Mark Ferrulo, director of Florida PIRG, called the situation "a ticking time bomb."

Many of the errors undoubtedly were the credit agencies' fault, but there are tons of horror stories created by consumers themselves. You can prevent errors and mix-ups on your credit report by following a few simple tips.

➤ Always use the same name. If your full name is Jeremy C. Bullwhistle III, don't write "J. C. Bullwhistle" or "Jeremy Bullwhistle" (without the "C"). Don't use "Jerry," or your last name without the three Roman numerals after it. The reason for this is that you don't want inconsistencies appearing on the report. You could get tagged with the bad credit of Jerry Bullwhistle-the-Credit-Card-Maniac who lives 2,000 miles away. You'd be amazed at how many folks commit that simple mistake, and wind up spending months or years fighting the credit agencies to prove they're the *real* Jeremy Bullwhistle III.

➤ Always use your Social Security number. You've got the only one like it in the world. This will help you prevent your name from being confused with folks with the same name.

➤ Always list your home addresses for the past five years. It will help you in the future if you move.

How to Handle Disputes

Let's say you check your credit report and you spot a $1,000 dispute with Max's Clothing Store from three years ago. You don't know anybody named Max, and the last time you bought a suit was five years ago.

The bad news is that it can sometimes take weeks or months of letters and phone calls to correct the report. But the good news is that you can do it if you follow these steps carefully, remembering to *always* keep a file copy of anything you send to somebody else.

1. If you think Max's Clothing Store is responsible for the error, send Max's a letter by certified mail, asking that it send a written statement to all three credit bureaus, telling them it was a mistake.

2. Write each of the three credit bureaus a certified letter, and enclose a copy of the letter you sent to Max's, to make sure the store followed through on the changes. Give the bureau all the details, describing the mistake, and include your full name with your middle name, address, date of birth, and Social Security number. Note whether you're a junior or senior or have three Roman numerals after your name.

3. Make photocopies of any documents that you think support your claims.

4. If you believe your name was mixed up with someone else's, include a copy of your birth certificate.

Under the Fair Credit Reporting Act, a credit bureau usually has 30 days to resolve the problem. If you feel the bureau is dragging its feet or not handling your situation fairly, contact the attorney general of your state or the Federal Trade Commission in Washington at (202) FTC-HELP.

Remember that a bankruptcy remains on your credit report for 10 years, while other negative information such as a judgment or lien stays on for seven years.

You Have a Right to Correct the Record

Many people aren't aware of it, but in case you find an error on your credit report or wish to dispute a creditor's charges, you are entitled to submit a 100-words-or-less statement to each credit bureau, explaining the situation. By law they must insert this into your report, so that anyone inquiring about you can see your side of the story. Be sure to send your statement by certified mail and keep a copy.

Don't fail to do this. Creditor after creditor tells us they are impressed when a consumer has taken the time and trouble to correct a report and insert their own version of what happened. It could make the difference in getting your next loan.

Protecting Yourself from Fraud

Americans lose more than $2 billion a year to credit-card-fraud artists. You can protect yourself by following these tips, advises Experian:

➤ Sign your new cards as soon as they arrive.

➤ Treat your cards like money. Keep them in a safe place.

➤ Shred anything with your account number on it before throwing it away.

➤ Don't give your card number over the phone unless *you* initiate the call.

➤ Don't write your card number on a postcard, or on the outside of an envelope.

➤ Remember to get your card and receipt immediately after every transaction, and double-check to be sure they're yours.

➤ If your billing statement is incorrect or your credit cards are lost or stolen, notify your card issuers at once.

Beware of "We'll Fix Your Credit" Operators

You come across these bozos in dozens of classified ads or even on television. They offer to "fix your credit" by claiming to be able to remove any negative information from your credit report. They also promise to "get you a credit card even if you have bad credit."

Forget those pitches. Never, but never, send those guys one dollar up-front. Otherwise, you'll learn a painful lesson that could cost you hundreds—or thousands—of dollars. The truth is, those "credit-repair clinics" can't do anything for you that you can't do yourself, for *free* or at a *minimum cost*.

If the information in your report is correct, by law no one can remove it. You can have inaccurate information removed at no charge. Credit agencies will supply you with a simple "dispute form." It's easy to fill out and mail back.

Lately there have been stories about these scam operators suggesting to people that they create a new identity for themselves by, for example, getting another Social Security number. The FBI would like to talk to you—and those guys—if you foolishly try to do this.

Helping Hands

Struggling under a heavy personal debt load? Contact the following sources for helpful information on consumer credit and how you can strengthen your credit report:

Bankcard Holders of America
524 Branch Drive
Salem, VA 24153
(703) 389-5445

The Banker's Secret Bulletin
P.O. Box 78
Elizaville, NY 12523
(800) 255-0899

National Center for Financial Education
P.O. Box 34070
San Diego, CA 92163
(415) 567-5290

Consumer Federation of America
1424 16th Street N.W., Suite 604
Washington, D.C. 20036
(202) 387-6121

Chapter 17

The Right Credit Card for You

In This Chapter

➤ A crash course on the credit card jungle

➤ How to find the card that fits your budget to a T—including one that will cost you NOTHING

➤ How to beat banks that are raising all their fees and charges

➤ How to stay out of the debt (and bankruptcy) trap with credit cards

➤ Where to get a card even if you have bad credit

There's no bigger rip-off than credit cards, and the odds are stacked against your not getting hurt by them. High interest rates have hardly budged in 20 years. Banks and other issuers have jacked up their already-ridiculous fees even higher. And there are new fees in addition to the old ones. As the number of personal bankruptcies soars past 1.3 million annually, banks try to make it harder for people to go bankrupt—but at the very same time they fill mailboxes with offers of easy credit for people already drowning in debt. In short, banks are getting away with murder—and you're their patsy, as credit card profits get bigger and bigger. You must now gain control of this ugly situation for yourself, or face the possibility of being taken for a bigger and bigger ride.

This chapter is a crash course in everything that's wrong with credit cards and how to escape their debt threat. You'll learn how and where to shop for cheaper rates, how to avoid those insane fees and charges, which type of credit card fits you to a T, why promoters' card tricks really aren't what you think they are, and how to see through the freebies and perks that banks keep dangling before your eyeballs. Your pocketbook and your debt picture will be saved!

Credit Cards: Personal Debt Enemy #1

Engrave this on your mind: Credit cards are the main reason so many Americans are up to their ears in debt, and why the bankruptcy rate is so high. The banks, of course, will refute this, but if you want to confirm it, ask any bankruptcy attorney what caused his clients' problems in the first place. The lawyers can even describe how more low-income senior citizens have turned to charging groceries on their credit cards in order to survive.

A big business? Oh, yes. Total bank-card debt reached $425 billion in early 1998, and unused credit lines (the additional amount consumers could charge on their cards) was another $1.8 trillion. There were 475 million cards in circulation, with many households having card debt of $5,000 or more. In one recent year, credit card issuers made $60 billion in interest charges.

Yet the card issuers' greed keeps growing, as cardholders keep getting slapped by a slew of new card fees, deceptive interest-rate practices, and especially higher charges to customers whose card behavior is not the greatest.

Can't Live with 'Em, Can't Live Without 'Em

Notice how more credit card offers have been bombarding you lately? Card companies send out 2 billion offers a year to consumers. Some folks with household incomes of $50,000 or more report they get two or more dozen direct mail pitches a year. Why? Credit cards represent enormous profits for banks. They sock you with rates averaging more than 17 percent while paying puny interest of 1 percent on checking and 3 percent or 4 percent on savings. In short, they have found a golden goose.

Yet Americans continue to be hooked on plastic, plain and simple, because of its convenience. We simply run to the mall, whip out our credit cards and say, "Charge it!" No money leaves our wallets. That's a good feeling—temporarily. Then later, when the bill comes in with all the charges and interest, it's pay-up time. Sure, the bank will let you get away with a teensy minimum payment, but that's how they make their money, by keeping you in debt forever. And if you're late with your monthly payments—by as little as one day—you pay a big penalty and wind up with an ugly mark on your credit record that'll haunt you for years.

It's time to take the bull by the horns, dear friend, and get rid of the debt monster!

Why Cards Keep You in Perpetual Debt

You can make purchases with your credit card up to a certain dollar limit decided by the card issuer. That's your maximum credit line. As you use the card, you're constantly borrowing against your limit and repaying the money. Say your credit limit is $1,000 and you buy a garment for $100, or take a $100 cash advance against the card. You have $900 left. When you repay the $100 (plus the interest charges), you again have $1,000 in available credit. That's called a "revolving" credit account, similar to a home equity line of credit (see Chapter 20).

Okay, say that you're a "revolver"—a person who doesn't pay off his monthly balance, but instead "rolls" part of the bill over to the next month. Nearly seven out of 10 cardholders do this, and the average amount they roll over every month is anywhere from $1,700 to $3,000, depending on which study you believe.

Let's set it straight one more time: Banks and other credit card outfits *want* you to do this. They make their profits by making it easy for you to finance your balance. If you paid off your bill every month, they wouldn't make a dime.

How expensive can a credit card get? Take the case of a cardholder with a balance of $2,500 who pays 18.5 percent interest. If he or she made only a minimum monthly payment of 2 percent of the unpaid balance, which many card issuers allow, it would take more than 30 years to pay the card off. Even worse, the total interest would come to $6,500. All for a $2,500 loan!

Just Try NOT Having a Credit Card

Skip credit cards entirely? Just try it. In today's society, a credit card is almost as important as a birth certificate. You need plastic to rent a car, buy an airline ticket, reserve a hotel room, order from a mail-order catalog or TV shopping network, or rent movies. A woman we know moved into a new town and tried to deposit $20,000 in a bank. She showed her driver's license and voter's registration card, but the bank insisted on seeing a credit card before they'd accept her as a new customer. She didn't have one, so they declined her business!

Credit cards definitely have a place in your personal financial life, although we know lots of wise people, especially older folks, who make a habit of paying cash, who aren't plagued by one cent of debt. The key to avoiding credit card trouble is to be smart about how you use credit, *before* you even apply for a card! Make up your mind that you're going to be disciplined—you're too smart to fall into that plastic trap!

1. Figure how much credit card debt you can afford to surely pay back in full each month. Then, don't charge a dime over that amount!

2. Don't fall for banks' come-on card deals. Read all the fine print in their hustle literature. Is the rate fixed or variable? Will a low-ball introductory rate jump to a higher rate in six months? What's the grace period—the number of days to pay of the balance before the interest charges kick in? What's the annual fee? The late-payment fee? The fee for going over your credit line? For cash advances?

3. Watch out for deceptive language. Many outfits offer you a "pre-approved" card, but they may reject you if you're unemployed or don't have an adequate income. Many promise a credit line "up to $100,000," but are more apt to offer $5,000 after reviewing the application.

4. Limit your number of credit cards to one or two—no more. Not only will this help keep your debt down, it will help your credit profile overall. Lenders monitor what your total possible debt could be if you ran up all your cards to the limit.

5. If you feel your card rate is too high (say, above 14 percent) or if your fees are grotesque, tell your bank you're considering moving your accounts to a different institution. They may cut the rate and lower or waive some fees.

Did you know that:

➤ In effect, your card is free if you pay off your balance each month?

➤ You can cut your card costs nearly in half if you have good credit?

➤ You can even get a card if you've had credit problems or haven't had a chance to build up a credit record of your own? (See "Secured Cards for Those with Bad (or No) Credit" in this chapter.)

The following will help you become a smart credit card user.

Kinds of Credit Cards

The main types of credit cards are:

➤ Fixed-rate cards.

➤ Variable-rate cards.

➤ Gold cards.

➤ Secured cards.

➤ Cards with gimmicks, such as cash rebates and air miles.

The sections that follow explain each of these types in more detail. Besides the standard cards issued by banks, thrifts, and credit unions, consumers may qualify for an American Express card—provided their financial condition is eligible for a minimum credit line of $5,000. You pay no interest rate with an American Express card, but the annual fee is $75. American Express makes its money from these fees, and from merchants and other businesses that accept the cards. The merchants pay them a small percentage of any amount charged on the card.

Retail credit cards (such as those issued by department stores) are also big business, but their interest rates tend to be higher than the rates banks charge on their standard cards. We've seen many stores slap customers with rates as high as 21 percent, which is almost as bad as paying juice money to a loan shark when you're only earning 4 percent or 5 percent on your CDs.

Remember: No matter what credit card you use, *your payment record on the card is going to wind up on your personal credit report, which can be accessed by any bank or company to which you apply for credit.*

Fixed-Rate Cards

This is your ordinary, everyday, plain credit card. The interest rate is *fixed* at a certain percentage. Whatever you buy, that's the percent interest you'll pay on the purchase. This type of credit card has become an ugly duckling because the average rate has stubbornly remained at about 17.5 percent, according to the newsletter *Bank Rate Monitor*. In cities such as San Francisco, the rate is even higher—an astronomical 19.5 percent!

To avoid paying these high fixed rates, shop the best card deals nationwide. You'll find rates as low as nine percent. Locating a cheaper out-of-state card is a perfectly safe and smart thing to do. After all, most big card-issuers are national anyway. The only catch is that the lower the card rate, the more difficult it is for people to get their credit approved. Nine-percent issuers tend to want only squeaky-clean credit records, so standards may apply. But if your credit is good, give it a shot!

Table 17.1 shows the best fixed-rate credit card deals in the U.S., according to the newsletter *Bank Rate Monitor*.

Watch Your Wallet

While credit card issuers make it tougher for people to qualify for a low-rate credit card, at the same time, many have offered higher spending limits to existing customers. Some bank executives deny this, but the overriding evidence is that more and more easy credit has been pushed on consumers.

Table 17.1   Best Credit Card Deals for Persons Who Carry Balances

Institution	Interest Rate	Annual Fee	Interest-Free Days/From
Pulaski Bank & Trust Little Rock, AR	7.99%	$35	25/billing
Wachovia Bank New Castle, DE	8.25%	$88	20/billing
USAA Savings Bank Las Vegas, NV	9.25%	$45	25/billing
Metropolitan National Bank Little Rock, AR	9.48%	$25	25/transaction
Huntington National Bank Columbus, OH	9.50%	$39	25/billing
Simmons 1st National Bank Pine Bluff, AR	9.75%	$35	25/billing

continues

Table 17.1   Continued

Institution	Interest Rate	Annual Fee	Interest-Free Days/From
Capital One Bank Richmond, VA	9.90%	$0	25/billing
First USA Bank Wilmington, DE	9.99%	$0	25/billing
AFBA Industrial Bank Colorado Springs, CO	10.50%	$35	25/billing
Amalgamated Bank Chicago, IL	11.25%	$37	25/billing
First Union Charlotte, NC	11.40%	$39	25/billing
AmTrust Bank Boca Raton, FL	11.75%	$18	25/billing
Ohio Savings Bank Cleveland, OH	11.75%	$18	25/billing
Central Carolina Bank Columbus, GA	12.00%	$20	25/billing
Pullman Bank & Trust Co. Chicago, IL	12.25%	$0	25/billing
Washington Mutual Bank Wilmington, DE	12.25%	$18	25/billing

Source: Bank Rate Monitor

It may be necessary to switch banks to get a better deal on your credit card. If so, fine. The new bank may give you a special "account-closing" check to pay off your balance at the old bank. The balance then will show up on your new card account at the outfit to which you switched your business—or you simply pay off your old balance and open a new account at another bank. Either way, cut your old credit card in half, and enclose it with your check and a letter to the old bank. Advise them you are closing your account (give the number) and keep a copy of the letter.

Variable-Rate Cards

Choosing a *variable-rate* credit card can cost you less in the long run. With this type of credit card, your interest rate changes according to an index used by the bank. Often, the rate is tied to the bank's prime rate plus six to nine percentage points. For example, if the prime is 8.5 percent (which it was in early 1998), the variable rate on your credit card would probably be 14.5 to 17.5 percent. More than 70 percent of all credit cards now are variable-rate.

Remember that your introductory rate on a variable-rate card can be as low as 3.9 percent to 9.9 percent. Six or more months later it will jump to the fully-indexed rate, which today averages 16.5 percent.

Variable-rate cards are great when the prime rate is low, as it was in the early 1990s when the prime stood at only 6 percent. Then, the average variable rate was only 12 percent. But when rates start rising, as they did in 1994, variable-rate plastic becomes less and less attractive.

Table 17.2 shows the best variable-rate credit card deals in the U.S. as of February 1995, according to the newsletter *100 Highest Yields*.

Table 17.2   Best Deals for People Who Pay Off Their Balances

Institution	Interest Rate	Annual Fee	Interest-Free Days/From
Capital One Bank Richmond, VA	9.90%	$0	25/billing
First USA Bank Wilmington, DE	9.99%	$0	25/billing
AFBA Industrial Bank Colorado Springs, CO	11.40%	$0	25/billing
USAA Savings Bank Las Vegas, NV	12.15%	$0	25/billing
Pullman Bank & Trust Co Chicago, IL	12.25%	$0	25/billing
Metropolitan Savings Bank Mayfield Heights, OH	13.90%	$0	25/billing
Ohio Savings Bank Cleveland, OH	13.90%	$0	25/billing

Source: Bank Rate Monitor. V = *variable rate*

Gold, Platinum and Titanium Cards

The secret to shopping for gold cards lies in their perks, such as emergency roadside service, buyer protection plans, and cash back if you spend thousands of dollars. All too often, though, cardholders are tempted to choose gold cards as a "status" symbol. The only thing a gold card *can* promise you is a higher credit limit—and sometimes expensive annual fees. Gold card applicants require a stronger credit record, and the cards come with mandatory benefits such as $150,000 travel-accident insurance.

Asset Advisory

"What credit card extras do I *really* need, or could do without?" That's the key question you should ask before you consider a Gold, Platinum or Titanium Card. Some, for instance, will offer credit card life insurance along with the card, when you may really find that term life insurance is a better deal. Similarly, you may not be a candidate for "job loss protection" or "credit card registration" because there are other options for you to explore. In many cases, all you need is a standard card, period.

In recent years, card issuers, catering to a strong economy, have also brought out upscale Platinum and Titanium Cards. If you put them under a microscope, they offer many of the same features as Gold Cards, plus a few more. But just as with standard cards, you're going to have your pocket picked if you don't pay close attention to the fine print. Here's a good example of why:

First USA offered a Platinum Card with a 3.9 percent "introductory fixed rate." The "fixed" part of the rate deal only lasted for several months, when the rate rose to a 9.9 percent variable rate. There was no annual fee, a credit line of $5,000 to $100,000, a 30 percent discount on a slew of different products and services, auto rental insurance, a $100,000 travel accident policy, and a 20-to-25-day grace period.

The shocker was that First USA's rate soared to 19.99 percent if the cardholder made two late payments within a six-month period, and to 22.99 percent if there were two consecutive late payments in such a period. In other words, a late payer with a $3,000 balance would pay about $393 in extra interest on an annual basis! Cash advances also cost 19.99 percent.

Secured Cards for Those with Bad (or No) Credit

There are more than 400 issuers of *secured* credit cards for folks with a poor credit history or no history at all. Anyone who's been hanging his head because he lost his card during bad financial times now has new hope.

A secured card works like this: You typically keep $200 to $500 on deposit with the bank. It issues you a card with which you can make purchases for up to your deposit amount. More and more institutions also pay you a small amount of interest on your deposit, such as two to four percent.

The interest rate you pay on a secured card is a little stiff, anywhere from 17 to 21 percent, but it's temporarily worth it for you to start rebuilding your credit. Banks used to charge an application fee of $20 to $40 on secured cards, but that's fading as competition heats up.

Why the boom in secured cards? Because banks have discovered a huge, new market of people with damaged credit, young people applying for a card for the first time, divorced people who don't have their own personal credit records, and new workers, including immigrants.

Who can get a secured card? Almost everybody, with a few exceptions. Requirements vary. Many card issuers will accept those with bad payment records; a few will even take customers with bankruptcies that are at least six to 12 months old. Others insist that you be employed for one year or have no excessive credit card debt or federal tax liens. Income requirements range from $165 a week at Key Bank & Trust, Havre de Grace, Maryland (800/539-5398), to $12,000 a year at First Consumers National Bank, Beaverton, Oregon (800/876-3262). First Consumers requires an opening deposit of $100 minimum; Capital One, Richmond, Virginia (800/445-4523) requires at least $199.

Is a secured card for you? Yes, if your credit needs repair and you don't mind paying the high interest. If you mind your manners and make your monthly payments on time, that will be a plus on your credit record. Six to 12 months later, you might be able to ask the bank to increase your credit limit, or apply for a standard card. For example, Key Federal Savings Bank allows you to apply for their unsecured credit card if you have maintained a good track record on your secured card for 24 months.

Table 17.3 is a rundown of the different outfits that offer secured cards, based on a *Bank Rate Monitor* survey. Note: Citizenship, age, employment, credit record, region, residency, income, current debt, bankruptcy record, account minimum/maximum, and other restrictions may apply.

Asset Advisory

Don't jump at the first secured card offer that comes along, no matter how plastic-hungry you are. With so many banks beating the bushes for business, you should shop these cards as aggressively as you would a standard credit card.

Table 17.3   Who Offers Secured Credit Cards

Institution	Rate	Fee	Grace period	Min. deposit
Amalgamated Bank Chicago, IL	16.50%	$50	25/billing	$500
Banco Popular Orlando, FL	19.80%	$35	25/billing	$200–$5,000
Bank One Tempe, AZ	19.99%	$25	25/billing	$250–$5,000

continues

Table 17.3 Continued

Institution	Rate	Fee	Grace period	Min. deposit
Chase Manhattan Wilmington, DE	19.90%	$35	25/billing	$300–$5,000
First Premier Bank Sioux Falls, SD	18.90%	$45	25/billing	$200–$10,000
People's Bank Bridgeport, CT	16.90%	$25	25/billing	$500–$1,500
Union Planters Bank Memphis, TN	18.90%	$35	25/billing	$500–$4,500
Wells Fargo Bank San Francisco, CA	20.05%	$35	20/billing	$500–$5,000

Source: Bank Rate Monitor

Rebate and Frequent Flyer Deals

Credit cards with bells and whistles are popping up all over, as every card outfit and its brother tries to get a piece of the credit card pie. The main gimmicks are discounts on merchandise and services, promises of cash rebates, and free airline miles. The more you use a particular card, the more rebates and freebies you get. These can range from discounts on new cars to free air travel and cut-rate hotel rooms.

That all sounds groovy, but in reality these card issuers have been cutting back on their deals because the market has been saturated and some outfits have lost money. Cutbacks have been in the form of offering a lower dollar value of the freebies and perks, and reducing the time period for which the offers are good. Once, these deals were so liberal that the General Motors Gold Card enabled customers to earn up to $7,000 toward the purchase of a new GM vehicle. Now, on its GM MasterCard, the maximum is $3,500 over seven years.

Watch Your Wallet

Beware of third-party outfits that "guarantee" to get you a secured credit card or "fix your credit" for a fee. The company may be a fly-by-night scam, and besides, you can easily handle your card application by yourself and deal directly with the bank. You do not need a third party to do this for you.

Ask yourself these questions:

➤ Do I really need or want the freebies?

➤ Could I get a better deal with another card that offers a lower interest rate and lower fees?

➤ Do I really need the "free" merchandise, discounts and whatever? If the card gives me points toward buying a Chevrolet sedan, but I'm in the market for a Ford pickup, it doesn't make much sense.

If you're not satisfied with the incentives, don't be afraid to ask the issuer for a better deal. The name of the game today with card issuers is, *negotiate!*

The offers have lots of different twists, the most popular being money-back gimmicks that rebate a percentage of your purchases. For example, Citibank Driver's Edge for Visa and MasterCard, Sioux Falls, South Dakota (800/967-8500), rebates 2 percent toward the purchase or lease of any new vehicle, regardless of make or model. That's up to $500 in rebates per year, with a maximum of $1,500 on one vehicle. Expiration is three years after the rebate is earned. Washington Mutual Bank (800/533-5600) offers a 3 percent rebate on net purchases when the balance is carried from one billing cycle to the next. Amoco Visa (800/858-3299) offers up to 3 percent rebate on purchases toward gasoline, credited automatically to the monthly statement. The Golf Card from American Express gives one point for every eligible dollar. Points may be redeemed for advance tee time reservations, golf equipment, clothing, gear, and instructions.

As with any credit card, it's not the gifts and pizzazz that count, it's what you wind up with in your pocket. Compare the bottom-line costs—after the rebates. Here are some typical deals:

Cash/credit rebates: Bank Americard Rewards has MasterCard/Visa programs for Gold and Classic cards issued by Bank of America, Phoenix, Arizona (800/200-7119). The six-month introductory rate is 5.9 percent, then it rises to a 15.49 percent variable rate with no annual fee. Customers in western states only get 0.5 percent to 2 percent cash rewards.

Also check out rebates and cash rewards offered by Chevy Chase Bank, Maryland (800/334-2378); Discover Card through Greenwood Trust Co., New Castle, Delaware (800/DISCOVER); and GE Rewards MasterCard through GE Capital Consumer Card Co., Mason, Ohio (800/437-3927).

Gasoline rebates: Besides Amoco, there's BP Visa via Bank One, Phoenix (800/278-4721); Citgo Companion through Associates National Bank, Wilmington, Delaware (800/462-4846); Exxon MasterCard through GE Capital Consumer Card Co. (800/554-6914); Gulf Oil MasterCard by Fleet Bank, Providence, Rhode Island (800/677-6677); Shell MasterCard via Chase Manhattan, Wilmington, Delaware (800/373-3427), and others.

Frequent-flyer miles: Most major airlines are tied in with at least one big bank. Read all the small print carefully. Note the exclusions and restrictions, such as blackout dates, when you can't fly, and the limitations on miles and the expiration dates. Some cards offer bonus miles when you sign up, and many businesses, such as rental car companies, hotels and phone companies will bait you with frequent-flyer miles. A few banks, such as First USA in Wilmington, Delaware (800/945-2023), will let you pick the airline you want, so choose a carrier whose free miles you've already been saving for. Be sure to figure the real bottom-line cost of these programs versus what a non-rebate card would cost you.

Ouch! Those Fees Hurt!

Okay, you've got the types of cards down pat. Now you need to know the *key cost factors* you could be hit with. The three main ones are interest rate, annual fee, and grace period. The kind of card you want depends on the way you pay off your credit card bills. If, as we said earlier, you're a "revolver," you want a credit card with a *very low interest rate*. If you pay your balance off in full every month, you want a card with *no annual fee*. This card will cost you nothing.

Remember, if you don't pay off the full balance, interest keeps accumulating on the unpaid amount. The meter begins ticking the moment you buy something with the card or more likely, the day the card issuer bills you for what you owe.

The interest could keep you in bondage forever if you don't use your noodle. For instance, says Bankcard Holders of America, it would take *eight years and eight months* to pay off a $1,000 balance at 16.5 percent if you only pay the minimum payment every month. (The minimum is normally only 2 percent of the amount owed.) You'd wind up paying $766 interest on your $1,000 loan. But you could pay off the debt in *three years* and pay *$500 less* in interest just by adding an extra $10 a month to your payment.

You pay the *annual fee* just to have the right to have the card for one year. The fee is usually $20 to $50, but many banks charge no fee at all. If you're the meticulous type and always pay your monthly card balance in full, you should carry a no-annual-fee card and nothing else. The card will cost you nothing. It will be like having a free card.

Asset Advisory

Double-check the rates and fees you're now paying on your cards. The rate may have gone up over the past year if you're carrying a variable-rate card that is tied to some index. If your rate today is 16 to 19 percent, you're being taken to the cleaners. You might have missed the fine print on a bank notice, stating that the card's annual fee has been raised. The most you should pay is $40.

The *grace period* is the number of days you have to pay off all new purchases without being hit by a finance charge. The usual grace period is 25 days. Typically, if you don't pay off your entire bill, all new purchases get clobbered by finance charges immediately.

For example, two brothers, Eenie and Meenie, both carry credit cards with an 18 percent rate. Each has a $1,000 balance on his card, on which there's no annual fee. Eenie pays off the entire $1,000 before the 25-day grace period is up. The card costs him zero. But Meenie only makes a minimum payment, $20, and gets charged 18 percent interest per year on the remaining $980. If you can't pay off your credit card entirely, always be sure to pay at least the minimum payment on your card before the grace period expires. Late payments will go over like a lead balloon at the next place you apply for credit. You'll probably get rejected.

Other niggling card costs:

➤ **Late fees**   You'll usually be nicked with a flat $15 charge, or two percent of your outstanding balance, if you don't make at least a minimum payment by the due date shown on the bill. Many banks have been raising their late fees even higher, charging even if your payment is one day late. Tip: Allow seven days for your payment to reach the card company.

➤ **Cash advances**   You can borrow money against the card, but the interest rate you pay for this type of transaction is apt to be higher. It's not uncommon for your regular rate to be, say 15 percent, but the cash advance rate to be 18 or 19 percent. Plus, there's usually no grace period and you may also pay a small fee.

➤ **Inactivity fee**   Some banks will nick you $15 to $25 if you don't charge anything on your credit card for six months. If you close your account, you might be charged another $25.

➤ **Over-limit fee**   These are going up, too, as banks penalize you up to $25 for exceeding your credit line by as little as $1.

Meanwhile, *grace periods* are getting shorter, reducing the number of days you have before the interest rate meter starts clicking on your card balance. When you take all these charges and tough new rules together, if you get the impression that card issuers are now really slamming it to the little guy, *you're right!*

The Biggest Secret of All—Watch Your Habits!

Americans are up to their ears in debt, and credit cards got them there, no matter what stories the banking industry tells you. Bad card habits have caused divorces, bankruptcies, lost dreams, and emotional wreckage. You can avoid the credit trap by following these simple rules:

➤ Know your credit limit based on your income, amount of current debt, and credit history. A rule of thumb is that your total monthly debt should not exceed 38 percent of your monthly income. For a review on managing your debt, check out Chapter 2.

➤ Carry only the number of cards you need, even though you haven't used up your credit line. Creditors look at how much you're able to go into debt based on your total lines of credit, when they review your record.

➤ Don't apply for more than one card at a time. Some creditors may think you're going to charge like mad and take off for Brazil.

➤ Consider joining a credit union to take advantage of their lower interest rates. In 1998, for example, the average credit union offered a fixed-rate credit card at 13.11 percent, versus the national average of 16.65 percent at a bank, according to *Bank Rate Monitor*.

➤ Remember that a bad credit record will dog you for years. Nothing can screw up your life faster than going overboard with credit cards. Your card payment record will shadow you in everything you do, including buying a home (or renting), getting a job, and opening a checking account.

➤ Pay against your balance ASAP. Don't let bills hang around. Every day you wait is going to cost you more in interest.

➤ If you can't make your payments on time, or if you want to dispute a charge, contact your card issuer immediately—and put everything in writing.

➤ Don't get fooled when card issuers lower your minimum payments. It only makes it easier for you to stay in debt, and increases the total interest you'll pay. This is a tar pit if ever there was one.

➤ If you run into severe financial problems, contact one of the personal-credit counseling organizations such as Consumer Credit Counseling Services (800/388-CCCS) listed in Chapter 16. They've helped millions of people, and can probably help you, at no charge or for a small fee.

The Least You Need to Know

➤ Credit cards are poison to your personal financial life. They're the number-one reason why more than 1 million people file bankruptcy each year.

➤ The basic types of credit cards are fixed-rate cards, variable-rate cards, gold cards, secured cards, and credit cards with gimmicks such as rebates.

➤ Banks are raising ALL their card fees—from late-payment and over-limit fees, to cash advances. They're especially making it rough on anyone who fails to pay exactly on time, and even penalizing customers who don't use their cards for six months.

➤ Never pay only the minimum balance due. It could take you decades to pay the whole balance off.

➤ The three most important things to shop are the rate, grace period and annual fee. Read the fine print in every contract and see how the bank can later jiggle the rate upward.

➤ People with bad credit will pay a higher rate, but you can get a secured credit card no matter how terrible your credit is.

➤ Cards that offer rebates, cash rewards and free air miles are a bummer unless you really need those services, and provided they'll honestly save you money.

➤ Don't carry more cards than you need (one or two, maximum).

To Lease or Not to Lease

Getting a car is probably the second-biggest money deal you'll ever make, right after a house. But should you lease or buy? *That's* the $64,000 question. Leases have become the rage as car prices keep rising, because the monthly payments are less and you can turn the car in for a new one in three or four years. Yet very few people know the behind-the-scenes tricks to negotiating the right lease or obtaining the best outright buy. The average Joe never learns how he's being taken for a ride by nervy salesmen, or how he could have easily saved hundreds—perhaps thousands—of dollars. Meanwhile, dealers keep using crafty showroom and backroom tactics to drive up the cost of your car, from verbal gimmicks to trapping you with charges on things you don't need.

Whether you know it or not, the way you handle yourself with the salesman—what you say and what you don't say—has everything to do with whether or not you'll get scammed. Your costs can be inflated without you ever knowing it. In particular, the average buyer knows zilch about the numbers behind a leasing deal, and that's where this chapter will help you. Although leasing today may appear to be the cheapest way to get behind the wheel, it's loaded with hidden mathematical schemes. You'll learn how to compare the bottom-line costs of a lease versus a purchase, the key questions to ask, and how to prevent the dealer from robbing you blind. The chapter exposes many of his biggest tricks, to enable you to come out ahead when you wheel and deal for your new wheels.

Knowing the Biggest Rip-Offs

When you go into a store to buy a television set or washing machine, they tell you the price and maybe the cost of an optional service contract. And that's about it, right? Not so with a new car. Auto dealers are the add-on champions of all time. Besides the financing rip-offs, which we'll discuss a little later, the list includes:

➤ Invoices and stickers that could have been created by somebody in the back room, not the manufacturer.

➤ An outrageous delivery charge. Shouldn't the cost of hauling the car from Detroit be included in your price?

➤ The dealer's "setup and preparation" charge. What did they do besides a wash and vacuum? After all, the car didn't arrive in bits and pieces from the manufacturer, did it?

The Money Line

You probably can't do much to avoid setup-and-prep charges, but there are other ways you can foil a dealer's adding to the price. For one thing, the window sticker on most new cars shows an "MSRP" price (Manufacturer's Statement of Retail Price) at the bottom. That's what the car maker has determined to be the optimum retail price for the options on the sticker. You won't be able to escape the delivery (freight) charge on the MSRP, but the dealer's charge for setup-and-prep is a tip that the dealer has that much more room to discount the selling price.

➤ A whole bunch of options—a power sun roof, for example, or power seats—all priced sky-high.

➤ Dealer maintenance, which you can buy cheaper somewhere else.

➤ Extended warranty plans that they scare you into buying because "Nick, the mechanic, does work at $70 an hour."

➤ Dealer interest rates that have been booted up higher than what you could get from a bank.

➤ Vehicle undercoating. Forget it. You don't need to spend the extra couple hundred bucks. Do you think manufacturers are stupid enough to build new cars that rust out overnight?

➤ Credit life insurance. You're not required to buy it, and you shouldn't. Insurance experts have pointed out that of every $1 people spend on this scam, only 40 cents is paid out in the form of claims. Most people are already covered by life insurance policies or other assets if the borrower dies.

➤ Trade-ins. The dealer promises to lower your monthly payment if you trade in Old Betsy. But he's already figured how much it will cost him to spruce up the car and how much he can sell it for at auction. He knows exactly how much money he has to play with to get your business. He'll take his cost of that old clunker out of your hide one way or another.

> **Asset Advisory**
>
> Dealers make money from the manufacturer that not even their salesmen know about. One is a "dealer holdback" that doesn't appear on the invoice. It may be 2 percent to 3 percent of the MSRP, so on a $17,000 car, the dealer would get $510 back from the manufacturer. Also, there may be special dealer "incentives" from the manufacturer that don't go through the salesmen. To wheel and deal on *these* incentives you'll have to talk directly to the sales manager or another higher-up.

You don't need all the extras the salesperson will try to load on you. They only increase the debt you'll have to finance, and boost the salesperson's commission. Even so, consider options carefully, and make your own decisions. You may wish to include certain attractive options if you plan to sell the car a few years later. Reason: Today many options—for example, power windows, cruise control, and a cassette player—have become almost-standard equipment that your future buyer will expect when he or she buys the car from you.

Used Cars: Buying Right and Selling Right

A new car depreciates the moment it is driven off the dealer's lot. The amount of depreciation can vary, but we've heard of as much as 20 percent to 30 percent in the first year.

When you finance a used car, expect to pay an interest rate of two to three percentage points above the rate you pay on a new car. If a new car costs 9.5 percent to finance, chances are, a used car will cost 11.5 percent to 12.5 percent in the same town. (If your credit is really bad, prepare to get hit with a rate that may be 15 percent to 18 percent or higher.)

One good source of information on what a used car is worth is the National Automobile Dealers Association's *Official Used Car Guide*. It covers domestic and imported cars and small trucks. On the pages of the guide you'll find three columns of numbers for each auto make and model:

➤ **Trade-In Value** shows what the car is worth in trade at the dealer—*if* the vehicle is in tip-top condition in both appearance and mechanics.

➤ **Loan Value** normally determines how much a bank will lend you to finance the car.

➤ **Retail Value** tells you what price the car will fetch in the marketplace, whether you sell it to someone or buy it from the dealer. The value assumes the car is in great shape. If it isn't, the value will be less.

Also try the excellent price guides on used and new cars offered by Edmunds on the Internet at www.edmunds.com/edweb. The site is loaded with prices, tips on buying and leasing, and gives you a great peek at all the incentives and rebates dealers work with to make a bundle off you.

How to Get Top Price When You Trade In or Sell a Used Car

First, look at the vehicle you're trying to trade or sell. Ask yourself, "Would I buy this car if someone offered it to me?" If not, invest a few bucks at an auto detail shop, a complete car wash (including wax), and a mechanic if necessary. On many used autos, this couple-hundred dollars of investment could bring an extra $500 to $1,000 in the selling price or trade-in value.

On a trade, the new car dealer is saying to himself, "Let's see, if I accept this clunker against the price I'm going to try to get from this customer on a new car, there's some fixin' I'm gonna have to do. Like new carpets, a couple of tires, wash and wax, maybe an engine tune-up and other stuff." The dealer figures he'll sell your slightly renovated car for, say, $5,000 at an automobile auction; he offers you $4,000 for Old Betsy. He spends $300 to get it in shape, and pockets the $700 difference.

Asset Advisory

You'll probably come out ahead if you negotiate the lowest possible price on a new car and sell your old car by yourself. Consider running a classified ad in the "Used Cars" section of your local newspaper, plus an inexpensive ad in *Auto Trader*, a small publication offered for free at newsstands, supermarkets, and other locations.

Now you know rule number one when you trade your car in on a new one: *Do some preliminary shopping around* before *you let a dealer know that you have a used car to trade.* Consumer experts differ on whether you should tip to the dealer that you have a trade-in *before* you negotiate for your car, but in this book, we're suggesting that you wheel and deal on Old Betsy first...after you've done some homework.

So you get Old Betsy polished and super-cleaned before you show up. You check out its real value on the Internet at www.edmunds.com/edweb/. The dealer's salesman at first will try to low-ball you and steal the car—guaranteed. He'll try to maneuver you up and down and inside out by working the old car numbers against the new car numbers, but you can't let him do that. Cut a clean deal first for Old Betsy based on what it's really worth. Better still, sell the car yourself. (Dealers know that many consumers don't know how to do this.) Otherwise, the dealer might try to grab your old $5,000-value car for $2,500.

Then, test drive the new car. If you like it, negotiate the new-car price at a discount off the dealer's sticker price. That "price" is nothing more than packaged smoke. It means absolutely zip, and it won't give you a clue about the dealer's true cost or the hidden incentives he secretly gets back from the manufacturer when he sells the car (which we discuss later in this chapter). Some dealers tell us that this discounted price may be at least between $1,000 and $1,500 less than what the sticker price shows. The sticker price is called the Manufacturer's Suggested Retail Price, or MRSP, in the trade. Don't expect a big discount if there is an industry shortage of a particular model. In that case, the discount will be less.

Negotiate each and every one of the options and extras you want for the new car. Don't just accept whatever numbers the salesman throws at you. You should wheel and deal on these items the same way you haggled on the price of the car. At least the dealer will know you're no idiot.

Only after that should you get into the financing subject—never before.

Keep in mind that the dealer's goal is probably to make a profit of 8 percent to 10 percent on the vehicle, but you really want to chew him down to 2 percent to 5 percent over his cost. (The first thing you should have said to the sales person in the showroom was, "I'm a serious buyer and I'm ready to buy today.") Don't get emotional over any new car you see; that's suicide. Take another person with you to keep the haggling better balanced. Remember, you're on the dealer's turf and the cards are heavily stacked against you. Every trick you can use will make it a more level playing field.

You always ask the questions, *not* the salesman. Ignore whatever documents the sales guy shows you during his spiel. Don't even look at them. Those papers don't count until after the deal is cut. Take a pencil and a notepad with you to help you with your own figuring.

Ignore the salesman's pet comments and shrewd language such as "What do I have to do to get you into this car?" or when he says, "You're wasting my time because you're not serious," or, "This is my last offer." You just say, "When I get the answers to all my questions I'll tell you whether I'm interested." Period.

Repeat: Stifle Those Emotions When You Go to Buy!

Follow these rules whenever you are buying a new or used vehicle:

➤ Don't get excited about the vehicle. The salesperson can read you like a book. If he or she senses you're falling in love with that little two-seater with the stick shift and double carburetor, it's going to cost you.

➤ Don't be anxious to close the deal on the same day. And don't be afraid or let any of the salesman's guilt-trip ploys get to you. No matter what little threat the salesman makes, you can always walk out and come back later!

➤ Shop at least one other dealer who offers the same car. Dealers know from experience you're going to do this and that's what will give you clout in negotiating the cheapest price.

Watch Your Wallet

Simple interest loans are commonly offered by banks, whereas many finance companies will charge higher interest through front-end loans. If a finance company does offer a simple interest loan, it will probably be at higher interest rates than you'd pay at a bank. If you have a poor credit history, the rate could shoot up even higher.

➤ Bargain on a lease just like you would if you were buying. Car shoppers make a big mistake by being too easy on the dealer when they lease a car instead of buying it. Later in this chapter, we'll explain how a lease works, and how to get the best deal. But when you read about knocking down the dealer's price, remember that this applies just as much to a lease as it does to buying a car that you finance.

Getting the Best Financing

Competition in the new car market is so ferocious that many dealers earn more of their living from the finance charges than from the profit they make off their autos. This section explains how you can avoid the pitfalls and walk out with the best deal.

Avoid Dealer Financing

Want to save one to two percent on your loan right off the bat? Avoid dealer financing altogether. And don't even think about going to an independent finance company where the rates are even higher—unless, of course, your credit is so shot that there's no other way out. Many dealers love to charge higher rates to poor credit risks.

Go to a bank or thrift institution and obtain a pre-approved loan for the amount you plan to finance. Better yet, join a credit union if you're not already a member. CUs are big in car loans, and their interest rates always beat what banks charge, as you'll see in Table 18.1, which shows what the average credit union charges for a new car loan versus what you'd pay at a bank or thrift institution, according to the industry newsletter *Bank Rate Monitor*.

Credit Unions Offer the Cheapest Rates

It's less expensive to finance a new car through a credit union than through a bank or thrift. Besides offering cheaper rates, a credit union will provide you with information on the dealer's *real* cost of the car. A CU also often arranges special mass car sales with local dealers who guarantee CU members special low rates.

When you walk into the dealer's showroom armed with a pre-approved loan, you'll have enormous clout for two reasons. First, the dealer knows you're a red-hot, live prospect—and he won't let you out the door until he gives you his best deal. Second, he won't try to flim-flam you with his own financing (which is more costly), because you already have a cheaper deal in your pocket. A nice position to be in!

Table 18.1   Auto Loan Interest Rates

Type of Institution	Interest Rate
Credit union	7.76%
Bank	9.04
Thrift	9.07

Source: Bank Rate Monitor

Get a Simple Interest Loan

With a simple interest loan, you'll be paying interest only on the remaining amount of the loan. How come? As you make your payments month after month, you'll be steadily paring down what you still owe on that original $15,000. Say you make 10 monthly payments of $373. At nine percent interest, your first payment of $373 is on the whole $15,000. Of the $373, $112 is interest and the other $261 reduces the principal you still owe to $14,739.

After the tenth payment, you will have whittled the principal down to $12,302. But your monthly payment will stay the same. Here's why: When the bank sets up your simple interest loan, it figures a flat amount of how much total interest you'll pay on the $15,000 you're borrowing. You can arrange your payments so that they'll still be $373 every month. That's easier for you, because you wouldn't want to start out with a gigantic payment and have it get smaller every month. You might not be able to afford the payment in the early months.

Example: On a four-year (48-month) loan, the total interest comes to $2,917. Divide 48 payments into $2,917 and you get a monthly interest payment of $61. The bank gets its $15,000 back, plus the $2,917 interest. You can budget for a steady monthly payment figure.

What you should avoid is a "front-end installment loan." Unlike the simple interest example you just read, with the installment loan *you pay interest every month on the original $15,000 you borrowed*. In this case, your total interest cost would work out to $5,400, or $2,483 more than with the simple interest loan. Your monthly payment would be $425 instead of $373. Better that money goes into *your* pocket instead of the dealer's (or the bank's).

Other Financing Secrets

The following tips will help you stay focused on the bottom line when you buy a car:

➤ **Don't slide into the low payment mentality.** This is where many folks never learn. Car dealers are no idiots. They know the average person is more concerned about being able to afford their monthly payments than they are about the total cost of the loan. So what do dealers—and banks—often do? Suggest you stretch the loan term to five years instead of three. They say it will "make it easier on you." Humbug. All lower monthly payments do is jack up your financing cost.

For example, a $15,000 loan financed through a bank at nine percent for three years comes to $477 a month, with a total cost of $2,172. But over five years, though the monthly payment drops to $311, your loan cost jumps to $3,683. Not much of a deal, huh?

➤ **Make as big a down payment as you can.** Generally, you'll be required to make a down payment of 10 percent to 20 percent when you buy a new car, although we've seen credit unions finance 100 percent of the price. Some banks will do that, too, but only on luxury models. Why a bigger down payment? Because the more you put down, the lower your interest rate is apt to be.

➤ **Check out manufacturer financing carefully.** Boy, are they enticing—those car dealer ads with low-ball financing and the promise that you can drive the car home by five o'clock! Car manufacturers have captive finance companies to help their dealers wheel and deal. They desperately want your business and they'll turn cartwheels to get it—including a super-low interest rate and same-day credit approval, even on Sundays.

However, this type of financing used to have several downsides. First, the low-ball rate only applied to certain models, like that little convertible with the purple stripes and no trim. Other regular models may have cost more to finance. Second, if you do get the dealer's low manufacturer rate, the dealer may take it out of your hide by charging you more for the car. Third, manufacturer financing is less apt to give you a simple interest loan.

But lately, because of enormous competition and the world economy, U.S. and foreign manufacturers have been pushing low-rate deals right and left. On some models, for instance, Detroit's Big Three automakers not only were offering cash rebates from $500 to $2,000, they also had low financing of 0.9 percent to 4.9 percent on terms of 24 months to 48 months. And the deals covered a broad list of models.

➤ **Stay away from variable-rate loans.** Most car loan rates are *fixed*—that is, you're charged the same interest during the entire loan term. Some car financing rates are *variable*—meaning the rate can go up or down, depending on which direction all bank rates are going. If rates rise, as they did in 1994, your car loan rate could go up by as much as two to three percentage points in a year.

If that happens, the bank may make it "easier" for you by keeping your monthly payment the same, but stretching the term of your loan. Result: Your 48-month loan could turn into a 50-month loan. You wind up paying a bigger finance cost.

➤ **Take advantage of car rebates.** If Bubba's Auto Showroom says the manufacturer has a special $1,000 "rebate" offer, you may want to grab it—that is, *if* the rebate applies to the exact auto you want. Here's why:

Say you're working with that same $15,000 example at nine percent bank interest for four years. The loan payment is $373 per month. The total cost of the car is $17,917. On the other hand, if you take the $1,000 rebate and apply it to your down payment, you'll reduce your monthly payment to $348. The total cost of the loan will be cut to $16,723.

➤ **Check whether you can pay off your loan early.** Some lenders will let you do it, others won't. So before you sign for a loan, ask if you can pre-pay the loan without a penalty. Are there any extra fees or charges? If a pre-pay is okay, be sure to note on your payment checks how much is going toward reducing the principal and how much is going toward the interest. This way you'll have proof if the dealer or the bank ever challenges you.

➤ **Get a tax deduction on the car by hocking your house.** It's a little bit risky, but lots of people do it. You can no longer get a tax deduction on a straight car loan—the IRS did away with that in 1990—but you can get one by borrowing against your home. How? By opening a home equity line of credit. First, you figure how much of your home you own—what the house is worth, minus what you owe on your mortgage. Banks, thrifts, and credit unions will usually lend you up to 75 or 80 percent of that amount (see Chapter 19).

For example, if your home's appraised value is $100,000 and you owe $40,000 on the mortgage, your equity in the house is $60,000. If the bank lends you 80 percent of that $60,000, the amount of the principal is $48,000.

If the interest rate on the home equity loan is less than the rate on a car loan, you'll save on your financing costs. Plus, if you're in, say, the 28 percent tax bracket, you'll save money compared to the taxes you'd pay on a straight auto loan. Reason: The IRS allows you to deduct the interest expense.

Watch Your Wallet

Some lenders have a complicated little gizmo built into the way they calculate your payments. It's called the "Rule of 78s." It's complicated as heck—and depends on state law—but it simply means that most of your early payments are going only toward the interest, not the principal. In that case, you won't save very much by paying off the loan in advance.

Watch Your Wallet

Banks like home equity loans because they're protected by holding a lien on your house. *This means that if you can't meet the payments, the bank could take your home,* never mind the car.

Buy or Lease?

How popular has leasing become? Today, nearly 40 of every 100 new car deals are a lease, up from 3 out of 100 a decade ago. And leasing will get bigger. Why the big growth?

There are several reasons. Auto prices have been going up; the average car cost $18,200 last year, versus $10,725 10 years ago. It's now cheaper for you to get into a leased vehicle. Plus there's no more tax write-off on the interest you pay to finance a car. Consumers also have less disposable income to play around with, and there's more competition for the dollars they have. And the idea of "turning in your car to get a new one every two or three years" has caught on in a big way.

Knowing that, dealers have learned how to gouge people with complicated lease agreements that only an accountant can understand. Dealers have been pulling so many shenanigans on customers that consumer advocate Ralph Nader and the attorneys general of 22 states have demanded that leasing laws be overhauled to protect the average Joe. Leasing was no problem when big corporations did most of the leasing, but now Joe is the key customer—and he knows zip about the subject. This section will help you figure out whether leasing is for you—and how to get the best deal on a lease.

How a Lease Works

In a nutshell, leasing is just like buying a car except that you pay only a portion of the principal with your monthly payments. When the lease expires, you can do one of two things:

➤ Walk away from the car and owe nothing. That's called a *closed-end lease*. It's outlawed in some states, but it's the most popular type of lease nationwide.

➤ Consider buying the car. That's an *open-end lease*. Your monthly payments may be lower, but you could wind up on the short end of the stick, as you're about to find out.

Fiscal Facts

The **residual value** of a leased car is the lessor's calculation of the value of the car at the end of the lease period. When your lease period is up, this becomes the **buyout price**, or what you would have to pay in order to own the car outright.

At the beginning of the lease, the dealer's figured how much your car will probably be worth at the end of the lease, say, in three or four years. That's called the *residual value*—what the dealer thinks the street price of the car might be at that time. When the lease is up, you can buy the car for the residual value, or *buyout price*.

Some dealers figure the residual value in two or three years, instead of four or five. That tips the scales in their favor. Why? Because a car can depreciate by 10 percent the moment you drive it home, and maybe by another 20 percent two or three years later. The younger the car, the higher the residual value. If you get a three-year lease and the dealer has figured the value after two years, you'll have to spend more than you should to buy the car when the lease expires.

Look at the Bottom Line

Let's say you're deciding between leasing or financing a $15,000 vehicle, but don't have the $3,000 down payment (20 percent) to go the financing route. Under a lease, the dealer will typically want—up front—the first month's payment of, say, $250 plus $15 in taxes—and another $250 as a refundable security deposit. That makes a total cash deposit of $515. Assume the lease is for four years, and the residual value is $8,000.

If you finance the car, you'll be borrowing $12,000 for four years after making your $3,000 down payment. Assume you pay 6 percent in taxes up front, and that your interest rate is 10 percent. Your monthly payment will be $350. So far, the lease gets the nod. But how will your wallet really make out in the long run?

With the straight loan deal, in four years you'll own the car outright after paying a total of $4,800 in interest, $373 in taxes and $12,000 on the principal. Had you leased, you'd probably make a $240-per-month payment and could simply turn the car in after four years and say good-bye. You wouldn't own a dime's worth of the vehicle and would still need new wheels. To buy the leased car, you would have to pay the dealer the $8,000 residual value.

But suppose the street value of the car has declined to only $6,500? You'd be out the $1,500 difference, because you could probably buy a similar car for $6,500. It would only be a good deal *if* the residual value were *less* than the street price. In that case, you'd be foolish not to pay the residual value and keep the car. You could sell it at a profit and use the money as a down payment on another set of wheels.

The key to getting the best deal on a lease is to do your homework. Check out these sources before and after you lease:

➤ You can get an excellent checklist and brochure on auto-leasing tips by sending a check or money order for $1 to Consumer Task Force for Automotive Issues, Reality Checklist, P.O Box 7648, Atlanta, GA 30357-0648.

The Money Line

Dealers may talk you into a lease by using language that sounds like you're purchasing the car instead of leasing it. For example, one Detroit auto maker instructs its dealer sales staff to never use words like *lease, interest rate,* and *residual* when they chat with you in a showroom. Instead, they're instructed to use words such as *buying, equity,* and *guaranteed future value.* And you have the option to *trade or sell* after a couple of years.

➤ What's your leased car worth now? Click onto the Internet at www.edmunds.com/edweb/.

➤ Go to the library and look up the market value of your car in the *National Automobile Dealers Association Used Car Guide.*

➤ Check the classified ads in your local paper to determine your car's value.

Don't Touch That Pen Until You Read This

Before you sign any lease, go over these points as though your life depended on them:

➤ Lease for no more than three years. That's the most you want to get stuck with if something unforeseen happens.

➤ Dealers are pushing shorter and shorter leases, such as two years. One reason: Their warranties from manufacturers to cover any possible problems with cars may only be for that long.

➤ If you turn the car in before the lease expires, the dealer will sock you with an early termination charge of $250 to $500. Insist that the charge be calculated by the *level yield method*, which means the dealer only recovers his charges for services and depreciation—no more.

Say you lose your job and can no longer make the payments. When you turn the car in, that's called *voluntary early termination.* You'll still be responsible for all remaining monthly payments, plus the pre-set residual value. In that case, the total due could be twice the value of the car!

➤ How many miles a year do you drive? If you've exceeded that estimated mileage when the lease ends, such as 12,000 to 15,000 miles a year, the dealer will hit you with an extra-cents-per-mile charge. Be honest up front. If they tack on a higher mileage cost at the beginning, it will probably be *less* than what you would be charged when the lease is up.

➤ A lease may require higher insurance limits. Insurance is your responsibility, not the dealer's.

➤ What does the dealer mean by "normal wear and tear"? If, when the car is turned in, it's dented and dinged all over, and the seat cushions are ripped and torn, it's gonna cost you.

➤ You may have to keep documents to prove that the car maintenance was done by a reputable outfit.

➤ Check all the fees and payments under the lease. According to the "Truth in Leasing Law," you have a right to see them.

➤ Negotiate. Dealers can wheel and deal on leases just as on a sale.

➤ If there's a chance you might move, check to see whether you are restricted from taking the car to another state. Some dealers are finicky about this.

The Least You Need to Know

➤ Haggle on a leasing deal just as you would if you were buying the car. Push the dealer to the limit: It's your money we're talking about, not his.

➤ Remember, you're on the salesman's turf. Go in prepared to buy, but volunteer very little information. You—not the salesman—should ask the questions. Car salesmen can read you like a book.

➤ Just say no to vehicle undercoating, credit life insurance, extended warranties, and other unnecessary charges.

➤ Get the deal on your trade-in done first before you begin discussing a deal on a new car. Then get the dealer's discounted price before you start haggling.

➤ Whether you're trading in your old car or selling it yourself, spend a few bucks to get the vehicle into top cosmetic and mechanical shape. Also check out the car's real current market value: You'll make more money on the deal.

➤ Don't show any emotion when you inspect a new car, and do not close the deal the same day you visit the dealer's showroom.

➤ Always shop the same vehicle at more than one dealership.

➤ A new car sticker price doesn't reveal the whole story. Dealers get special "holdback" money and incentives from the manufacturer they'll never tell you about.

➤ Get pre-approved for a loan through a bank or credit union before going to the dealer. You'll save money on interest rates by not financing through the dealer, *and* you'll have more negotiating power because you have the money in hand.

➤ Other ways to save on finance costs include getting a simple interest loan, paying a higher down payment, and taking advantage of manufacturers' rebates.

➤ Leasing a car is not as simple as your dealer may lead you to believe. Make sure you're aware of all the terms of the lease and compare the lease to the cost of buying the car outright.

Chapter 19

Mortgage Shopping: Let's Make a Deal

In This Chapter

➤ Which kind of mortgage is best for you, considering your personal financial situation

➤ The key differences between fixed rates and ARMs: Their pluses and minuses

➤ How the right mortgage can save you *tens of thousands of dollars*!

➤ Where to get cheap government-backed financing with only 3 percent down

➤ What's more important—rates or "points?"

➤ The quick, easy way to find the best mortgage deal

"Hey, where do you think mortgage rates are going?" That's one of the most frequently-asked questions in the world of personal finance. Rate guessing—knowing when, or when not to, make your move on a new mortgage loan or a refinancing—has turned into a giant crapshoot. No one knows for sure where the numbers will be in one week, a month or a year from now. The average homebuyer is bedazzled by the interest rate jungle, different types of mortgages, and a list of fees as long as your arm. Yet a mortgage loan is probably the single biggest hunk of money you'll ever have to borrow and pay back. It's for the number-one asset you'll ever own—your house. Dollar-wise, you're talking about an investment that will probably cost you $200,000 to $300,000 over your lifetime. But if you don't buy your mortgage wisely, it could easily cost you tens of thousands of dollars more!

This chapter explains the tricky, complicated mortgage process in simple language. It tells you step-by-step what to watch out for, what kind of mortgage will fit your personal money situation like a glove, and when it's time to grab the right interest rate. You'll learn how to strengthen your credit record so your loan application will be approved, and how to get into a new home with little or no cash down even if you're a first-time buyer. On top of that, you'll learn super-easy ways of tackling mortgage math, and short-cut ways to shop for the best deal.

The ABCs of How Mortgages Work

A *mortgage* is nothing more than a loan. If you don't have the money to pay all cash for a house, a mortgage lender may loan you up to 95 percent of its appraised value. You deposit the rest up front as a down payment. The lender holds a lien on your home until you fully repay what you borrow—meaning that if you default on your payments, the lender can take the house.

We're not talking about small change in mortgage loans, folks; we're talking hundreds of thousands of dollars. That's the total tab of a 30-year mortgage when you add up the amount you borrow plus the huge interest you'll pay on the loan.

You'd think that with that kind of dough involved, more people would understand what makes mortgages tick. Not so. The guys in the mortgage business have made loans so complex that it takes a mathematical wizard to figure them out. What you need to do is dissect this monster one piece at a time.

Asset Advisory

Always compare APRs—with the points included—when you shop, so that you're comparing the *total* costs of mortgages that offer the same interest rate.

The key to getting the right mortgage is learning which type of loan will fit your present and future budget to a T. There are two major types of "conventional loans" (as opposed to government-insured loans, also discussed in this chapter).

They are *fixed-rate* and *adjustable-rate mortgage* (ARM) loans. Trying to compare the two appears complicated, but it isn't. You can do it. Just keep asking yourself this one basic question: How will each mortgage gimmick impact my pocketbook, today and several years from now? The answers will come to you, as mortgage lenders knock themselves out trying to get your business.

Mortgage-ese You Should Know

Let's start with the lingo. The mortgage process is chock-full of confusing terminology. The following definitions should help clarify things a bit:

Appraisal: A professional estimate of what a house is worth, based on its style, appearance, construction quality, improvements, usefulness, and the comparable value of nearby properties.

Up-front charges: What you are charged at the beginning of the home buying process, such as for an appraisal of the property.

Closing: The final settlement of the transfer of property. It involves the buyer's signing of the mortgage and mortgage note, and a change of title to the home.

Closing costs: Fees and other charges paid by the buyer and seller at closing.

Conventional mortgage: A mortgage *not* insured by the government (such as an FHA or VA loan).

Deed: The document that transfers the title from the seller to the buyer.

Down payment: The buyer's payment to the seller at closing. The payment is based on a percentage of the purchase price required by the buyer's mortgage loan.

Earnest money: Money paid by the buyer to the seller at the time an offer to purchase the home is presented.

First mortgage: A mortgage that is a first lien on the property pledged as a security.

Mortgagee: The lending party under the terms of the mortgage.

Mortgage note: A signed promise to repay a mortgage loan in regular, monthly payments under pre-agreed terms and conditions.

Offer to purchase: A legally-binding, written contract that declares how much a buyer will pay for the property, provided certain conditions are met.

PITI: Principal, interest, taxes, and insurance—the four main parts of a monthly mortgage payment.

Points: One point equals one percent, or one one-hundredth, of the total mortgage amount.

Qualify: To meet a lender's mortgage-approval requirements.

Sub-prime loan: A loan made at higher interest rates to less creditworthy individuals.

Title: The right of ownership and possession of a property.

Title insurance: A policy that protects a buyer against errors, omissions, or defects in the title.

$64,000 Question: Should You Get a Fixed-Rate or an Adjustable-Rate Mortgage (ARM)?

Here's the difference: A *fixed rate* is typically for 30 years or 15 years. It locks in your interest rate—and your monthly payments—for the entire life of the loan. You don't have to worry about the payment suddenly shooting up. The rate is carved in stone.

An *adjustable rate (ARM)* starts out lower than a fixed rate—with lower monthly payments—but usually is only good for the first year of the loan. Then the lender hikes the rate and payment based on the index it uses. It can increase the rate again and again, up to a maximum of 5 or 6 percent over the starting rate, according to how often the index changes.

Which rate is for you?

Suppose you borrow $100,000 at 7 percent interest, which was the approximate average fixed rate at the beginning of 1998. The $100,000 is called your *principal*. With a 30-year term, your monthly payment would be $665, and your total *interest cost* over all 30 years would be $139,511. But suppose that instead of a 30-year loan, you took one for 15 years at 6.75 percent. The monthly payment on the 15-year loan would be higher—$899—but the total interest over 15 years would be sensationally less—$61,789. You'd save a whopping $77,722 with the 15-year loan! Now that's what you call *saving!*

Fiscal Facts

An **index** is a known benchmark used by a lender to set its mortgage rate on a variable-rate (as opposed to a fixed-rate) loan. The lender adjusts the homeowner's rate when the index goes up or down. When the index rises, the interest rate increases; when the index declines, the rate is adjusted downward.

But hold on. A 15-year loan is a good option for middle-aged and older buyers who can afford the higher monthly payment. It will save you a ton of money in interest, and it builds up your equity a lot faster. The disadvantage is that there's less tax-deductible interest on a 15-year loan. Plus, people with low incomes probably won't qualify as borrowers because their budgets can't handle the stiffer payments.

A 30-year fixed-rate loan has its advantages, too. It's a good investment when interest rates are low. Also, there may be considerable tax benefits, especially in the early years. Your payment stays the same even if rates rise, regardless of inflation. The one disadvantage is that your equity builds up more slowly with a 30-year loan.

Table 19.1   How Much You Can Save with a 15-Year Fixed Rate, Assuming the Rate Was the Same

	30-year	15-year
APR	7.5%	7.5%
Monthly payment	$874	$1,159
Paid after 15 years	$30,717	$125,000
Total interest paid	<u>$189,644</u>	<u>$83,577</u>
Interest saved		$106,067

ARMs' Initial Payments Are Lower but Could Shoot Up Later

Suppose someone lends you $1 today. He charges you a dime in interest this year, but next year he starts working with a different formula that could increase your interest to 15 cents in the second year, 20 cents in the third year, and so on, until it gets up to 80 cents or a maximum of a dollar. That's sort of how adjustable-rate mortgages (ARMs) work. You start out paying cheap interest, but later, the rate can skyrocket.

The only thing ARM rates have in common with fixed-rate mortgages is that they're both usually for 30 years. But unlike a fixed-rate mortgage, the ARM interest rate can adjust periodically—typically every year or six months. The adjustment is based on which index the lender ties its ARM rate to. The rate can go up or down according to the index—and so does your monthly payment. But your indexed rate may not start showing up until the second year of your loan, after the first adjustment.

What kind of mathematical nonsense is this? Lenders discount their first-year ARM rate as a low-rate ploy to get you in the door. As a result, their introductory ARM rate looks mighty good to you—it's probably a half-percent to a full percent or more, less than the interest on a fixed-rate. So far, so good. But at the beginning of the second year, as we just explained, the ARM rate jumps to the index rate plus a margin (for example, markup) that the lender tacks onto the index. This produces your indexed rate. If the index continues to rise, your ARM rate keeps going up as well. But if the index goes down, the ARM could fall, too.

The ARM indexes that lenders use have complicated names that consumers aren't aware of. But don't let it throw you. The main thing is, by knowing the lender is basing your ARM rate on a publicly-known index, it's better than having an index that the bank secretly concocted in its kitchen. You're better protected.

Asset Advisory

One index may change more often or more slowly than another index, and that can affect how long it takes the lender to change your ARM rate—and your monthly payment.

Here are the most common ARM indexes.

➤ **The 1-Year Treasury Bill Index.** This index is for ARMs whose rates generally change once a year. The lender will notify you of your new rate 30 to 45 days before it takes effect.

➤ **The 11th District Cost of Funds.** This gets its name from the Federal Home Loan Bank's 11th District which is based in San Francisco, but whose index is used by lenders nationwide. It's used mostly for ARM rates that are adjusted monthly. Your new rate is usually determined by the index value 30 to 90 days before the next rate change.

➤ **LIBOR—the London InterBank Offered Rate.** This is the most volatile index; it can jump up or down more frequently, with no set pattern as to how often. When mortgage rates are bouncing up and down erratically, lenders like the LIBOR index, because it protects them against wild rate swings

Watch Your Wallet

Beware of *negative amortization*! This is the ugliest of all types of mortgages, and it is usually found on adjustable-rate loans. Negative amortization is a little confusing, but basically it works like this: When you make a monthly payment, you may not get all of your interest, or any of your principal, credited against your loan because of the mathematical formula the lender uses.

Every ARM Wears a 'Cap'

Just because the lender can change your ARM rate whenever his index changes, doesn't mean he can keep increasing your rate forever. There's a limit to high he can go. This limit is called a "cap." There are really two caps on every ARM loan: A 2 percent cap per year, which means the rate can only rise by 2 percent in any given year, and a 6 percent cap over the life of the loan. If, for example, your ARM loan started out at 6.5 percent, it can never go higher than 12.5 percent.

But that's pretty scary, considering the fact that if your lender raises the rate by 2 percent a year, in four years' time you could be at the 12.5 percent level—when fixed rates might be only 7 percent, 8 percent or 9 percent. That's why ARMs are best for people who plan to move within four years, or for younger, first-time home buyers who may be short of cash for a few years.

The Big Benefit of Newfangled Mortgages: Cheaper in the Early Years

Two hot options are called 5/1 and 7/1 mortgages, where you lock in a fixed rate for five or seven years, then switch to whatever ARM rate exists at that time, plus a cap. While the starting rate will be a tad above the standard ARM, it's nevertheless lower than that on a 30-year fixed. That makes these loans ideal for folks who don't plan to remain in their home for many years, or who expect their future income to grow.

For example, one big lender was charging 7.25 percent on a 30-year fixed-rate mortgage, and on the same day had a 6.25 percent first-year introductory rate on its ARM loan. At the same time, it had a 6.5 percent rate for new home-buyers taking out a 5/1 or 7/1 loan. But for people who wanted to refinance their present mortgage, it charged 6.625 percent for a 5/1 refinance and 6.75 percent for a 7/1 refinancing.

All those numbers are enough to boggle the mind and frighten you away from mortgages entirely, but don't worry. Before you're through reading this chapter, you're going to learn the simple way to cut through the confusion and shop for the best deal!

Or Maybe You Need a 5/25 or a 7/23?

These are a couple more flexible mortgages that might fit your financial situation. They're very similar to the 5/1 and 7/1 plans just outlined, with a minor variation.

Say you can only afford a low monthly payment, and don't plan to stay in the home for more than a few years. Let's suppose interest rates are rising, and you prefer to lock into a fixed rate instead of gambling with an ARM rate that could increase by two percentage points a year. A *5/25* or *7/23 mortgage* may be for you.

With these loans, you take out a 30-year mortgage for which you pay a fixed rate for the first five or seven years. At the end of either term, your rate adjusts to a new fixed rate (which may be higher) for the remaining 25 or 23 years. Some lenders offer customers an option to convert to an ARM mortgage after five or seven years. Either way, these types of mortgages are good for first-time homebuyers with more income ahead.

Another Possibility: Cheap Government-Agency Financing

Can't afford a big down payment and four-figure closing costs? There are ways to get into a new home through government-agency programs that are ideal for new, young families and folks who don't have a lot of cash. One reason lenders are pushing the programs is this:

The federal government is clamping down on lenders—especially banks—if they fail to help provide affordable housing for low and middle-income families. They've set aside billions of dollars for these efforts—and in hundreds of cities across America, local governments have come up with "free money" for down payments and closing costs. Some of the deals are the following:

➤ **Fannie Mae "Flexible 97" Program**   It charges a market rate for a 30-year fixed-rate mortgage, but has a minimum 3 percent down payment. That money can come from a confirmed gift or a family loan, whereas under other low-down-payment programs, the 3 percent must be your own cash. Also, with Flexible 97, the seller can contribute up to 3 percent of the total mortgage amount toward your closing costs. In other words, if the costs were $3,000 on a $100,000 loan, you wouldn't have to put up any closing money. So if the down payment were a gift from Uncle Joe, you'd get into the house without having to use any of your own cash. Plus, the program has a loan ceiling of $227,150, and there's no limit on maximum household income. For details, call Fannie Mae at (800) 732-6643.

➤ **Federal Housing Administration (FHA) Loans**   The federal government doesn't actually *lend* the money for these loans; rather, it insures, or guarantees, the loan for the lender under several different mortgage programs. The down payment may be only three percent or less, and the fixed rate is lower than what you'd pay for a conventional 30-year loan. But the big news is that ARMs are back in the

FHA program. The downside is that the credit limit on how much you can borrow is limited by the median home prices in different areas. The loan term can be from 15 to 30 years.

➤ **Veteran's Administration (VA) loans**   These loans are also federally insured or guaranteed, with no down payment and have some of the same features as with an FHA loan. Borrowers must have current or previous military service. Loans may be for a 30-year or 15-year fixed-rate, or a 30-year ARM, and 100 percent financing is available. Rates are in the same ballpark as FHA loans.

➤ **Community Home Buyer's Program**   This may be the cheapest deal of all. Lately, there's been a new thrust toward 100 percent financing, but traditionally the CHB down payment requirement has been only 5 percent, with 2 percent of that allowable as a gift from family or friends. The 2 percent doesn't show up on your credit report, so it doesn't count as a debt you owe. Plus, you don't need cash reserves to cover two months' worth of mortgage payments (normally you need them with other low-income loans).

When Are Fixed or ARM Rates Best?

Timing is everything when you choose a mortgage. When interest rates are low, more homebuyers choose a fixed-rate because it locks in their monthly payment for 15 or 30 years. When fixed rates start approaching 10 percent, more people tend to shift to ARMs because the low introductory rates are then typically two to three percentage points below a fixed-rate.

For example, when the average fixed rate was 6.8 percent nationwide a few years ago, and the ARM rate was 4.0 percent, almost all homebuyers chose the fixed rate. Buyers avoided ARM rates because, despite the cheap 4.0 percent financing, the rate could rise to as high as 10.01 percent (6 percentage points above the starting rate). But a few months later, however, the fixed rate had climbed to 9.1 percent and the ARM was at 6.8 percent. Then the reverse happened; most consumers began choosing ARM mortgages instead.

Table 19.2   How Rates Go Up... and Down... and Up

Mortgage Type	1990	1991	1992	1993	1994	1995	1996	1997	1998*
ARM	8.17%	7.02%	5.46%	4.42%	6.18%	6.73%	5.64%	5.61%	5.71%
30-year fixed-rate	10.01%	9.09%	8.27%	7.18%	8.99%	8.95%	7.76%	7.57%	6.99%
15-year fixed-rate	9.67%	8.76%	7.80%	6.66%	8.50%	8.58%	7.28%	7.16%	6.66%

First half of 1998
Source: Bank Rate Monitor

To understand how an ARM might work, let's look at this example. Pretend that the average fixed rate is 7 percent, but in the first year, the average introductory ARM rate is only 5.50 percent. You choose the ARM because it's cheaper. Your monthly payment on a $100,000 mortgage would be $567.79 in the first year. But in the second year, the lender starts to set your new rate based on an index such as the one-year Treasury bill. Say the index is 5.2 percent. The lender adds its margin, typically 2.75 percentage points. That increases your rate to 7.95 percent (5.2 plus 2.75), but because of the two-percent-cap-per-year, your new rate can't go any higher than 7.5 percent. That's the maximum rate you pay in the second year, so your monthly payment increases to $696.21.

In year three, let's assume the index has now gone up to 5.4 percent. Add the 2.75 percent margin again, and your ARM rate becomes 8.15 percent (5.4 plus 2.75). Because that rate is below the two-percent-per-year cap maximum, your new rate stays at the 8.15 percent level. Your monthly payment jumps to $739.36 in the third year.

Play out that same scenario through the fourth year. The lender hikes your rate again, to a new index of, say, 5.6 percent plus 2.75 percent, or 8.35 percent. That becomes your new rate because it's within the two-percent-cap limit, and payments rise to $752.57 this year. At this point, four years after you took out your ARM loan, which type of mortgage would have been the better deal—the ARM or a fixed-rate? Obviously the fixed rate. Table 19.3 shows you why.

Table 19.3 ARM Costs Can Rise

	ARM	Fixed-Rate (7%)
First year	$5,466	$6,968
Second year	$7,365	$6,894
Third year	$7,925	$6,816
Fourth year	$8,038	$6,731
Total interest cost, first 4 years	$28,794	$27,409

Of course, ARM rates can go down as well as up, depending on what happens to the index. The indexes that ARM rates are tied to will change periodically. The higher the index, the higher your ARM rate (based on a formula the lender uses). In strong economic times, and during periods of inflation, the index will probably rise. During a recession, such as the one between 1990 and 1993, the index will fall. Table 19.4 illustrates by how much two popular ARM indexes changed between 1990 and 1998. (Remember: An index is only a benchmark that the lender uses to figure the ARM rate you are charged.)

Table 19.4 ARM Index Changes

Adjustable Index	1990	1995	1998
1-year Treasury	8.09%	5.47%	4.97%
11th District Cost of Funds	8.48%	4.59%	4.88%

Worst-case scenario: If the fourth-year ARM rate in the example we gave stayed at 8.35 percent for the remaining 27 years, you'd wind up paying a total of $167,776 in interest over the life of the loan—*plus* the $100,000 principal you owe. By comparison, had you grabbed the 30-year 7 percent fixed rate at the beginning, you'd pay a total of $139,508—a savings of $28,268.

What's It Gonna Cost Me?

Except for low down-payment government programs (described in this chapter), you'll probably make a down payment of between five percent and 20 percent on that little house with the picket fence. You'll also have closing costs that run 2 percent to 5 percent of the amount borrowed. And you'll be forking over money for not-so-incidental things such as moving, new-house fix-ups, and any outside legal fees attached to the purchase.

Watch Your Wallet

Be forewarned: Lenders provide you with a "good faith estimate" of the total costs of a mortgage loan at the time you apply, but the real final cost can be a lot more than the "estimate." There's no federal law that forces these guys to make the estimate 100 percent accurate.

That's a lot of cash outflow. So it's not wise to plunk down *all* your money into a down payment. There's a better way around it. To budget for the house, you should ask yourself these questions:

How low do I want my monthly payment to be?

How long do I plan to stay in the house?

How much out-of-pocket is required for incidentals to move into the house and stay there over the next three to six months?

Don't forget, you also need to take rates, points, APR, fees, and closing costs into consideration when figuring out how much your mortgage is really going to cost you.

Which Should You Watch Most—Rates or Points?

So far, we've discussed only rates. However, there's another little animal in the mortgage jungle that directly affects the cost of your loan. It's *points*. A point is one one-hundredth of your loan amount. On a $100,000 loan, each point is $1,000. Lenders charge points to cover the costs of completing a mortgage application and to earn income. The buyer pays the points at closing, for example, when buyer and seller sit down together and close the sale. If a $100,000 mortgage comes with three points, that's $3,000.

Mortgage shoppers often ask, "Which is more important, rates or points?" It depends on your situation. The *rate* is probably the key because it determines your monthly payment of principal and interest. But points can directly influence the rate you pay, even though the two are completely different things.

Points come into play when the lender determines how much of a monthly payment you can afford. Since that payment is influenced by the interest rate, one way to bring the rate (and your payment) down is to increase the number of points. Many lenders have five or more rates-and-points combinations; some may have a dozen. For example, a lender that quotes a rate of 8 percent with no points might also have quotes of 7.5 percent with one point, 7.2 percent with two points, and 6.8 percent with three points.

As you can see, rates and points move in opposite directions. The higher the rate, the lower the points, and vice versa. If you want to lower your monthly payment, you can "buy down" the rate by paying more points. The lower rate can also reduce your interest expenses. On $100,000 borrowed at 7.5 percent for 30 years, the monthly payment would be $699. Over the first five years of the loan, total interest would be $3,121. If you lowered the rate to 7.2 percent by paying more points, the monthly payment would drop to $679 and total interest for five years would decrease to $2,994. Besides having the lower payment, the lower rate would save you $127 in interest, but the benefit would apply only to the first five years.

Asset Advisory

The longer you plan to stay in your house, the more you should pay points in exchange for a lower interest rate.

That five-year period is important. Why? Because it takes at least that long, and more likely seven years, to recoup the cash outlay of more points with lower monthly payments. If you don't have a lot of ready cash or aren't planning to stay in the house for more than five years, taking fewer points and a higher interest rate would probably be the better strategy.

The "APR" Tells You the REAL Cost!

What's an "APR?" It stands for "Annual Percentage Rate," a complicated term that throws almost any mortgage shopper for a loop. An APR is simply a percentage number that includes the rate plus certain fees and charges, It helps you compare apples with apples when you try to stack two loan offers side by side to decide which one is the better deal. The Consumer Credit Protection Act requires that lenders disclose their APRs.

The APR is almost always higher than the rate, but it reflects *the real cost of your loan on a yearly basis*. That creates a more level playing field for you to judge all the different mortgage deals. For one thing, the APR includes the points *and* many of the fees you're charged on your loans. Starting to get the idea?

Asset Advisory

If you can afford a higher rate with higher monthly payments, some lenders may offer you a no-points deal.

Suppose (as in Table 19.5) that Megabuck Bank offers a 30-year fixed-rate loan at 7.5 percent. Friendly Federal's rate is only 7 percent. That makes Friendly's offer the better deal, right? Maybe not. You could pay three points for Friendly's loan, compared with only one point at Megabuck. Plus, Friendly might have forgotten to tell you about other fees, such as mortgage insurance premiums, prepaid interest, and its cost of originating the mortgage. That could total a few thousand bucks. On the surface, it *looks* like Friendly Federal has a cheaper mortgage based on the rate alone. But when all the costs are figured into the APR, the cheaper mortgage is Megabuck's.

Table 19.5   The Lowest Rate May Not Be Your Best Deal

	Megabuck Bank	Friendly Federal
Rate	7.5%	7%
Interest	$7,469	$6,968
Points (based on a $100,000 30-year mortgage)	$1,000 (1 point)	$3,000 (3 points)
Closing costs	$500	$2,500
Total cost in first year of mortgage	$8,969	$12,468

Asset Advisory

When you shop, always ask lenders for their APRs on fixed-rate loans versus ARMs, and compare those with other lenders' APRs in the area.

Learn the Up-Front Fees and Closing Costs

Besides the cost items that go into your monthly payment, there are other costs on the front end and back end of a mortgage loan. Ideally, you want to do business with an outfit that doesn't rook you at either end. Most lenders will charge you up-front fees; others may not charge anything at all to get your business. Beware of lenders who load on extra costs like photos, document charges, notary, and so forth. These can run into hundreds of dollars.

Typically you should only pay:

Up-front: Appraisal and credit report.

Closing costs: Points, recording fees, documentary stamps, mortgage insurance, document preparation, and inspection.

Remember that you must have enough cash for closing costs, which have to be paid when the final papers are signed. Most lenders will provide you with a "good faith" estimate of these costs in advance. Typically, closing costs run between 2 percent and 6 percent of the loan amount.

The Quick, Easy Way to Find the Cheapest Mortgage

Okay, so now you know all the major costs of getting a mortgage, but you're probably thinking, "How am I going to remember all this stuff? I feel like I'm drowning in an ocean of rates, points, formulas, and other mathematical gobbledygook. There's gotta be an easier way!"

There is. Try this simple solution. It works like a charm, and there's probably no better way to shop a mortgage, even if you have three college degrees in math. First, pick out a half dozen or more of the lenders in your area that seem to be offering the best combination of rates and points.

Second, assume you'll be in your new house for five years—which is about the average length of time most families stay. (Five years also happens to be the magic cut-off point for deciding between a fixed-rate and an ARM, remember?)

Then ask each lender to tell you—*in dollars and cents, not percent*—the following:

➤ Total up-front fees *and* charges on the types of loans you'd consider.

➤ Total interest charges (not counting the principal) for the first five years.

➤ Total closing costs, including points.

Got that? Three dollar items from each lender. Then add up the total cost of the mortgage—those three items—for the first five years at each lender, and compare the various deals. Voilà! You immediately see who offers the best deal! When you shop for the lowest mortgage cost among several different lenders, add up the three main cost areas (shown in Table 19.6, the Mortgage Shopping List) for each lender, and compare. Be sure each lender covers ALL the costs. Don't let them get away with saying, "Then, of course, there are certain other fees and charges." You want them all—now—period.

Tip for the cyber crowd: Two good places to find the latest mortgage rates, and calculators that help you figure what different loans will cost you, can be found on the Internet at www.bankrate.com, and www.interest.com/calculators.html.

Here's what your shopping list should look like:

Table 19.6 Mortgage Shopping List

	Lender A	Lender B	Lender C	Lender D
Up-front charges	$_____	$_____	$_____	$_____
Interest cost (first 5 years)	$_____	$_____	$_____	$_____
Closing costs	$_____	$_____	$_____	$_____
Total cost (first 5 years)	$_____	$_____	$_____	$_____

The Money Line

Lenders are super-hungry for business. The sharp cuts in interest rates have increased the number of buyers and created dog-eat-dog competition. As a result, many lenders are waiving fees, reducing their down payment requirements, discounting their financing costs (for example, a $250 cash bonus applied to closing costs), approving loans for buyers with risky credit records, and often permitting buyers to lock in their rate 30 days *before* closing instead of *at* closing.

To get lenders to bid against each other for your business, it's possible to submit loan applications to two outfits at the same time. This may enable you to get a lower rate and lower fees, but when the lenders discover what you're doing, don't be surprised if they give you poorer service.

Who Lends the Money?

Lenders fall into one of three categories:

➤ **Financial Institutions, such as Banks, Thrifts, and Credit Unions**   Sometimes the institution offers the loan, sometimes it's a mortgage company owned by the institution. You can't tell the difference offhand in most cases; it's more a technicality than a real difference anyway. For example, if your bank directs you to a loan office somewhere else, you'll probably be dealing with a mortgage company owned by the bank. Provided the lender is legally licensed by the state, it doesn't make any difference anyway, because most lenders sell off their mortgages to a secondary market.

➤ **Mortgage Companies**   The term may be loosely applied to an organization that specializes only in mortgages, or to a bank or thrift that has an affiliated mortgage company (hence the term "mortgage banker"). Mortgage companies can be big national outfits such as Countrywide Mortgage or Norwest, or small home-grown lenders. They make the same loans that banks make. Size isn't important, especially if you're getting a standard 30-year loan.

➤ **Mortgage Brokers**   They're like mortgage bankers (although they are not connected with financial institutions), but they can be part of a national loan company. But there's an important distinction: *Brokers don't actually fund mortgage loans.* Instead, they put borrowers and lenders together. They call on a number of loan sources to arrange the best possible match. Brokers can be a great help if you've had past credit problems because they can locate lenders who will be more flexible than others.

Remember: No matter how charming the broker is, remember that he or she is representing the seller, not the buyer. That's where they make their money. Since the lender and the broker sometimes split some of the fees you're charged on a mortgage, it shouldn't cost you any more to borrow through a broker.

Should you choose one over the other? Not unless you have a special circumstance. If a bank will give you a better break because you're already a customer, that's good. If a mortgage banker will cut its rate to get your business, that's fine. And if a broker can get you a loan when others have turned you down, that's even better.

No matter whom you do business with, you should always shop around for the best possible lender. When you talk to a bank or mortgage company, ask for references from other customers. In the case of mortgage brokers, talk to lenders the broker uses regularly. Those are your best references, nobody else.

Asset Advisory

Doing business at a bank where you have a checking account or another loan can be an advantage. Why? You may be able to apply at the same branch where people already know you. Plus, because you have the other accounts, the bank may discount your mortgage rate by (say) one-quarter of a percentage point if you agree to have your monthly payments debited automatically from checking.

How to Play the Mortgage "Lock-In" Game

Unpredictable mortgage rates can drive homebuyers batty. They nervously watch rates dance up and down, week after week. But knowing exactly when to lock in their rate is like a cross between playing Blind Man's Bluff and Las Vegas craps. Even the "experts" can't tell you how high or low rates will be a week or a month from today. So what do you do if you want the best possible rate on the day you're supposed to close?

If you believe rates will drop between now and the closing date, skip, postpone, or shorten the lock-in because you might cut a better deal later. If you think rates are going up, tell the lender you want to lock in the current, lower rate for a certain number of days (such as 30, 60, or 90). But it will cost you something in return.

As part of the game, the lender may tempt you with different rates and points for different lock-in periods. For an extra half-point or so, you might be guaranteed the current rate for "X" number of days. For every $100,000 borrowed, that would cost the borrower $500. (Remember: A point is one one-hundredth of the loan amount.)

You say you'd rather gamble and save the $500? Consider what happened to a couple we know. Their builder promised them their new home would be ready in 45 days. So they skipped paying the $500 to lock in a lower rate for 60 days. Guess what. The builder didn't finish the house for 90 days. Meanwhile, mortgage rates climbed by more than a half percent. That added thousands of dollars to the couple's total mortgage cost.

When you play the lock-in game, follow these rules:

➤ When rates are rising, lock in immediately. When they're falling, stall for as long as you can.

➤ Learn the lock-in choices and how much each one costs. In general, the longer the lock-in period, the higher the points. You may discover that the lender won't lock in the rate.

➤ The lock-in period should be spelled out in a document provided by the lender. You will likely be required to sign this sheet. The document should explain what would happen to your rate if the lock-in expires before you close on the house purchase.

Watch Your Wallet

Be careful. Some lenders lock you in the day you apply for a loan. Others start the clock the day you receive your credit approval.

What happens when the lock-in expires? Your rate should then float up or down to the current rate at closing. Sometimes, if rates have fallen, you'll pay the original rate that was in effect when you applied for your loan. If rates have risen, you'll pay the new, higher rate.

How to Speed Things Up

Beware of lenders who drag their heels in processing your loan. It could happen, especially when rates are going up, because that increases the lender's profit. The result is that the rate jumps and you'll be forced to make higher monthly payments.

Bear down on your loan officer. You don't have to be a pest, but you should keep on top of your application. Call in regularly with questions about your loan status. Find out if the appraisal has been ordered, completed, and reviewed. Ask the loan officer if he or she needs any additional information from you.

You may find that the appraisal has been done, but it mistakenly got routed to Joe or Sally, or it's still in that big stack on Harry's desk. A couple of phone calls can get things back on track. Each step of the way, note in writing what the lender tells you. Keep a complete record; give the loan officer a report each time you talk. That way the lender will know you're ahead of the game.

Get Your Credit Record in Shape Now!

What mistakes do lenders think home buyers make when they set out to buy a house? They'll tell you that *too many consumers wait until the last minute to get their credit in order*. The process, they say, should begin six months before you apply for the loan (unless, of course, you have megabucks in the bank and have a squeaky-clean credit record). Here's what to do:

➤ Get a copy of your credit report. (To learn how, see Chapter 16.)

➤ If you have four or five credit cards, trim the number down to only one.

➤ Pay off as many of your debts as possible.

➤ Don't apply for any more credit until you go for a mortgage. A bunch of new inquiries could show up on your credit report; that's a no-no in the eyes of lenders who are considering you for a mortgage loan.

➤ If Aunt Matilda promised to give you a present of $20,000 next year, ask Auntie to help by letting you have the money now, to build up your bank balance before you go for a mortgage.

You Pay Through the Nose in the Early Years

The way lenders calculate the payback on your mortgage loan, you get socked with tons of interest in the early years of the loan. Very little of your monthly payment amounts go toward your principal. It's not until the later years that your monthly payments begin to reduce the principal substantially.

Assume you borrow $100,000 for 30 years at a 9 percent fixed rate, with a monthly payment of $805. In the first five years, the picture looks like this (Table 19.7):

Table 19.7 The First Five Years of a Mortgage ($100,000 at 9 Percent)

Year	Principal Still Owed	Principal You've Paid	Interest You've Paid	Total Payments You've Made
1	$98,984	$1,016	$6,698	$7,984
2	$97,895	$1,089	$6,895	$7,984
3	$96,727	$1,168	$6,816	$7,984
4	$95,475	$1,252	$6,732	$7,984
5	$94,132	$1,343	$6,641	$7,984

Asset Advisory

The way the math works out, the higher the interest rate, the greater the amount of your early payments that go toward interest. Conversely, the lower the interest rate, the less the amount of early payments that go toward interest.

In other words, after five years of the 30-year loan, you've reduced your $100,000 principal by only $4,120 ($100,000 minus $95,880), but have paid a total interest of $42,157 (the sum of the five numbers in the column headed "Interest You've Paid")! Yet you've been making a monthly payment of $805 all along.

But as the loan gets older, more and more of your monthly payment will start being applied toward the principal, and less toward the interest. Use the example in Table 19.7. Although it's not shown, by the time you get to the twenty-third year, about the same amount will go toward the principal and the interest. In your final (30th) year of the mortgage, you will have paid off the original $100,000 loan and paid a whopping $189,658 in interest. Your total payments for principal and interest will be an astronomical $289,658!

The Law Cracks Down on "PMI"

To protect themselves from homebuyers who default on their mortgages, lenders insist the buyer take out Private Mortgage Insurance (PMI) if they have less than 20 percent equity in the home. PMI normally adds between $20 and $100 to the monthly payment, or as much as $1,200 a year. But crafty lenders often didn't tell homeowners when their equity hit 20 percent, and PMI continued on and on.

Now, by federal law, the lender must discontinue charging for PMI when the owner's equity reaches either 22 percent of either the original purchase price or the appraisal value at closing, whichever is lower.

Don't confuse PMI with credit life insurance, which pays off the mortgage on behalf of the surviving family in the event of the homeowner's death.

Putting the Tax Savings in Your Pocket

The one bright side to the staggering cost of a mortgage is that you can deduct certain items on your personal tax returns. That will effectively reduce the cost of your mortgage. For the deductions, you should obtain the help of a professional tax consultant, who can also bring you up to date on the Taxpayers Relief Act of 1997. For one thing, it liberalized the tax benefits for people who had to sell their homes after living in them for less than two years.

The main tax deductions are these:

➤ The interest costs that you pay per year on the loan.

➤ The points you pay at closing, but only in the year in which the loan is made.

➤ Your (the buyer's) prorated portion of items such as property taxes and other statements that are finalized at closing.

➤ State and local taxes that are associated with the loan.

Using the example from Table 19.7 (a 30-year, $100,000 loan at a 9 percent interest rate), assume you are in the 28 percent federal tax bracket. Table 19.8 shows you what you can deduct from your federal tax returns over the first five years.

Table 19.8   What Uncle Sam Will Let You Deduct (28 Percent Tax Bracket—$100,000 at 7 Percent)

Year	Annual Int. Payment	Tax Savings Per Year	Your Net Cost After Deduction
1	$6,968	$1,951	$5,017
2	$6,895	$1,931	$4,964
3	$6,816	$1,908	$4,908
4	$6,732	$1,885	$4,847
5	$6,641	$1,859	$4,782

If you also deducted state and local taxes from these numbers, you'd be able to save even more. It gets a little complicated, but again, let's assume you're in the 28 percent federal tax bracket. When you factor in state and local taxes of six percent on top of the federal tax deduction, the formula comes out to a total deduction of 32.32 percent.

Your total payment in the first year, for the example in Table 19.7, is $7,984. Of that, $6,968 is interest (see Table 19.8). Multiply 32.32 percent by $6,968 and you arrive at a tax deduction of $2,252 for federal, state, and local taxes in the first year.

The Point Is—Points Add Up!

When they shop mortgages, many homebuyers look only at the interest rate, and forget to figure in the points as part of their total cost.

The true annual percentage rate (APR) on a loan should include the points as well as the rate. On the same type of loan, the greater the number of points, the higher the APR. Table 19.9 shows you how the points you pay can affect your APR on a $100,000 fixed-rate loan at nine percent for 15 or 30 years.

Table 19.9   What a 7 Percent Loan Really Costs

Points	APR (15 Years)	APR (30 Years)
1	7.16%	7.10%
2	7.33%	7.20%
3	7.49%	7.30%
4	7.66%	7.41%
5	7.83%	7.52%

The Least You Need to Know

➤ The two major types of mortgages are fixed-rate and adjustable-rate (ARM).

➤ A fixed-rate is best when interest rates are low, so you can lock up that rate for the full life of the loan. ARMs are generally a better deal if you don't have extra money to cover a big down payment and high closing costs, or if you only plan to remain in the house for less than four years.

➤ There are government-backed mortgage programs for first-time home buyers and others with low incomes, for as little as 3 percent down.

➤ The easy way to shop for the best mortgage is to ask a half-dozen different lenders for the total *dollar costs* of their upfront charges, finance cost over the first five years, and closing costs including points. Then add those three numbers for each lender.

➤ The Annual Percentage Rate (APR) is a good way to compare mortgage deals, apples to apples, because it includes fees and charges in addition to the rate.

➤ You can really negotiate better rates and fees with many lenders. You may also be able to swing a better deal at the bank, thrift, or credit union where you are now doing business.

➤ Make sure your credit is in order at least six months before you apply for a mortgage. Chapter 16 provides more information how to do this.

Chapter 20

The Biggest Advantages—and Dangers—of Home Equity Loans

In This Chapter

➤ How home equity loans can consolidate debts at cheaper rates

➤ Which type of home equity loan is best for you

➤ The real upsides and downsides, if you borrow this way

➤ Why you should beware of low rate offers

➤ Tricks and traps your lender won't tell you

➤ How to figure the real cost of your loan

➤ How to be aware of scam operators pushing home equity

How enticing can it get! Famous sports celebrities in television commercials, urging you to call a toll-free 800 number to get fast cash through a home equity loan. In your mailbox the next day, an unsolicited letter with a humongous $50,000 check, made payable to you. The check isn't negotiable, but the letter says "up to $100,000 is waiting for you" and "perfect credit is not required." In fact, the letter goes on, you can get up to 125 percent of what your home is worth! And you can use the cash for whatever you wish—paying off credit card debt, home improvements, medical bills or college tuition.

Home equity is the banks' hottest product these days. In fact, about 3 million Americans a year now take out a home equity loan to pay off 100 percent of what they owe on credit cards. It looks like the greatest deal that ever came down the pike, because the interest rate on these loans is much less than it is on credit cards. Getting their hands on a slug of fast cash could sure help many debt-riddled consumers out of their jam. But there are dangers and traps galore. This chapter explains what they are, and guides you so you won't trip up and make the biggest mistake of your life.

Home Equity in a Nutshell: Your Nest Egg Is on the Line

With a home equity loan, you borrow against the amount of equity you have in your home. The bank either gives you one lump sum of money, or it sets the money aside for you in a reserve account—called a home equity line of credit—that you can tap into at any time. You can access the funds by check, ATM or even by phone. Your interest rate will be cheap—only 10 percent on average, versus the 18 percent that your credit cards are probably costing you. But, unlike borrowing with a credit card, or taking out an auto loan, you'll be able to deduct 100 percent of the home equity interest from your taxes, up to $100,000. But, you have to pay the money back. If you don't, the bank can foreclose on your house. What you've really done with a home equity loan is hock the farm, probably the single biggest, most important asset you'll ever own. Plus, because of inflation, that little abode you bought back in the 1970s is probably worth a lot more today.

Hence, for the unsuspecting home owner, the loan can be a time bomb that one day could explode in their face. Before you jump at this kind of borrowing, you mustn't just think about the big benefits, but also of the possibly terrible consequences.

Why Banks Love Home Equity Loans

Home equity lines of credit (HELOCs, for short) are the banks' darlings because they're collateralized loans. In case you default, the institution has something of value, your house. Also, HELOCs are bigger loans than, say, the piddling $3,000 loan on which the bank makes less money. It takes a lot of those little loan customers to equal what a bank can make off a single home equity customer. Plus, these borrowers tend to be more upscale than people with lower incomes who don't own a home.

No wonder every time you turn your head you see a bank hustling HELOCs. Because competition among banks and finance companies is so fierce, they're all wheeling and dealing to get your business. Many are even waiving up-front fees and closing costs.

How a Home Equity Loan Works

Say you still owe $25,000 on your mortgage, and appraisers figure that the market value of the house is $125,000. Subtract what you owe from what the house is worth to get your equity—in this case $100,000. That's your "loan-to-value" figure, or LTV. Famous Finance Company says it will lend you up to 80 percent of that amount. Get the calculator out. Wow! That means you can get your hands on as much as $80,000!

Think that's impressive? The plot gets thicker: Now lenders are offering loans of up to 125 percent of the value of your home! In other words, on a $200,000 house with a $175,000 first mortgage, you'd get a $75,000 equity loan. (Your two loans would total

$250,000, which is 125 percent of what the house is worth.) Hopefully you're not foolish enough to borrow that much without being sure you can pay the money back, because you'll be, as they say in the trade, "upside down" (owing more than the house is worth). Unless you have a steady source of income, the two payments could strangle you.

What does Famous Finance require from you before it hands over the money? Some collateral, such as a *lien* that gives the bank ownership of your house in case you default. That's right. If you can't pay the bank back, it can grab the home that you busted your hump for all your life. Welcome to the dangerous, fast-growing world of home equity borrowing.

The Money Line

The two biggest reasons why Americans get a home equity loan, according to Consumer Bankers Association, are debt consolidation, cited by 40 percent of respondents to a survey, and home improvement, mentioned by 23 percent.

Type A and Type B

Famous Finance will lend you the money one of two ways: A *home equity loan* or a *home equity line of credit*. If you take a plain home equity loan, it will usually lend you at least 80 percent or 90 percent of your equity in your house—or, in some cases, as much as the 125 percent LTV we mentioned. You get the money all at once and make fixed monthly payments, just like paying back a second mortgage.

But if you take a home equity line of credit, Famous Finance will give you a credit line in the same amount, which works like a revolving credit card account. As you pay back the amount, you're rebuilding the credit line so you can keep borrowing from it. In effect, the credit line works like a giant credit card. You access the amount you need, whenever you need it, simply by writing a check against the account or getting the money from an ATM. Typically, a home equity line is for 10 to 15

Watch Your Wallet

Trouble all over again: In the 1996–97 two-year period, 4.2 million people used home equity loans to pay off their credit card debts. But after that, two out of three of those people got into debt again by running up their credit card bills.

years. By having access to the money when you need it, you don't have to keep going back to the bank and reapplying for loans.

The big downside is that with either type of home equity loan, you're not only robbing your nest egg, you're also swapping short-term debt for long-term debt.

How One Family Blew It

Here's a lesson on how *not* to handle your financial life after you take out a home equity loan. It's the sad, painful story of Tom and Marla:

They bought a home two years ago for $100,000 with 5 percent down. They borrowed $95,000 at 7.5 percent for a monthly payment of $654. Their mortgage balance was $93,180. The home value had appreciated by 5 percent per year to $110,000, and the equity in their home grew to $17,000.

The couple bought a new car one year ago, for which they financed $18,000 at 8 percent for a monthly payment of $440. The loan balance had subsequently been reduced to $14,000. Tom and Marla carried a credit card balance of $8,000, at 18 percent, for an annual interest cost of $1,440 ($120 per month plus paying off 2 percent of the balance every month, for a total of $280 per month).

They needed $5,000 per year for the next four years for their child's college education. At this point, their monthly obligations, counting a $416 college payment, came to $1,800, against total monthly family of $4,167 ($50,000 a year). Tom contacted a finance company that agreed to give them a 125 percent loan, which amounted to $42,000. That reduced their monthly payment on debts to $440, a drop of about $700 from the earlier figure of $1,136.

But now, two years later:

➤ The balance on the home equity loan is $39,320.

➤ Credit card balances are back up to $5,000, with a minimum monthly payment of 2 percent of the balance plus interest at 18 percent, for a total of $175.

➤ Total family debt has risen to $44,000, and monthly payments other than the mortgage have increased to $615 from $440.

➤ The only good news is that, counting the mortgage payment, total monthly payments are $1,280, which is *less* than the $1,800 per month the family was paying before. But the family is *now more in debt than before they got the home equity loan!*

And Another Family Got Hit by a Balloon

You think Tom's and Marla's case is bad? Check what happened to another couple, Jim and Jane. They borrowed $20,000 via a home equity loan for five years at 10 percent interest. They can't afford a $400 per month payment, so what does the bank do? It offers them a balloon payment deal.

All Jim and Jane have to do is pay the *interest* on the loan every month; they don't have to pay on the principal (the $20,000) until the very end of the five years. Then, BOOM! They must pay the $20,000 all at once—just like a balloon being inflated. But suppose they can't come up with the twenty grand? They'll lose their home to the bank. Goodbye American dream!

On a $20,000 loan ,at 10 percent interest for five years, the loan will cost them a staggering $20,000 if they only pay back the interest over that period. They'll still owe the $20,000 principal after the five years are up. In other words, they'll have to pay back $40,000.

Right this moment, millions of consumers who've taken out home equity loans are caught in that trap. They're like time bombs waiting to go off. Assuming their credit is still okay five years from now, Jim and Jane could roll the first loan over into a new loan at the same bank. But that would only cost them more interest on top of the outrageous $20,000 in interest they've already paid.

However, balloon payments aren't a threat if you plan to sell your house before the loan matures. You could pay the loan off with the proceeds from the sale.

Watch Your Wallet

Some banks hide in small print the fact that they have a "base rate" on variable-rate loans. This sets a floor below which your rate will never go, regardless of what happens. For example, if the base rate is 9 percent and the bank's prime rate plunges so low that your loan rate should be 7 percent, you'll still pay the floor rate of 9 percent!

The Interest Adds Up

A home equity line of credit is a revolving account. Money goes out, money comes in; that's how the account revolves.

Your monthly payment is generally two percent of the total P&I (principal and interest) you owe. If the amount you borrow over a year (P) is $5,000 and your interest rate (I) is 10 percent, the interest is $500. Therefore, the total P&I is $5,500. Two percent of that is $110. That's your monthly payment.

Fixed versus Variable Rates, and the "Introductory" Teaser Rate Come-On

The interest rate you pay is critical because it could knock your wallet for a loop. With a fixed rate, you lock in your cost over the full life of the loan. The rate won't ever change and you'll know your costs in advance. With a variable rate, the rate can go up or down according to whatever "index" the bank ties the rate to.

Most home equity lines charge a variable rate that's based on the bank's prime rate plus anywhere from one to three percentage points. If the prime is 8.5 percent and the rate is prime plus 1.5 percent, then you'll pay an indexed rate of 10 percent.

Now, here's where the sneaky ploy comes in:

Just about every bank in the land uses artificially low introductory "teaser" rates to get you in the door. For example, Megabuck Bank might feature a giant 9 percent rate in a newspaper ad or in the bank's lobby. However, the fine print at the bottom of the ad says, "Nine percent introductory rate is only good for the first six months, after which the rate will revert to Megabuck's prime rate in effect at that time, plus three percentage points." Translation: If you take this loan at 9 percent on July 1, next January 1 your real home equity loan rate will jump to 12 percent. Big difference? You bet. The interest cost on a $10,000 loan will go from $900 a year to $1,200.

Never borrow on home equity without finding out for how long the rate is good and what the real rate will be after the introductory period.

Keep these tips in mind when playing the rate game:

➤ Often, the more money you borrow, the lower your starting rate will be.

➤ When interest rates are rising, avoid variable-rate loans or lines at all costs. Get a fixed-rate loan instead. That will tell you your cost from Day One until the loan is paid off. But when rates are falling or you don't think they'll rise soon, you should go with the variable rate.

➤ Stay away from variable rates when you borrow for a longer term, such as 10 or 15 years.

➤ In a rising-rate environment, you can keep your monthly payment budget intact by asking the bank to stretch the number of months to repay the money or by asking the bank to lower the payment—or both. However, remember that the longer you have the loan, the more interest you'll pay.

➤ If you're considering a fixed rate, tell them you want to be able to switch to the future current rate in the event that interest rates start shooting up. Some lenders will allow you to convert to a fixed rate once or twice during the loan term without paying any extra fees.

➤ Most variable rates have a cap (a maximum amount, or ceiling) that the rate can rise to. Be sure to ask what that is.

Asset Advisory

If you opened a home equity loan several years ago and interest rates have declined in the meantime, try to renegotiate a lower rate with your lender.

Pros and Cons of Home Equity Loans

Taking out a home equity loan isn't all bad. Consider these advantages:

➤ It's cheap. Ten percent beats 18 percent credit cards any day. Plus, you can try to negotiate an even cheaper rate with the lender.

➤ The interest can be 100 percent tax-deductible for up to $100,000.

➤ It's a fast way to get your hands on a good sum of cash to consolidate your debts at a lower cost, or for urgent big-ticket items such medical bills and tuition. For example, if you owe $5,000 on credit cards at 18 percent interest, and you take out a $5,000 home equity loan at nine percent to pay them off, you've chopped your financing cost in half, from $900 a year to $450 a year.

➤ You can pay back only the interest on the loan for several years or until it matures (such as in 10 years). Banks are flexible on this, but there's a built-in booby trap, as you'll discover in this chapter.

➤ Here's what big banks and thrifts in large U.S. cities were charging on home equity lines of credit, compared with fixed-rate credit cards:

Asset Advisory

If you're not sure about your future job security, it might be better to get a home equity loan or line of credit now, while you still qualify. Then if you get laid off, you'll be better able to pay off high-rate credit cards.

Table 20.1 How Home Equity Credit Line Rates Compare with Credit Card Rates:

	Home Equity	Fixed-Rate Credit Card
New York	8.52%	17.01%
Los Angeles	7.87%	16.61%
Chicago	8.92%	N/A
San Francisco	8.28%	13.99%
Philadelphia	8.68%	16.90%
Detroit	8.91%	15.37%
Boston	8.60%	N/A
Washington	8.68%	12.17%

N/A= Not available at largest institutions
Source: Bank Rate Monitor

Before you dash off to the bank to get your home equity loan, keep in mind that a home equity loan isn't for frivolous folks. It's for disciplined people who will use the money wisely (not for vacations, second honeymoons, or a wild spending spree in Las Vegas). In other words, the rabbit should not go near the lettuce. You should not take out such a loan unless you are 100 percent certain you will be able to repay it on time.

The downsides of the loan are these:

➤ It reduces or eliminates your equity in the home.

➤ Your total cost over the life of the loan can be expensive.

➤ If the value of your house depreciates, the amount you owe on the loan stays the same.

➤ The bank can grab your house if you don't pay back the money on time. That's called a foreclosure. In fact, if you use home equity loan proceeds to buy a car and don't make the payments, they may take the house instead of the car.

➤ The biggest danger is that borrowers won't discipline their spending habits after paying off their debts, and get in over their heads all over again.

They Make It S-o-o-o-o Easy

Banks keep giving you more ways to access the money in your home equity credit line. Besides issuing you a bunch of checks to tap into the cash, some let you use your credit card or let you access the credit line by telephone or an ATM. Why?

Those cunning outfits don't make a dime off you unless you actually *use* the cash available in your account. That's why many of them charge an "inactivity fee" if you don't touch any of the money within a year's time. The fee could be anywhere from $50 to $150. (When was the last time anyone ever billed you for doing nothing?)

Other banks require that you borrow a minimum, such as $300 each time you draw on the equity line. Others will insist that you take an initial cash advance when you first set up the line to get your debt rolling—a foxy move on the bank's part.

Right this moment, millions of consumers who've taken out home equity loans are caught in that trap. The loans are like time bombs waiting to go off. Assuming their credit is still okay five years from now, Jim and Jane could roll their first loan over into a new loan at the same bank. But that would only cost them more interest on top of the outrageous $20,000 in interest they've already paid.

However, balloon payments aren't a threat if you plan to sell your house before the loan matures. You could pay the loan off with the proceeds from the sale.

Fee-Fi-Fo-Fum...but Mostly Scads of Fees

Fees range all over the lot, regardless of whether you're getting a straight home equity loan (a lump sum all at once) or a home equity line of credit so you can write checks for what you need.

But it all boils down to this: The bank or finance company charges you what it wants to charge you, and the numbers range all over the lot. We've heard of closing costs, alone, running from $150 to $800. Some lenders will waive points (a point is one-hundredth of the total loan amount, or $10 for every $1,000 you borrow). Others will charge between one and three points.

On the straight home equity loan, fees could total a few thousand dollars for credit checks, appraisal fees, legal fees, title insurance, and closing costs when the loan is finalized. Always ask the bank these three questions before you take out the loan:

1. What are my up-front fees and charges?
2. What is my total financing cost (the interest amount on the loan)?
3. What are my closing costs including points? (A point is one-hundredth of the loan amount.)

Get those amounts in dollars and cents, not percent.

We know a couple who thought they were breezing through a home equity loan, only to discover that their total fees (not even including the interest) came to $6,000!

On home equity lines of credit, the fees can be a lot less. Because banks are fighting their competition with brass knuckles for new home equity customers, many will waive their fees and closing costs. You'll see lots of "no-fee" deals in ads. Others will waive their annual fee in the first year and start charging you in the second year. A few will even offer you a cash bonus of $100 or $200 (added to your credit line) to get your account.

A fixed-rate home equity line is rare, but if you find one, there could be extra fees and formulas, such as a $75 "finance charge." Or the fee could vary depending on the amount of your credit line and/or the bank's rate formula that's tied to its prime rate. For example, you might get a loan with no fee if your line is more than $20,000—or if you borrow less than $20,000, but agree to a rate of the prime plus two percent. Or you might pay a $200 fee if you choose to pay the prime rate plus 1.5 percent. It's not much different then the mortgage game: If you get a low rate and cheap fees, they'll take it out of your hide by charging higher points.

Beware of Home Equity Scam Operators!

Be leery if someone comes knocking at your door and says his company will build you a new room, or put new siding on your house, and all you have to do is take out a home equity loan to pay for it. The Federal Trade Commission has caught a lot of those guys preying on homeowners—particularly the elderly, minorities, and those with low incomes or poor credit.

You could wind up owing tens of thousands of dollars more than what you thought you signed up for, and lose your home. The scam operator may encourage you to "pad" your income on the application to get the loan approved, or may leave blank spaces on the application, which he falsely fills in later. Or, he may offer to help you find financing, but request that you first deed your property to him, claiming that it's a temporary step to prevent foreclosure. Once the lender has the deed to your property, he may borrow against it or even sell it. You could wind up in the street!

The FTC has case after case where people lost their homes—or went bankrupt after paying through the nose—to scam lenders who stripped them of their assets. One woman was conned into taking out four successive loans, each one bigger than the other, until she couldn't make her payments and the lender foreclosed on her house. For an important consumer fact sheet on how to avoid these home equity schemes, write to: FTC, Bureau of Consumer Protection, 6th & Pennsylvania Avenue N.W., Washington, D.C. 20580. Or find the FTC on the Internet at www.ftc.gov.

The Least You Need to Know

➤ Don't borrow what you don't need and can't pay back.

➤ Always read the fine print in the ads and in your contract. If anything is not absolutely clear, ask for a straight answer in plain English.

➤ When you shop, don't be dazzled by gimmick rates and freebies. Consider the total cost of the loan based on how much you borrow, plus the up front fees and closing costs.

➤ Don't get tricked by low-ball rates. Almost every bank uses that tactic in its advertising.

➤ With a credit line, the bank considers how much money you could wind up owing if you use all the available credit.

➤ If you only need a small amount of cash for two or three years, home equity probably isn't the answer. You'll be better off with a regular short-term fixed-rate loan.

➤ Get your credit record in order before you apply. Despite the fact that the bank will hold a piece of your house until you repay the loan, it's still going to be nosy about your income, other debts, job, credit payment, record, and so on.

➤ Most important, remember that your house is on the line.

➤ Beware of scam operators who falsify contracts and are out to steal your house from you.

Chapter 21

Getting Out from Under Debt

In This Chapter

➤ You *can* control the debt monster, believe it or not!

➤ Tricks on how to pay your bills to avoid problems

➤ The biggest mistakes to avoid in straightening out your financial life

➤ How your "debt-to-income ratio" lets creditors size you up

➤ What to do in a *real* debt crisis—where to go for help!

➤ How to beat ugly, bothersome collection agencies

Consumer debt. It's a subject that's becoming more terrifying every day. More than $1.5 trillion is in revolving loan accounts—of which 450 billion is in credit cards alone, as of 1998. Card volume has been growing by nearly 17percent a year. Americans are on a borrowing spree, the likes of which the country has never seen before. Yet in 1997, there were 1.35 million personal bankruptcies, a nearly 25 percent increase over the year before, with the main culprit being credit cards, according to experts. But while credit card industry lobbies are making it tougher for Joe Doaks to file bankruptcy, and although it swears it's clamping down on easy credit, the industry stuffs 3 billion tempting credit card offers a year into mailboxes. Meanwhile, the debt-ridden middle class is being squeezed by low savings rates, high credit card rates and steadily-mounting fees—while big-balance bank customers escape paying most of those charges. The rich are getting richer, while the poor are getting poorer.

As the debt monster gets bigger and bigger, most people—no matter how close they are to financial disaster—haven't come up with a plan to rescue themselves. Nine out of 10 haven't asked to see their personal credit report from a credit bureau, few have sat down and figured out their debt-to-income ratio, which banks use to determine whether they're creditworthy or a deadbeat. In this chapter you'll learn how to escape the foul clutches of the debt monster—or avoid being caught by it in the first place.

The Whole Thing Could Go *B-O-O-M!*

Consumer debt is a ticking time bomb. If the economy ever turns upside down, millions of folks and their families will quickly go over the edge—especially those living from paycheck to paycheck. This chapter tells you the danger signals and suggests ways you can get the debt monkey off your back, starting at the very beginning. It explains how to take a cold, hard look at your financial situation, take the necessary steps to solve your problems and avoid bankruptcy. Plus—you'll find out why you should avoid "Fix-your-credit" scam operators who are only after your wallet, or what's left of it.

What's been behind the staggering rise in America's consumer debt? You get different answers, depending on whom you talk to. Probably the most accurate analysis comes from economists, who say it's a combination of high consumer confidence in the roaring bull market between 1994 and 1997, and this country's atrociously low savings rate, one of the lowest in the world. The credit industry offers a different excuse. They say it's because more people have switched to the convenience of plastic credit cards for their purchases. But if you ask a bankruptcy attorney why he's been gaining more clients, he'll point to credit cards as the number one reason.

There's an Answer—If You Try

A retired man we know was really in the pits a couple of years ago. His wife of only three years had left him after running up thousands of dollars in credit card debt. Altogether he owed about $8,500, had only his Social Security checks and a part-time job in a grocery store to show as income, and was convinced he had no choice but to file bankruptcy. He mentioned that decision to a lawyer who immediately told him, "I'll get the papers together."

A friend told the man there was an alternative: Go chat with the local Consumer Credit Counseling Services office, and maybe their counselors could work out a payment program with creditors. Reluctantly, the guy went, and listed his debts and income on a sheet of paper. The CCCS counselor assured him she could arrange a plan to avoid a bankruptcy, but the man didn't believe her. He went ahead and filed a Chapter 7 bankruptcy anyway. It wiped out his debts—but his credit report will show the bankruptcy for 10 years, virtually assuring that he won't be able to get any credit, anywhere, during that time.

That's an extreme case of a debt situation. And a foolish one. The man's total debts were less than those of clients that CCCS normally sees; he could have easily gotten out from under his debt with the agency's help. Better still, had he done a little early homework, he could have controlled his financial situation a lot better, even if his wife had already bought her plane tickets to Las Vegas.

There Are No Easy Answers

Let's get one thing straight right off the bat. There's no easy answer to getting your money life in order if you constantly spend more than you make and keep running into malls waving your credit cards as you yell "Charge!" You shouldn't idiotically pay outrageously high interest rates that only make the banks richer. But we assume that, because you're reading this chapter, you're serious about whipping the debt monster and are willing to do what it takes to get there. With the right steps and some will power, you have a good chance!

Check Your Credit Competency

Every person's situation is different, but somehow, through a combination of increasing your income and shaving your expenses, you should get to a point where you'll have enough money every month to pay your bills. First, however, you need to be able to detect the early warning signs of financial trouble. Ask yourself these questions:

➤ Are you always late with your payments?

➤ If you lost your job, would you be in immediate financial difficulty?

➤ Have you withdrawn money from your retirement account to pay current expenses?

➤ Are you getting calls from creditors about overdue bills?

➤ Do you regularly use credit card advances to pay off other creditors?

➤ Do you put off medical or dental visits because you can't afford them right now?

We're going to look at five key areas, one by one, to help you take the first steps toward strengthening your financial position. They are:

1. Figuring out where you stand financially, and keeping track of what you do.
2. Learning how creditors look at you. These are the guys who count in your financial life and they can mess it up in a heartbeat.
3. Deciding which creditors to pay first, including how to pay them and when.
4. Learning how to cut your cost of debt.
5. Learning how to handle a debt crisis, including collection agencies.

Don't Be Afraid to Know Exactly Where You Stand

Let's face it. No one wants to put their spending habits under a spotlight and be told they have to change them. Well, that's not quite what we have in mind, and you'll never read the words, "You've gotta go on a budget!" here. But to help get you out of any debt mess you're in, we first have to convince you that a few basic steps are a must, no matter who you are.

Even if you think you already have a good idea of where your money goes, please do the following exercise anyway—it'll be illuminating, at the very least.

Get yourself a big notepad and write down, each day for 30 days, what you spend. Arrange the pad in columns labeled "Food," "Entertainment," "Travel," and so on. Jot down every penny, day by day, including when you cash a check or take emergency money out of an ATM. When you pay a bill, such as making a mortgage or car payment, write that down, too, under the appropriate heading. Of course, you can't carry a big notepad around with you all day, so just tuck a tiny, check-size piece of paper in your pocket, wallet or purse and transfer the amounts to your notepad every night. It'll only take a moment.

After the 30 days, multiply all your expense numbers by 12 to come up with estimated *annual* expense. Are there other expenses that don't occur every month, such as medical costs? If so, estimate the annual cost and be sure to add it to your totals. Can you think of anything you've left out? In your opinion—making your best guess—how might these figures compare with, say, what you probably spent last year and the year before?

You had better prepare yourself. You're going to be shocked at how high some of those dollar amounts are. The reason is, almost no one thinks in *yearly* cost terms when they have a few nice dinners at the local bistro, or withdraw a fast 40 bucks from an ATM. Psychologically, it's the same thing we pointed about realizing your checking-account fees in Chapter 10. You're mainly aware of the *one-time* cost.

Next, your income. Beside your annual expense total, write down your estimated net income after taxes for this year. Be sure to include money not just from a regular job, but also other, residual income, such as from moonlighting.

How do those two totals—income and expense—compare? We thought so. Time to get to work.

Bye, Bye, Unnecessary Expense

Now, if you *had* to identify which expense items, in your personal judgment, were the most frivolous—which ones, if reduced or eliminated, wouldn't hurt you very much—what might they be? By how much might you be able to cut them *per year*? How would that translate *per month*? What would you have to cut or pull back on to meet that figure on a day-by-day basis?

Next, look at your expense list again. Which bills must *always* be paid? What's the total they come to? Put a check mark beside the name of each of those creditors. Got that? How much money is left over from your income after deducting those bills? Now, what other kinds of expense do you regard as essential or

Asset Advisory

If you feel you need some emotional and psychological support to help you through this period, contact Debtors Anonymous, P.O. Box 400, Grand Central Station, N.Y. 10163, and ask for the phone number of the chapter nearest you. They're people like yourself, who meet on a regular basis and help each other.

nearly-essential, such as haircuts or the health club? How do you think the remaining funds should be divided up among those expenses?

Pay Highest-Rate Credit Cards First

Hopefully, you have only one or two credit cards at the most. Anything more than that is inviting real debt disaster. When you pay your monthly bills, care for the highest-rate cards first, because that will save you the most money. For example, the annual-interest-cost difference between a 12 percent card and an 18 percent card, on a $3,000 balance, is $180!

So Long, Small Bills

With the cutback in the frivolous expense we described two paragraphs ago, how much of that money could you divert on a month-by-month basis to pay off some of the smallest, recurring bills, such as the water or gas? Why should you pay the smallest bills first? Because a creditor is a creditor. If you have 10 creditors and can get rid of three of them extra-fast, those are three fewer guys who will yap if they don't get paid on time. In effect, you erase three potential headaches a month.

Not enough money to handle those items? Don't panic; millions of people are in the same boat. So where else can you cut? You have two choices. The first is to borrow money. But your credit record may not be strong enough to get a loan, and you don't want to do business with a high-rate finance company. So, consider your second choice. Instead of carrying the yoke of debt forever, you can make some additional sacrifices for the next year or two, depending on how deeply in debt you are.

Actually, there's a third thing you can do—get a payment extension from the creditor, something we describe in this chapter. Remember that getting out of debt is going to involve a *series* of steps, not just one, and eventually they'll all interrelate to ease your load. The more you can exercise some real will power on the series of points, the faster you'll be out of a bad situation!

Your Creditors Are Watching You

The companies you owe money to aren't going to give you any gifts, such as wiping out your debt. Banks won't lend you a dime if you have a late-payment record and your credit file is also shot full of other holes. And Uncle Louie is probably still wondering when you're going to pay back the two grand he loaned you 18 months ago.

The more deeply you fall into debt, the tighter the noose, it seems. You do have some options, however. But before you do anything, obtain a copy of your personal credit report from one of the three major credit bureaus. This is critical. If anything in the report is erroneous or in dispute, correct it. *See Chapter 16 for phone numbers of the bureaus, and instructions.* After that, here are your choices:

Take out a straight loan from a bank or credit union: This can be a secured loan, where you put up assets as collateral against the loan, which will have an interest rate of about 11 percent to 13 percent. Or, you can try for an unsecured loan (without collateral) at about 15 percent. Those rates are relatively expensive. Join a credit union if you're not already a member. They offer the cheapest loan rates of all.

Go for a home equity loan or home equity line of credit: It's one of the best ways to trade high-rate debt, such as 18 percent credit cards, for low-rate debt at perhaps 9 percent. You consolidate all your expensive loans and pay them off at the cheaper rate. Plus, in most cases the interest is tax-deductible, which it isn't on auto loans or credit cards.

Assuming you have equity in your home, most banks will lend you 75 percent to 80 percent of that figure. If your equity is $50,000, you can borrow from $37,500 to $40,000, but there'll be fees and closing costs to pay. Some outfits will lend up to 125 percent of the equity—which is dangerous because you'd owe more than the house is worth, and you won't be able to write off interest on anything above 100 percent of equity.

Home equity is great for cutting costs through debt consolidation, or for paying for big-ticket items such as college tuition or medical bills. The negative side of home equity is that you'll be trading unsecured debt for secured debt, which means if you can't pay the money back the bank could take your home. Plus, even though you've paid off your credit cards, you'll still have the home equity debt to contend with. Although it reduces your monthly payment, it will cost you money in the long run because the interest will be stretched over five years or more.

Now for the really bad news: Research shows that just a few years after many people pay off their debts with a home equity loan, they're once again head-over-heels in debt with credit cards! There's a message in that for you!

Don't Stop at Repaying—Rebuild Your Good Credit

If you've acquired a bad credit rating after running up too much debt, you'll want to repair it quickly. There are a number of ways you can rebuild your credit, but all of them require discipline on your part. Here are some of the best ways to regain good credit standing.

A Secured Credit Card Can Help Rebuild Your Credit

This is discussed in depth in Chapter 16. A good way to recapture a good credit position is to open a secured credit card account if you've been denied a standard card. Credit cards in general are an invitation to debt-disease, in our opinion, but to overcome your problems you may one day need money help from a bank. And that may require establishing some good marks on your credit report by proving you can pay credit card bills on time.

To get a secured card, you deposit money at a bank, which gives you a credit line in the amount of the deposit, or slightly more. The interest rate will be high, and the fees fairly stiff, but you'll have a chance to prove that you make monthly payments on time. For a free list of secured cards nationwide, go to the Internet at www.bankrate.com.

And use any extra cash to pay off high-rate bills. Let's say you have $2,000 stashed away in a bank Money Market Account that's earning a miserable 2.5 percent interest, which comes to only $50 a year. But you also maintain a balance of $2,000 on an 18 percent credit card, which costs $360 a year. Instead of financing the card balance, you should pay the card off by tapping into the bank account. The move would save you $310. When you view all your possible strategies in this light, you begin to pare down your debt problem.

Here's how higher monthly payments can slash your interest, assuming you have a $1,000 debt at an interest rate of 18.11 percent:

Table 21.1   Pay more, save lots more

Monthly payment	Total interest	Term to pay off bill
$20 (minimum)	$893.12	8 years
$30	$406.40	4 years
$50	$198.08	2 years

Source: CardWeb, Gettysburg, Pennsylvania. (www.cardweb.com.)

Negotiate More Time to Pay Your Bills

Many creditors today are apt to be lenient in extending your payment period, rather than face the possibility of you going bankrupt and never paying them anything you owe. They may agree to string out your overdue amounts under a payment plan, but insist you pay all new bills on time. Besides arranging a payment program, they often will settle the whole bill for only a percentage of what you owe. Insiders tell us that some credit card companies will settle for 50 percent of the amount. If you remember only one thing from this book, it should be this: *Never hide from creditors if you can't pay your bills. Contact them and explain the situation. If you don't, then the collection agency will take over—and those cold-blooded guys never negotiate with anybody!*

Stay Away from Finance Companies and Debt Consolidation Promoters

The growing debt problem in America has created a new breed of entrepreneur who offers to repair your credit history, get you a new credit card and help you consolidate debt to reduce your monthly payment. The first thing you should do is check the firm out with the local Better Business Bureau. Too many consumers have been victimized by these outfits, some of which are out-and-out scams.

The truth is, no one can remove accurate and timely negative information from a credit report. Here's how to spot the shady credit-fix operators, says the National Foundation for Consumer Credit. They:

➤ Want you to pay for credit repair services before any services are provided.

➤ Don't tell you your legal rights and what you can do yourself for free.

➤ Recommend that you do not contact a credit bureau directly.

➤ Advise you to dispute all information in your credit report or take an action that seems illegal to you, like creating a new identity. If you follow illegal advice and commit fraud, you can be subject to prosecution.

Two reasons to stay away from finance companies: One, their interest rates can be sky-high because they're pretty sure you weren't able to borrow from a bank because of your credit history; and, two, when a finance company name appears on your credit report it's considered as a negative mark on your record.

Your Debt-to-Income Ratio Is How They Size You Up

When banks, in particular, review your loan application, they look at your debt-to-income ratio more than anything else. That, plus your personal credit report, is going to influence whether they say "aye" or "nay" to your request.

Most folks know diddly about the ratio. Here's how they figure it:

They take the total amount of all your monthly bills, except your mortgage payment or rent, and utilities. Then they divide your monthly gross income (before taxes) by your monthly bills total and come up with a percentage figure. For instance, a $2,500 monthly gross income versus $750 in bills is a 30 percent debt-to-income ratio (2,500 divided by 750). Normally, most lenders will want a ratio of 28 percent to 35 percent, but some may go higher. Mortgage lenders use what they call a "28/36" desirable combination—a 28 percent ratio not counting the mortgage, and 36 percent with it. When any loan company sees a too-high debt-to-income ratio, it's a sure sign the consumer is already overextended and may not be able to pay back any new loan.

Bottom line: The lower your debt-to-income ratio, the more creditors will love you. The higher the ratio, the more they want to disappear out the door. This is another good reason to make sacrifices on your expense items to strengthen your credit position.

Attention college students: Many credit card issuers set traps to get you to open a credit card account, which can be your first step toward painful debt. Recruiters will offer you everything from free T-shirts to Frisbees if you apply for a card. But surveys show that students who get cards through tables set up at campuses have an average unpaid balance of $1,039 versus $854 who did not. One national credit card is all you need. Pay the bills on time and build up your credit record. If you must carry a balance, pay as much as you can afford every month. You don't want to start your job career with a giant debt monkey on your back!

What to Do If It's Panic City!

Okay, so you're thinking to yourself, "Listen, Buster, everything you're saying *sounds* good, but you don't know how bad things have gotten around my house. My car has just been repossessed, I'm two payments behind on my mortgage, the phone company is threatening to shut me off, overdue bills are covering my whole kitchen table, and two guys with deep, gruff voices from collection agencies are parked across the street. How do I handle *that?*"

The first thing you do is not to ignore the problem, but at the same time you positively must not panic—because either of those things is as bad as the other. Instead, immediately go back to that cost-cutting exercise we described earlier. And, as we advised, immediately get a copy of your credit report so you'll know exactly what kind of situation you're dealing with.

Come Clean with Your Creditors

Lay out your note pad with all your monthly-bill-paying notes on it, and figure out how much income you have coming in over the next several months. Decide which bills you can pay the minimum amounts on, and when you can do this. Two weeks? A month? Two months? Some outfits will be happy to get "something now, and the rest later." At this stage of the game, you must stretch out your payments as much as possible, until your circumstances change. You don't want to just pay off one creditor in full and give zero to the other guys.

Call each creditor and explain your situation. Level with them. Buy more time by negotiating the absolutely lowest minimum payment they'll accept right now. From these calls, make a list of who gets paid first, second, etc., and how much. Whatever you do, do not be embarrassed or afraid to phone every creditor and arrange a payment program. Get the name and phone number of the person you spoke to. Follow up with a certified letter confirming your new payment arrangement, and keep a copy. If you don't do this with each creditor, it's like sending out engraved invitations to collection agencies inviting them to come pound on your door. Calling the creditors is easier and less frantic.

Slash Your Spending

Good. You've just bought yourself some time. But if you don't immediately begin to slash your spending, cut up your credit cards, and keep your word on the payments you promised. You'd better prepare to face the music: You may have to file bankruptcy, the most negative thing of all, that stays on your credit record for 10 years.

Call for Help

There's one more last effort we urgently advise: Phone Consumer Credit Counseling Services, a non-profit organization with a network of hundreds of offices nationwide, at (800) 338-CCCS and get the location of the office nearest you. CCCS helps nearly 1 million people a year, many with problems as big as the one we just described. It can arrange payment programs with creditors, often getting them to stop charging interest on accounts, and in some cases, reducing a debt. In most cases, CCCS is able to stop any legal action and develop a solution that will satisfy everyone. If you maintain your payment arrangements with CCCS, the majority of phone calls will stop.

Some CCCS offices work for free, others charge an average of $9 a month depending on where you go. A counselor will review your whole debt situation with you on a confidential basis, and help you set up a Debt Management Program based on what you can afford. There's no embarrassment, none whatsoever. Granted, CCCS is partially funded by the credit industry, including banks and other credit card issuers and finance companies, but so what? Don't let that worry you. CCCS has more clout with creditors than you do, and can negotiate a better deal than you can on your own.

Meanwhile, for tips on handling credit problems, click onto the Internet for the National Foundation for Consumer Credit, which is CCCS's parent organization, at www.nfcc.org. NFCC is a national network of 1,450 non-profit community organizations that provide consumer credit education, budget and debt counseling, and debt repayment programs for families and individuals. Another helpful, respected site is Debt Counselors of America (DCA) at www.dca.org, or call (800) 680-3328.

The Money Line

In 1997, a record 1.8 million Americans picked up the phone and called NFCC and its CCCS network offices for help. The number one reason they had debt problems, consumers said, was overspending, followed by job loss, medical problems, divorce or separation. "Those factors," said NFCC, "are often the last straw for consumers carrying high debt loads and credit card balances."

Other tips to rebuild credit: If you don't have a checking account, open one (preferably a free or low-fee account that doesn't pay interest), and don't bounce any checks. Apply for credit at a local department store or credit union, but make sparing use of the department store card because the high interest rate will be atrocious.

When the Bill Collector Comes Calling

No one wants collection agencies on their neck, and many people could have easily avoided those bloodsuckers if they had used their noodle earlier. But if and when those guys do descend on you, you need to know your rights so you don't get pushed around. As it is, lots of folks are frightened to death by collectors—avoiding their phone calls, not opening their mail, and losing sleep—but there's absolutely no reason to be.

Your Rights in Collection

Granted, having a collector on your tail is worse than being dunned by the original creditor, because collectors are trickier and nastier. Your strategy should be to never allow your bills to get to the debt collection level in the first place. And believe it or not, the original creditor has more leeway to be tough because the collection agencies are restricted from doing certain things under a federal law known as the Fair Debt Collection Practices Act.

Some of the things they can't do are:

➤ Call you before 8 a.m. or after 9 p.m., or phone you at work if you tell them your employer disapproves.

➤ Fail to identify themselves truthfully, or pose as somebody else with another organization, like "Sergeant Renfrew of the Amalgamated Private Police League."

➤ Tell other people about your debt, not even your brother or Aunt Agatha.

➤ Harass you by threatening to do something violent through some criminal act to you or your family, use abusive language, or bug you with constant phone calls. One of their favorite tricks is mailing you an official-looking letter that walks, talks and quacks like it came from an attorney, but really didn't. It's meant to scare you, natch!

Get the collector's name and mailing address the next time they call. You can send a certified letter to the collection agency, telling it to leave you alone, and that you're not paying the debt. Once they receive the letter, they must either stop trying to contact you, or notify you they're taking legal action. You can sue them if they do anything else.

Yet, a collection agency can still make your life miserable. Chances are they were hired by the creditor after you were 60 or more days late with your payments. The collection agency will be paid something like 25 percent of whatever it collects from you. But if it fails to get any money from you after many months have passed, the bill might be assigned to yet another—maybe tougher—outfit that will get a higher commission, such as 50 percent, if it succeeds. Not all collection agencies are big organizations, by the way, no matter how official they sound on the phone. Some may be smaller than your garage.

Negotiation Pays Off

Are you stuck with negotiating with a collection agency after it starts pursuing you? In all likelihood, yes. We've heard of some debtors getting back in the good graces of the creditor after the collection hounds got on the case, but odds are, once the collection agency has taken over, you must deal only with them. To repeat: You don't want your situation to get that far!

If you're caught in the collection web, make sure you make complete, accurate notes of every phone conversation you have with them. If you're freaking out because of their nasty, intimidating methods, write them a certified letter telling them so, and propose a solution which you know you can live up to. And keep a copy of the letter.

Oh, one more thing: Drag your heels. Instead of ever agreeing to any settlement deal proposed by the collection agency, tell them their offer sounds too high, that you need to think about it. (Those guys are taking notes, too.) Wheeling-and-dealing, cat-and-mouse style, is the name of the game in the collection business. They're *always* open to a compromise settlement, no matter what kind of excuses and malarkey they've been handing you in all those phone calls. If they get at least *some* money instead of *no* money, they'll probably go away satisfied.

Whatever you do, never agree to any repayment schedule that you don't feel you can handle, because it will only put you back in the soup. And, whatever you do agree to do, put it in writing with all the "I"s dotted and the "T"s crossed. Better yet, have an attorney write the letter.

Get the Watchdogs on the Case

If, after all that, you still believe the collection agency is doing something mean, shady or ugly, and is possibly breaking the law, contact your state's attorney general's office as well as the following organizations:

➤ **Federal Trade Commission**. It handles complaints about any kind of deceptive sales, marketing or credit practice, ranging from collection agencies and telephone solicitations, to finance companies and credit cards. You can find the nearest FTC office by looking in the phone book under "U.S. Government, Federal Trade Commission," or write to Correspondence Branch, Federal Trade Commission, Washington, D.C. 20580.

➤ **Comptroller of the Currency**. This agency handles complaints against nationally chartered banks, and that probably includes the biggest banks in your neighborhood. The Comptroller is also listed in the phone book under "U.S. Government." Or, write to OCC, 490 L'Enfant Plaza SW, Washington, D.C. 20219. Phone: (202) 622-2000.

➤ **American Collector's Association.** This trade organization oversees its debt collection members, and wants them to engage in only ethical practices and procedures. Write to ACA, P.O. Box 35106, Minneapolis, Minn. 55435. Phone: (612) 926-6547.

The Least You Need to Know

➤ Relax. All is not lost, regardless of how difficult your debt problem is.

➤ Get ready to exercise a little discipline to get your expenses and income in balance. It's not hard.

➤ Get rid of high-interest-rate bills first. Also pay down small bills fast to get more debt monkeys off your back every month.

➤ You can rebuild your credit with a secured credit card.

➤ Banks use a special formula to determine how far you are in debt.

➤ You can handle a bad debt-crisis situation if you know how.

➤ Consumer Credit Counseling Services can work out a payment deal with your creditors for free or a low fee. But you shouldn't do business with "credit-fix" outfits that may scam you.

➤ You can stop collection agencies from annoying you, if you know how.

Part 5

The Biggest Secrets to Retiring with Enough Money

The savings rate of American consumers has shriveled to almost nothing, putting it at the lowest level since the Great Depression.

So says the Commerce Department in July, 1998. What have you got to say about it? How much money are you saving for your future?

The amount of money you have earmarked for your retirement probably will be insufficient in relation to your needs. But there's something you can do about it...today.

Company plans, such as 401(k)s, are becoming the most dominant retirement savings vehicle. Your employer and even Uncle Sam offers incentives for you to sock away your dough for your future.

Let's hop on the retirement plan bandwagon and create a financially sound future for you and your heirs.

Chapter 22

You're Never Too Young to Think About Retiring

In This Chapter

➤ Why it pays off to start socking away today

➤ How to button down a plan that really works

➤ Learning the nuts and bolts to retirement accounts

➤ Getting the inside scoop if you're already retired

How many of you had a piggy bank during your childhood? That big, plump, porcelain pig that held all your loose change was the only method of saving you knew about. You knew you were supposed to save for a rainy day, but not many people understood *why* they were supposed to do it.

That rainy day is closer than you think. So why save for it now? The earlier you start saving for retirement, the less you'll need to save to have enough money to live well. Many people live an average 15 to 20 years in retirement, yet only save enough money for about half of that.

If you're counting on Social Security, forget it. Given the funding problems in the Social Security system, benefits are projected to provide only 21 percent of your current income. If you earn $26,000 a year, expect to receive an average estimated monthly benefit check of $455.

You may think you're young enough or ambitious enough to avoid thoughts of retirement. Perhaps you're counting on Uncle Milty to leave you a fortune in his will. But that's not always the case. Planning for your future does *not* mean you're expecting something terrible to happen. Buying a life insurance policy doesn't mean you're going to die right away, does it? This chapter explains what you can do for retirement starting today, some common mistakes you should avoid, and the different types of investment products that will get you from here to there.

Why Can't We Think About Tomorrow?

The statistics on how we relate to saving money are not encouraging. A Merrill Lynch study concludes that if Americans continue to save at the rate they do now, they may end up with only 36 percent of the money they'll need to maintain their current standard of living. Why have we developed such a nonchalant attitude toward the future, anyway?

Saving money for the future is B-O-R-I-N-G, many folks tell us. Put an extra $100 bucks in a savings account to earn a few pennies? Big deal. Credit cards have cured this boredom by enticing consumers to charge now and pay later. This bad habit hurts you in the long run because you'll be so busy climbing out of debt that you won't have any money to sock away for the future, let alone even think about it. Get rid of the credit cards. Make the transition from "see-it-buy-it" to "save-it-for-tomorrow." No matter what you may think, a $25,000 line of credit does not make you a millionare.

Many consumers think they can count on a company pension. After all, their parents had one. But you can't always count on a pension. Alarmingly, only 45 percent of all men receive a pension. Women? Just 23 percent—and those who do, only get about two-thirds as much as men. Companies are doing away with traditional pension plans, either by reducing the amount of benefit payments or eliminating the plans alto-gether. Instead, many companies offer other types of retirement savings programs (you'll learn about a few in this chapter) that shift the burden of saving onto you, the employee. There are, however, alternative or additional means of saving for retirement that work just as well—and sometimes even better!

Finally, people think that retirement is far, far away. A 25-year-old person, working hard to make ends meet, never ponders what life will be like at 65. But tomorrow always comes, you know. Know that if you delay any longer, you're going to have to come up with more money down the road for the same end result. Keep reading to learn how you can start saving today.

The Power of Saving

Read these motivating facts:

➤ A 25-year-old woman who saves $100 a month until she retires will have six times more money when she retires than if she were to begin saving $100 a month at age 45.

➤ A 50-year-old woman who contributes $500 a month to a retirement plan will never catch up with the 30-year-old woman who has been socking away $100 a month.

➤ If you save $2,000 a year at 6 percent for 30 years in a regular savings account, you'll have close to $120,900 after paying taxes. However, if you shelter your $2,000 each year in your IRA at six percent, your savings increases to almost $168,000 because of the tax-deferred feature.

Let's get started.

Excuses, Excuses, Excuses

Each person's situation is unique. Perhaps you don't have access to a company-sponsored program. Or you're saving your wad of dough for your children's college education. No matter what the excuse (because that's what they really are), you can still save for retirement.

Don't think that you don't have enough money to save. If you don't take advantage of saving your money from taxes, then you *really* don't have money to save! Sure, you may be saving for a child's college education or saving your money to buy a home, but that money is typically in taxable accounts. So, you're paying "extra" taxes by keeping your money in those accounts. Of course, you must continue to save for those financial goals, but *your financial goal of retirement is important, too*. Scholarships, Pell grants, and student loans are available for your children, but Social Security won't provide for you the way a scholarship can provide for your child. You can save for retirement if you reduce some of your current living expenses.

Just because you contribute to a retirement plan doesn't mean that you'll never have access to your money until you're older, either. Although the IRS will hit you with a penalty if you withdraw your money before age 59 $^1/_2$, you can access your money, depending on the circumstances. For example, if you contribute to a 401(k), some companies will allow you to borrow against your cash balance—but that's up to the company. There are also hardship withdrawals you can take—not for a whirlwind vacation, but for when you're in a financial pinch (as a result of a medical emergency, for example).

Finally, don't count on your cash value life insurance policy to take advantage of tax-deferred growth. True, cash value life insurance policies provide tax-deferred growth, but there's no tax deduction. And you don't "benefit"—your heirs do. You can borrow against your life insurance policy, but if you die with the loan outstanding, your intended heirs will receive less than you planned.

Turn These Must-Do's into Can-Do's!

Part of your everyday money management should include planning for retirement. You don't need to go overboard and deny yourself day-to-day necessities (like food) because you fear you'll wind up impoverished if you eat today. That's not the point. But if you have the benefit of time when it comes to evaluating your retirement plan, take advantage of it.

The earlier you begin to plan for your golden years, the less money you'll have to save to live well in the future. Why is this? Because the sooner you begin, the more your money has time to compound.

If you have more than a 10-year time frame, invest your retirement money for the long term. Younger people can take advantage of the potential growth that some investments offer, especially equities. Obviously, you don't want to gamble your retirement savings when you get close to retirement, but if you have time on your side, take advantage of more aggressive investments that offer higher degrees of potential growth.

Don't be *too* conservative in your retirement savings. This tip is aimed especially at the younger generation saving for retirement. Too often, younger people make the mistake of being conservative in their retirement-savings strategies. The biggest mistake is when they invest their 401(k) money in a Money Market fund as their long-term retirement choice. Bad move, especially when the Money Market rates usually do not keep up with inflation. Even if you are close to retirement, don't forget that you will probably live for a long time as a retiree, so your funds will still need to grow.

Take advantage of *every* opportunity to shelter your retirement money from current income taxes. These opportunities, which will be discussed in detail later on in this chapter, are different types of investment products that offer a tax-deferred feature. You can shelter your money from current income taxes through an individual retirement account, a company-sponsored retirement plan, or an annuity.

Even if you have a retirement program at work, open and contribute to an IRA to take advantage of tax-deferred growth. Depending on your income level, if you are covered by a company-sponsored plan, you may not receive a tax deduction on your IRA contributions. Are you *not* going to open an IRA because you don't receive a tax deduction? You still get the tax-deferred growth, just not the perk from Uncle Sam.

Retirement Accounts Explained in Simple English

The most common type of retirement account is an *Individual Retirement Account*. An IRA is available for you to make an annual contribution of $2,000 or 100 percent of earned income that year, whichever is less, up until the year you reach age 70 $1/2$. In other words, your contributions must come from a salary, wages, or self-employment income. Even alimony counts.

What if you're a non-working spouse? If you are part of a couple with one spouse working and the other not working, the working spouse may contribute an extra $250 (for a total of $2,250). The contributions must go into separate accounts, however—one bearing the name of the working spouse, and one bearing the name of the non-working spouse. The account held by the non-working spouse is called a *spousal IRA*. Spouses who work part-time and have no company benefits can open up their own IRAs. The same rules apply.

Ironically, an IRA causes a lot of confusion, as the most common question people ask is, "Should I invest my money in a mutual fund *or* in an IRA?" The truth is that you should invest your money in a mutual fund *inside* an IRA. An IRA is an account that shelters your contributions from current income taxes. The contribution you make should be made by your tax-filing due date.

So Who Is This Guy Roth, Anyway?

Similar to the traditional Individual Retirement Account, the Roth IRA shares the upside in the strategy of tax-deferred growth, but not the tax deductions, depending on your taxable situation.

Hands down, the Roth IRA is one of the most difficult types of retirement accounts to understand, not because of the way it's designed, but because there is so much contradictory information that exists on this type of account. It's a wonder anyone can get a straight answer.

So, rest assured. Here is a bullet-point basic that aims to please.

➤ Most of the rules that apply to traditional IRAs, such as the types of investments you can have within the account (no commodities, for one), also apply to Roth IRAs.

➤ You can contribute to a Roth IRA even if you are over age 70 ^{1}/$_2$ and even if you participate in a 401(k) plan or other employer plan. But you or your spouse must have taxable compensation income, and your modified AGI (adjusted gross income) must not exceed certain limits.

➤ You're not eligible to make annual contributions to a Roth IRA unless you have taxable earned income (from wages, for example); however, one caveat is that alimony income is included as taxable earned income.

➤ First-time homebuyers, who hold their Roth IRAs for at least five years, can withdraw a limited amount of earnings tax-free even before the age of 59 ^{1}/$_2$.

For more information on Roth IRAs, check with your tax adviser or financial professional.

They're for Your Benefit

The range of retirement plan alternatives is broad, but most plans fall into one of two major categories:

Defined contribution plans provide an individual account for each participant (that's you), and for benefits based solely upon the amount contributed to the participant's account. These include—but are not limited to—money-purchase plans, profit-sharing plans, and 401(k) plans.

Defined benefit plans are retirement plans other than an individual account plan (like a defined contribution plan). Retirement benefits must be definitely set. For example, a plan that entitles you to a monthly pension for life equal to 25 percent of monthly compensation is a defined benefit plan.

Another Way to Save for Retirement

Socking away $2,000 a year into a retirement program is great. But for those of you who have more money to invest, and want to take advantage of tax-deferred growth, you may want to think about an annuity.

What exactly is an annuity? You already know what CDs and no-load mutual funds are, right? Well, an annuity is an insurance company product with fixed-rate CDs and no-load mutual funds in it.

It's like creating an IRA that you can contribute an unlimited amount of money to. Plus, you are not obligated to take out the money by age 70 $1/2$, as you are required to do with an IRA. However, unlike an IRA, you cannot deduct your contribution on your income tax returns, but you can still take advantage of their tax-deferred feature. The money you invest in an annuity is made with *after-tax* dollars.

Once you put your money in, you must leave it there until you turn 59 $1/2$. If you dip into the money, watch out! You'll get nicked with a 10 percent federal tax penalty on any interest earnings to date—but not your principal. Plus, the insurance company hits you with *surrender charges*—sometimes as high as seven percent in the first year, although they do gradually decline one percent each year, until they vanish.

They come in two different types: an immediate annuity and a tax-deferred annuity. With an immediate annuity, you give a lump sum of money to the insurance company. Based on your age, life expectancy, and current interest rates, the insurance company calculates how much they'll send you each month—no matter how long you live—and invest it accordingly to provide for these specific dollar amounts.

The Money Line

There's one great advantage to a variable annuity that goes beyond the tax-deferred compounding: a *guaranteed death benefit*. This means the insurance company guarantees that when you die, your beneficiaries (which you name on your annuity contract) will receive *at least* as much as you invested in the original annuity or the current account value, whichever is greater. Make sure whoever sells you your contract explains how this works.

To set up a tax-deferred annuity, typically, you give the insurance company a lump sum of money to invest, and it grows on a tax-deferred basis over a number of years.

The beauty of a tax-deferred annuity is that you don't pay any taxes on the earning or profits that are built up in the annuity until you take the money out. If you want, you can add money to your tax-deferred annuity in various amounts over time. This is known as a *flexible-premium deferred annuity*.

Within a tax-deferred annuity, you have two options: a *guaranteed-rate* or a *variable* annuity. Guaranteed rate is just like it sounds—it pays a fixed interest rate that is guaranteed for a period of one to ten years (it's up to you). A variable annuity, though, allows you to choose among a wide range of mutual funds, such as stock, bond, or money market funds. Obviously, because these types of investment products don't guarantee a rate of return, your return in a variable annuity can fluctuate.

Most often, if you have more than a 10-year time horizon, and want to take advantage of tax-deferred growth, a variable annuity is a great place to begin. But there are some questions you should ask the insurance agent before you invest your cash.

➤ **Find out what the total expense, including all fees, would be for maintaining this account.** Even though there are no up-front sales commissions or loads that are charged (remember, these are no-load funds), there are still expenses involved. Find out what the surrender charges are, management fees (no-load funds have them, although they vary), and mortality fees, which take into account your projected life span.

➤ **Have the agent explain what funds are available within the annuity.** Just as you do when you are mutual fund shopping, check out what types of funds are available and the performance history of each. Within each variable annuity is a pool of mutual funds. Make sure they're well-established funds that you have heard of from your research.

➤ **Determine up-front if you can add more money to the annuity.** If it's possible, find out how much the minimum amounts are and if the additional money you invest will also extend the period of surrender charges. You don't want that to happen. Additionally, find out if the annuity will allow an automatic investment program similar to an automatic investment plan set up by a fund company. This way, you can have your monthly investment electronically transferred from your bank account to your annuity. Discipline, discipline, discipline!

If you need help annuity shopping, call Independent Advantage Financial Services at (800) 829-2887 for more information. Depending on your objective, they can research and find an annuity that best suits your financial goals and retirement needs.

You're Retired—Now What?

For the past thirty-some-odd years, you've spent a lot of time doing your homework—and contributing as much as possible to retirement accounts. After all, you want your retirement lifestyle to be comfortable, right? Right! But there are some rules you still have to follow *during* your retirement to keep the money growing, so it can keep on flowing.

> ➤ Continue to have your money grow and compound tax-deferred as long as possible.

> ➤ Be flexible with your funds so you can cushion yourself against any changing market conditions.

> ➤ Monitor the changing tax laws and how they affect your distributions.

> ➤ Keep a small portion of your retirement assets in growth investments (depending on your risk tolerance).

Your retirement income is probably based on how much you decide to receive in *distributions* (the money you eventually take out from your retirement plan)—and when. You must begin taking distributions from your IRA by April 1 of the year *after* you reach age 70 ^{1}/$_2$. It's okay if you start taking distributions before you reach 70 ^{1}/$_2$, but not before 59 ^{1}/$_2$, if you want to avoid the penalties imposed by the IRS. There are no limitations on how much or how little you can take out.

Once you turn 70 ^{1}/$_2$, it's a whole new ballgame. IRS rules dictate that you must take out enough money in distributions each year to use up your IRA account over your life expectancy. So how does the IRS know how long you're going to live? It's based on IRS mortality tables; your IRA *custodian* (the firm or company where your IRA is held) can help you calculate the amount.

You should have other retirement savings that you have put aside if you outlive your IRA and the IRS' mortality table. If you want to make your money last longer, have your annual distributions based on the joint life expectancy of *both* you and your spouse. If your spouse is much younger than you are, that would extend the payments over a longer period of time. If you are not married at the time, your calculation can be based on the life expectancy of you and your beneficiary (although there is a 10-year maximum age difference allowed).

The Early Bird Gets...

Imagine being 65 years old and living on $22,000, with almost a third coming from Social Security benefits. Many of you might spout off, "Oh, that's not going to happen to me!" yet it's a very real statistic for the 13 million seniors who live on that type of fixed income. So ask yourself: Can you live on that?

It's no secret: Rumors of the depletion of the Social Security fund in 20 years are nothing new. But government funding could change. Whether Social Security is here or not, don't consider benefits to be your only means of paying for your living expenses. Studies indicate that average-wage earners can expect Social Security benefits to replace 42 percent of their income—and those are today's figures. What about tomorrow?

As you work and pay FICA taxes, you earn Social Security credits. The number of credits needed for retirement benefits depends on your date of birth. If you were born January 2, 1929 or later, you need a total of 40 credits.

To learn the secrets of the Social Security system and make the most of your benefits—be informed, but don't let Social Security be the end to your means. The following are a few tips that will help you get the most out of your Social Security benefits when the time comes.

Secret #1: No Matter How Old You Are, Get an Idea of What Your Retirement Benefits Are NOW

Call the Social Security Administration's toll-free line (800/772-1213) and ask for an *Earnings and Benefit Estimate Statement*. The SSA will send you a form asking you how much you earned last year, your estimated earnings for this year, the age you plan to retire, and your estimated future annual earnings.

Based on this information, you'll get a complete earnings history, along with estimates of your benefits for retirement at age 62, 65, or 70. It includes estimates of disability or survivor's benefits and lists total Social Security taxes you have already paid.

Secret #2: Verify Your Social Security Record Every Three Years

Make sure all the taxes you have paid are credited to your account. Errors identified early are easier to correct. If you happen to run across an error, have your past tax returns and pay stubs available for proof.

Secret #3: Delay Retirement and You'll Increase Your Social Security Benefits

Age 65 is considered to be full-retirement age for receiving full benefits. Benefits are reduced if you retire sooner and collect them; they are increased if you delay retirement. You can start collecting benefits at age 62, but check out Table 22.1, which shows how it pays off to retire later.

Table 22.1   How Early Retirement Reduces Your Benefits (For Retired Workers Born Before 1938)

Retirement Age	% Reduction in Benefits	Benefit If Full Benefit Is		
		$600	$850	$1,100
65	0%	$600	$850	$1,100
64 1/2	3 $1/3$%	$580	$822	$1,063

continues

Table 22.1 Continued

Retirement Age	% Reduction in Benefits	Benefit If Full Benefit Is		
		$600	$850	$1,100
64	6 $2/3$%	$560	$793	$1,027
63 1/2	10%	$540	$765	$990
63	13 $2/3$%	$520	$737	$953
62 $1/2$	16 $2/3$%	$500	$708	$917
62	20%	$480	$680	$880

It may pay to wait if you...

➤ have sufficient financial resources and do not need Social Security benefits to meet living expenses.

➤ earn so much from your income that it triggers a tax on your Social Security benefits.

➤ earn so much from your income that you will lose benefits due to an earnings limit.

You may be better off using your savings or investments for living expenses. By spending your savings, you'll have less interest income to push benefits into the taxable range. Plus, waiting to collect Social Security will mean bigger benefit checks in the future. The following scenarios may help you understand how to determine when the best time is to start collecting your Social Security benefits.

Scenario #1: Milton, age 64, was forced to take early retirement. Currently, he receives $1,800 a month in pension benefits and about $650 a month from his well-established investment portfolio; his asset allocation is spread among stocks, bonds, and CDs. Plus, his home and car are all paid for. Even though he's 64, he hasn't applied for Social Security. If the total $2,450 he receives in monthly income covers his living expenses, he's done a smart thing—delayed his Social Security benefits today as a way to possibly increase his future benefits.

What he could do: He's doing the right thing. He should, however, contact the Social Security office to receive a copy of his estimated benefits now and when he turns 65.

Scenario #2: Norman and Merna, ages 64 and 62, are approaching retirement and are toying with applying for benefits. Norman has had commission-only sales jobs all of his working life, and, unfortunately, has no retirement benefits from any of his jobs. Merna works part-time and also has no retirement benefits. Their combined salaries are almost $55,000, and they have worked hard at accumulating almost $100,000 in their IRA.

What they could do: Even though Norman is approaching 65, his salary alone almost makes up the total $55,000—wiping out Social Security benefits. No reason for him to apply yet. What about Merna? Because she works part-time, she could file now because she is eligible to receive a year's worth of benefits.

Scenario #3: Sheila just turned 62, and wants to know if she should take her early retirement. She's married to Lester, who retired at age 63 from his job. Currently, they both receive pension benefits of $2,200 a month, Social Security benefits (from Lester) of $700 a month, and about $1,500 a month in investment income from their retirement nest egg. As his wife, she could start collecting benefits on the basis of on her husband's work record (there are special spousal rules—check with the SSA). They don't really need the extra income, but the couple hundred extra bucks per month would allow them to play a lot more Bingo games and take dance lessons at the local Y.

What they could do: Because she's only 62, Sheila would be better off waiting until she turns 65. Why? Because the extra money per month would put them over the income limit and subject a substantial percent of their Social Security benefits to taxes.

Whatever your situation, understanding the quirks and rules involved in applying for Social Security benefits will only make the system work for you. After all, you'll be working for it for quite a long time, right?

Count on You!

Average-wage earners can expect Social Security benefits to replace only 42 percent of their monthly income, according to the Social Security Administration. (Maximum-wage earners can expect benefits to replace 28 percent of their income.) So where can you get the remaining 58 percent if you're an average-wage earner?

Don't count on bonuses, commissions, stock options, severance pay, or even vacation pay. These all chalk up to income that will count toward the Social Security earnings limit, which can eventually reduce your Social Security benefits. That's why the following income sources are so important—they don't count toward the earnings limit.

➤ Pensions and retirement funds

➤ Investments (unless you are in the brokerage business)

➤ Individual Retirement Accounts (IRAs)

➤ Social Security and other types of government benefits

➤ Annuities and some tax-exempt trust funds

➤ Rental properties

➤ Gifts or inheritances and lottery winnings

➤ Money received from a reverse mortgage plan

So, even if you've built up a sizeable IRA and take distributions from it as a source of income, you don't have to fret about not getting your full Social Security benefits.

269

A Final Word

Geez, all these calculations and numbers in the retirement world? It doesn't have to be intimidating. No matter if you're single, married, divorced, or widowed, you should do something to prepare for retirement. Much of your fear will quickly disappear once you realize how easy it is to make your savings grow for retirement. The name of the game is to take one buck and turn it into two (then four, then sixteen, etc.) for a financially healthy tomorrow.

The Least You Need to Know

➤ Company pensions and Social Security won't cover all your financial needs for retirement. In order to be fully prepared, you need to start a retirement savings plan now.

➤ Take advantage of company retirement plans such as the 401(k). If you're not sure where to begin, contact your Employee Benefits or Human Resources department for information about company plans.

➤ If you don't have access to a company retirement plan, or if you are looking for tax-deferred growth, consider opening up an Individual Retirement Account (IRA).

➤ No matter how old you are, get an idea of what your retirement benefits are now. Call the Social Security Administration's toll-free line (800/772-1213) and ask for an *Earnings and Benefit Estimate Statement.*

Chapter 23

Maximizing Your 401(k) Benefits

In This Chapter

➤ Why you may be part of the nationwide savings crisis

➤ Understanding the benefits to a 401(k) plan

➤ Why you should aim for growth in your retirement account

➤ What you can do if you're self-employed

While this may not have the same shock value as Howard Stern, the fact that Americans, as a whole, are not saving enough money for their retirement is resulting in a nationwide savings crisis. Many employers offering company retirement programs agree that employees are not saving enough money to maintain their current standard of living when they retire.

Sure, we're all saving more than any one time in history—but the fact is, it's still not enough. Projections indicate that those of us between the ages of 35 and 52, in particular, are saving an average of only one-third of what we'll need to maintain our current lifestyle.

Why is this? Well, it's possible that many of us don't understand the benefits we can receive from employer retirement programs, such as the 401(k). According to the Merrill Lynch Baby Boom Index, benefits managers say that fewer than 68 percent have a good understanding of defined contribution plans; even fewer—25 percent—have a good understanding of Social Security or Medicare benefits. But they better start understanding: In the year 2000, there will be almost 94 million Americans who will face retirement.

Even with $7.9 trillion allotted in the U.S. retirement market, it's still not enough. What can you do to help thwart the problem? Well, you can't save the world, but you can save yourself. This chapter will help pinpoint the benefits available to you at work through the three little numbers with a little letter after them—the 401(k).

401(k) Is the Way to Play

If Merriam Webster could define it, it'd go something like this:

The 401(k), named for the relevant section in the tax code, is a tax-deferred investment and savings plan that acts as a personal pension fund for employees. This plan lets you defer taxes on a portion of your salary until you retire. Taxes on investment gains are deferred until you withdraw money from the plan. You can begin withdrawing from a tax-deferred investment account without penalty at age 59 1/2. Unlike pensions, 401(k) accounts are portable, in that you can "roll over" the account, take it with you and continue building it at your next employer with no penalty.

Because you get to deduct a portion of your earnings—before taxes—and put the money into various investment options, the money that comes out of your paycheck is in *pretax* dollars and it grows tax-deferred until you take it out at retirement. Also, you usually can make changes to how you allocate the percentage of money you contribute to each investment option every quarter—some companies offer the chance to do so every month.

Compared with other types of defined contribution plans, such as profit-sharing, 403(b), SEPs (simplified employee plans), and stock ownership plans, the 401(k) far outweighs these plans in terms of asset size.

The Inside Goods

In recent years, employers have expanded the range of employee investment options, offering five investment types in nearly half of all plans. By comparison, only three investment types were offered in the early '90s in about half of all plans. In fact, companies now appear to offer employees the option of more frequent investment selections, with 53 percent of large firms allowing their employees to change investment selections on a daily basis.

Many 401(k) plans offer a wide range of investment choices, with the most common being a money market fund, an index-based stock fund and an actively managed growth fund. Corporate bond funds, government securities funds and balanced stock and bond funds are typically offered. Company stock, although offered, is the most infrequent type of investment option offered to plan participants, according to the Merrill Lynch Retirement and Financial Planning Survey of Employers.

Show Me the Money!

Still not convinced of the greatness of the 401(k)? Well, then, it's time to forego the talk; let's show you the money.

	401(k)	**Taxable Account**
Amount contributed:	$15,000	$15,000
Less your taxes, 30%:	0	$4,500
Invested amount, plus employer's match:	$22,500	$10,500
Total amount, assuming 10% average return:	$30,220	$12,920

Convinced enough to hightail it right to your employee benefits department? Go ahead, but for those of you who think you can allocate a huge chunk of your salary to a 401(k) plan, unfortunately, the IRS says that's a no-no. The IRS does limit the amount you can contribute annually. The figures vary for different employees, typically following the trend—the more you make, the less you can contribute. Make sure your employee benefits department fills you in on this.

What happens if you leave your job and you want to take your money with you? The money you invest is yours, but beware, in order to avoid the tax monster there are rules to moving your money. You must have the transfer made directly from your old plan to your new plan. If you take possession of the money yourself—even if you plan on "rolling it over" into a new plan, whether it's at your new employer or in an IRA—you will get hit with a 20 percent federal income tax penalty. And, unless you replace the 20 percent penalty with new funds put into the new plan, it will be treated as a withdrawal. You will owe ordinary income taxes on the withdrawal.

Sure-Fire Investing Program

When you sock away money in your 401(k), it's in pre-tax dollars. Couple that with the market growth in the '90s and you could find you and your friendly 401(k) sitting on a slight windfall of money for your future.

Case in point: Let's say you have saved $9,000 a year in a taxable investment account. Well, you have to pay taxes on the contribution first. Depending on your tax bracket, that means you really invest only about $6,000. But if you put the $9,000 in a 401(k), you get to invest all $9,000 and reap the earnings of that tax-free contribution until you withdraw the funds. Plus, when you factor in the matching contributions that some companies kick in, you have guaranteed returns for your investments, no matter what the stock market does. Check with your Employee Benefits or Human Resources department to see if your employer offers a matching program.

A Brief Word About a 401(k) Versus an IRA

The name of the game is tax-deferred growth, and both contenders, the 401(k) and IRA, offer both. But is there one that is better?

It all depends on your tax situation. However, there are several benefits to investing in a 401(k). Even with the new tax laws, you can still contribute more tax-free dollars to your 401(k)—up to $9,240 a year, depending on your salary. Also, many employers will contribute (match) to your 401(k) plan, which is free money to you. So, if you have an employer that pays 20-cents on the dollar, that's like earning a 20 percent *guaranteed* return. Where can you get that these days?

Other benefits to a 401(k) versus an IRA:

➤ Also, investing in a 401(k) is done with pre-tax dollars; with an IRA, your contributions are done with after-tax earnings.

➤ You can also borrow money from your 401(k), but there are rules you must follow, as you'll learn later in this chapter.

➤ The only limitation to participating in your company's 401(k) program is if its investment choices are severely limited, such as it only offers a money market fund and its company stock. At that point, an IRA would definitely make sense.

Go for the Gusto

Despite the increase of investment options in 401(k) plans, the most frequently found type of investment choice is a money market fund, a vehicle typically used as a "safe haven" during turbulent market conditions.

Here's the paradox. If the goal for investing in a 401(k) is long-term growth, why do most participants choose these overly cautious investments for the long haul?

Call it long-term anxiety. Over the short-term, Americans are optimistic about their financial future, with 70 percent of consumers expecting to be better off financially in the next five years, either due to finally ridding themselves of credit card debt or finding more lucrative employment. But there is a deep-seated apprehension about long-term prospects. Even armed with the belief that their retirements will be financially more difficult than their parents and kicking themselves for not saving for retirement sooner, the typical Baby Boomer fears outliving the money they have put away, or plan to put away, for retirement.

That's why it does not pay to be too conservative with your retirement strategy. With the majority of 401(k) participants putting 60 percent or more of their contributions into bonds or money market funds, the wake up call on retirement day will require more than earplugs. Sure, stocks are riskier, but over the long run they have far greater growth potential than Money Market funds. Even small stocks have outperformed large-company stocks over the years, and, depending on which time frame you look into, foreign markets beat U.S. markets in some periods—as they did in 1993. Unless you expect to retire in the next five to seven years, many money managers advise you to put almost all your 401(k) money into stock funds. If that seems a bit too risky for you, as of this writing, you do have one low-risk next egg out there—Social Security.

The bottom line is that ideally your 401(k) plan should have at least half a dozen investment options. Unfortunately, there are still some employers that limit you to three or fewer—although that is changing. If your plan falls short, complain to your Employee Benefits department.

Rules, Rules, Rules

You must leave your contributions in the plan (or roll it over into an IRA if you leave the company, or take it with you to a new employer's plan) until age 59 $^1/_2$. There are hardship cases when you can withdraw money, such as purchasing a home, emergency medical expenses, or college tuition.

What constitutes a hardship? The withdrawal must be made on account of the participant's (that's you) immediate and heavy financial need—and the withdrawal must be necessary to satisfy such need. Check with your employer to find out exactly what your company's plan will allow.

What happens if you leave your job and you want to take your money with you? You *must* have the transfer made directly from your old plan to your new plan, or roll it over into an IRA account. If you take possession of the money yourself—even if you plan on "rolling it over" into a new plan (whether it's at your new employer or in an IRA), you will get hit with a 20 percent federal income tax penalty. Wait—there's more. Unless you replace the 20 percent penalty with new funds put into the new plan, it will be treated as a withdrawal and WHAMMO! You'll owe ordinary income taxes on it.

If You're Self-Employed...

You can create your own retirement savings program! Plus, you can contribute much more than the $2,000 IRA maximum. There are *Keogh plans*, which fall under two types: *defined benefit* and *defined contribution* plans. The choice is yours, but make sure you review the paperwork about requirements, especially if you have employees—then you *must* include contributions for them as well.

There's a lot of legal mumbo-jumbo to the paperwork when you set up a Keogh plan, but most mutual fund companies and brokerage firms (full-service, discount, and deep-discount) just need you to fill out the basic paperwork to set one up. A Keogh plan must be set up by the end of the year, and contributions must be made by the tax-filing due date.

As a self-employed individual, you also have access to opening up a SEP-IRA, which is a Simplified Employee Pension IRA. A SEP is easier to understand and administer success-fully than a Keogh. Sometimes dubbed an "easy-to-manage retirement plan for indi-viduals," a SEP-IRA can be opened and contributions can be made up until the last day of your tax filing deadline, including extensions. You can contribute up to 15 percent of your compensation or $22,500, whichever is less.

The Least You Need to Know

➤ A 401(k), named for the relevant tax code, is a type of tax-deferred retirement plan offered by employers to its employees. Some employers offer a matching program where for every dollar you contribute they will contribute a percentage up to 100 percent on the dollar.

➤ You can contribute pre-tax dollars to a 401(k), thereby reducing your tax liability to good ol' Uncle Sam.

➤ Don't be too conservative with your investment options. Unless you're retiring within the next five to seven years, go for the gusto and allocate a large portion of retirement monies to equities, as they tend to perform well over the long haul.

➤ Self-employed consumers can create their own retirement plans through Keoghs and SEPs, also known as simplified employee plans. Check with your tax adviser to determine which plan is best for you and your employees.

Part 6
Getting a Handle on the Rest of Your Money Life

Most of us don't have to "try" to go to work everyday. We just know we have to, so we do. It is comical, however, that to work out at the gym or manage our finances, we have to "try" to fit it in. Why not make it part of our day just like brushing our teeth or going to work each morning?

Just think if we didn't try, but rather did get a hold of our financial lives. Any emergency requiring instant cash could be covered. All the bills would be paid on time. And we could even plan for our future so retirement seems possible. Sounds like a plan!

We can't escape our responsibilities—rent or a mortgage, car payments, clothing expenses, groceries—but we can control them rather than having them control us. This part will show you how you can help you and your family in the event of a financial emergency, take advantage of your employee benefits at work, protect your health and wealth through insurance, and tackle taxes.

Chapter 24

You, Your Employer, and Your Paycheck

In This Chapter

➤ How to squeeze more out of your paycheck

➤ The best perk you'll ever receive from your boss

➤ Dipping into your 401(k)? Watch your fingers!

➤ Emergency plan if you're fired

You have the world at your feet. Two different prospective employers you interviewed with last week offer you positions in their company. Here's the lowdown.

Job Offer #1: You have your own office with a view that faces Lake Michigan. Your boss doesn't expect you to clock work hours more than 9 to 5. You have two executive assistants, a company car, $65,000 in income, and weekends off. You're allowed 10 sick days a year, and two weeks vacation. They offer you a reimbursement feature for your health-care costs and there's no retirement savings program.

Job Offer #2: Your office faces north—no window. You have a secretary, a parking space (no company car), $64,000 a year in income, 2 sick days a year, and 1 week vacation for the first year (which increases to two weeks after 12 months). You have access to a major medical plan, a 401(k), an employee-stock-purchase plan and a pension.

Which do you choose? The lake view? No way. You get the gold star if you chose Job Offer #2. Why? Because of the opportunity to earn 50 to 100 percent on your money. This chapter will explain all the opportunities that you can receive working 9 to 5.

Squeezing More Out of Your Paycheck

Don't have time to trek down to your local bank to buy savings bonds? Look no further than your paycheck. Most major companies offer you a chance to purchase Series EE savings bonds through automatic payroll deductions. Although the money is not deducted on a pre-tax basis, these deductions are a great way of breaking the "see-it-buy-it" mentality because the money is deducted automatically from your check. Plus, you can use the opportunity as an avenue to stash your "safe" money—money that you can't afford to lose.

You can have the deductions taken out weekly, monthly, or quarterly. Since savings bonds are purchased at a discount from face value (a $100 face value bond has a purchase price of $50), they're a great way to invest your safe money for the future. Over the years, the value of the bond will increase as the interest accrues.

One woman who works for a major brokerage firm in Chicago tells us she has $50 deducted from each paycheck to buy $100 savings bonds each month. "They're for my two-year-old daughter's future," Pam tells us. Good thinking, Pam. In just one year, you'll have invested $600 for $1,200 face value worth of bonds for your daughter's future. (Tip: You can use these as a way to pay for her college education and possibly *not* pay taxes on the interest you'll receive.)

Here's one more tip for getting the most out of your paycheck. Have your check directly deposited. This sounds so simple, but many consumers aren't doing this. They should take advantage of this paperless transition. No bank lines or traffic to wait in. Plus, direct deposit guarantees immediate access to your cash at most banks and thrifts. As you learned in Chapter 10 about checking accounts, it can take several days for your deposited check to clear. Why wait?

Besides the added convenience, you can make a little extra money off direct deposit with this little strategy: Have your paycheck directly deposited into a Money Market Account to earn the better rate of interest than a savings or checking account. You'll earn interest on payday since your check was directly deposited. When you need money, write a check to yourself and deposit it in your non-interest-bearing checking account to pay the bills.

Asset Advisory

If you have at least 10 years until you retire, invest in your 401(k) for growth instead of stockpiling your money into the Money Market Account.

Working 9 to 5—It IS a Way to Make a Living!

You have access to one of the most convenient and important investment resources—right at your employer's doorstep. It's your employer's *retirement plan*, which is one of the most important asset-building tools available to consumers. Once you participate in your employer's retirement savings program, you avoid one of the biggest mistakes people make: doing nothing.

The younger you start, the better—your money has more time to grow, and you might have to save less overall. Look at a couple of examples:

Sylvia gets her first job at age 21. Over the next eight years, she accumulates a bit more than $10,000. Eight years later, she gets married, has two children, and decides to put her career on hold. She stops investing and lets her money ride, earning around eight percent (compounded monthly) on her $10,000 until she retires at age 65. She has accumulated $176,448.

Myron doesn't invest a penny until he's about 29 years old. On his 29th birthday, he decides to stash $70 a month into an investment account that earns the same amount as Sylvia's: eight percent. He does that for 36 years, all the way to age 65, contributing a total of $30,240. His total accumulation? $174,771.

Who's better off? They both have relatively the same amount of money by age 65. But Sylvia's initial wad of dough was only $10,000. Myron contributed *three times* that amount—$30,240. Why is this? *Because Sylvia started earlier and had more time for her money to grow*.

Even though Americans socked away more than $7 *trillion* into some type of company-sponsored retirement program in 1997, such as a 401(k) or a pension or other type of defined benefit plan, there is solid evidence that young Americans are not saving enough. Of all the employees that have access to a retirement savings program, only 60 percent contribute. They're really behind the eight ball.

The Money Line

The Merrill Lynch Baby Boomer Index measures the savings shortfall of that generation of America. Most recent estimates indicate that America's 77 million baby boomers have saved only 36 percent of what they should have saved for retirement.

Why the problem? Because many people are living moment to moment and can't think about the future. Others don't want money taken out of their check because "they need it NOW." Ya know what? These people who can't afford the deduction now won't be able to afford retirement. Still others do not contribute because they just don't understand how the dang thing works.

Another culprit is that many people *are* savers, and a company retirement program sends chills down the spines of Americans who couldn't stand the thought of losing money by investing. Saving is something you used to do when you were a kid, often dropping coins into a piggy bank. Sure, you can save today. A prime example is the emergency fund you should save in a SAFE place (such as a money market fund), that will cover three to six months' worth of living expenses.

Asset Advisory

If you have a defined benefit plan, check whether the plan is insured by the Pension Benefit Guaranty Corporation. The PBGC guarantees to cover retired workers and the "vested portion" of current employees.

Contributing to a retirement plan practices the strategy of tax-deferred investing. Stocks, bonds, and mutual funds are purchased within a qualified investment plan, such as a 401(k) and pension plans (which you'll learn more about in this chapter).

By deferring your income taxes, you can increase your investment returns. For example, look at Table 24.1 for comparison, assuming a $2,000 per year investment at an average nine percent return in a tax-deferred versus taxable account.

Table 24.1   Advantages of Deferring Taxes

Years	Investment Dollars in a Tax-Deferred Account	Investment Dollars in a Taxable Account
10	$33,150	$28,725
15	$64,200	$51,500
20	$112,000	$83,100
25	$184,700	$125,100
30	$298,000	$184,600

Investing is a different story; you create goals and work toward those goals. True, whenever you invest in a product, there is a potential of risk. If you look at the facts, however, you can see how investing in a company-sponsored program is the best investment deal in America today. For example, here's how much you can save by sheltering your contributions from taxes. If you contribute $2,000 a year in your company's plan and your account earns a modest six percent a year for 30 years, you'll have about $168,000, which would be $48,000 *more* than if your $2,000 investment went into a taxable account.

The Fabulous 401(k)

A 401(k) plan, which was dubbed for the section of the tax code it represents, allows you to make contributions on a pre-tax basis. The money is taken out of your check and invested in several different options, all of which you choose. The money grows tax-deferred until you take it out.

282

The upside of a 401(k) is that you decide which investments you want to put your money in (unlike other company retirement plans, such as a pension). Your investment choices in a 401(k) plan are strictly up to you. Typically, you'll have a choice between a Money Market Account, a general growth or equity stock fund, a fixed-income choice, and an investment in your company's stock. As you learned in Chapter 23, any money you contribute is yours, even if you leave the company, and you can roll it over into a tax-deferred IRA when you leave the company. The biggest allure, however, is that you don't pay taxes on the money you contribute.

So what exactly is a 401(k)? It's sometimes known as a *salary reduction plan,* because when you enroll your employer deducts a percentage of your salary—usually between two and 10 percent, the percentage is up to you—and deposits the funds in your plan account. The money is deducted from your paycheck before being taxed federally, state, locally and even before Social Security takes its chunk. So, the earnings you report (your wages/salary) to the IRS on your income tax return are lessened by the amount of your contribution.

What a perk, huh? Many times, your employer matches the money you set aside. For example, some plans will pay 50 percent for every dollar that you contribute; others may even match your contribution 100 percent. Meaning, for every dollar you put in, your company matches your contribution and contributes a dollar to your retirement account in the plan. Where else can you earn 100 percent on your money like that?

The IRS does limit how much you can contribute annually, although this figure increases each year with inflation. Currently, the limit for 401(k) plans is $9,240. Now, that figure is not for *all* employees; typically the more money you make, the less you can contribute—it's known as "rank-and-file"—and rules vary. Make sure your employer spells this out for you.

So what's all this *vesting* talk? It's not a clothing phenomenon, rather it tells you how much of your employer's matched contributions and earnings in a retirement plan you can take with you if you leave your job, get laid off, get fired, or retire. You can keep all of *your* prior contributions and earnings, but your company's vesting schedule will determine how much of the company's money you can keep. Vesting schedules differ among employers, so check with your boss to make sure what the company rules are.

Dip into Your 401(k)? Sure, but Watch Your Fingers

You can borrow against your 401(k). But is it worth it? Many 401(k) programs offer this option to its contributors. All you do is borrow from your tax-deferred savings program and pay interest into your own account. Kind of like "paying yourself back" plus interest. What a great loan customer.

The rates are low—about a point lower than what banks charge on secured personal loans, but the hidden costs are high. The largest hidden cost is the lost opportunities of the earnings you might have gained on your tax-deferred savings. Consider it like transferring the money from one pocket to another; the money you borrow is not collecting any interest or increasing in capital growth. But, if you need the money, it is a source you can count on.

The loan must be repaid quarterly and within five years, unless you're using it to buy a house, usually your principal residence. The vacation home in Bermuda is not an exception. If it is your principal residence, you may have up to 30 years to repay, often through payroll deductions. If you borrow from your 401(k), follow these rules:

➤ There are hardship rules you will have to follow—and it's usually up to the company to decide—such as uninsured medical costs. If it's to buy the flame red Maserati, forget it.

➤ Try not to leave the company with a loan outstanding. Why? Because the balance will be subtracted before you receive your 401(k) funds. What does this matter? Enter Uncle Sam, who says if you don't pay back the loan within the 60-day grace period, you have to roll the funds over into another qualified plan or an Individual Retirement Account (IRA), or he'll take a chunk out. The IRS considers it an early withdrawal, and will hit you with a 10-percent penalty as well as income tax.

➤ If you take a leave of absence from work, see if you can still make your loan payments. Even though most companies will allow you a grace period of one year, once you return, your loan payments are raised in order to meet the five-year time frame requirement.

The drawback of a 401(k)? The dollar amount you contribute each year is subject to a limit set by your employer as a percentage of your salary. The other drawback is that it's completely voluntary. You don't have to participate and many people don't, for various reasons. The biggest one is that they don't understand what a 401(k) is. You shouldn't necessarily be *forced* to invest, but take a look at why you should.

If you contribute $2,000 a year every year for thirty years into a 401(k) (which is a company-sponsored plan) instead of a taxable account, you will have accumulated almost $50,000 *more* in the 401(k) than a taxable account in the same amount of time. And that's not even including the matching contributions your company makes. If your company doesn't offer a 401(k), lobby for it.

Fiscal Facts

A *403(b) plan* is a pre-tax savings plan offered to employees who work for non-profit or tax-exempt organizations, such as a school or even a hospital. A 403(b) plan is like a 401(k) since your contributions grow on a tax-deferred basis and the money taken out of your check is in pre-tax dollars. In most 403(b) plans, however, you are allowed to contribute a higher amount than most 401(k)s. Check with your employee benefits department.

Take Advantage of Other Company Plans

Most large companies offer a traditional pension plan, known as a *defined benefit plan*, but about 30 percent fewer companies are offering such plans to employees these days. Instead, they're shifting the burden of saving for retirement onto you, the employee, through the 401(k) plan. Make sure you understand all the benefits you are garnering under your company's plan. Most large companies have an employee benefits officer who should be able to explain to you in plain language how their plan works.

A *defined benefit plan* guarantees that you receive a fixed monthly sum at retirement and for the rest of your life. That's why it's called *defined*; the benefit you'll receive at retirement is defined in advance. Typically, it is based on the average of the last five years' salary, the number of years of employment, and your age at retirement. You don't make any contributions—the employer makes them each year, so that when you reach retirement age there will be enough money in the plan to pay your lifetime benefits.

If your company offers a *defined contribution plan*, you'll have more flexibility than a traditional pension plan (*defined benefit plan*), but not as much as a 401(k). There are two types of defined contribution plans: a money purchase plan and a profit-sharing plan.

So how does a *money purchase plan* work? You must usually work at your job for at least one year to participate. The maximum annual deductible contribution is 25 percent of your salary or $30,000, whichever is less. The reason it's called a money purchase plan is that the retirement benefits amount to whatever the assets in the account will purchase at the time you retire. The only employer obligation is to make a defined contribution for each worker each year, regardless of profits. These plans are different than defined benefit plans in that there are no guaranteed benefits at the time you retire.

A *profit-sharing plan*, on the other hand, obligates the company to contribute part of its profits each year, if any, into each worker's account. However, the company can change the rate of contributions, based on profits, or eliminate them in any year. Monthly benefits are whatever the money you have in your account will buy when you retire. You still contribute to this type of account: 15 percent of your salary or $22,500, whichever is less.

Your contributions are made with pre-tax dollars to defined contribution plans, and the money grows tax-deferred, which is a great advantage. Look at Table 24.2 to see how much your pre-tax contributions can grow over five years if you save $3,000 a year for five years and your employer matches 50 cents on the dollar. This table also assumes a 10 percent average annual rate of return.

Asset Advisory

If you want to know what your savings bonds are worth today, call (800) US-BONDS to find out.

Table 24.2   How Pre-Tax Contributions Can Grow

	401(k)	Taxable Account
Amount contributed	$15,000	$15,000
Less your taxes (30%)	$0	$4,500
Invested amount, plus employer's match	$22,500	$10,500
Total amount, assuming 10% average return	$30,220	$12,920

No Matter what type of plan is available to you, make sure you ask your employee benefits officer the following questions:

1. How are my retirement benefits computed?

2. How long will it take until I'm *vested*? (That's how long it will take for plan contributions made by the company to be owned by you.) By law, your pension benefits must be fully vested in a maximum of seven years.

You're F-I-R-E-D

Before the pink slip arrives, make sure you have an emergency fund. About three to six months' worth of living expenses is the rule. Keep this money in a Money Market fund that has a check-writing feature. This way, as you're adding to your emergency fund, you can take advantage of the higher rates. *Do not keep this money in a checking account.*

Unless you live under a rock, you're probably aware of all of the layoffs that have taken place in Corporate America in the past decade. Whether or not it is due to technology or companies tightening their belts isn't the point. The point is what *you* should do if it happens to you. You have an overwhelming amount of decisions to make. This section will help answer some questions about what to do with all the financial issues you face.

Does your company provide continued health insurance coverage in the event you leave voluntarily or involuntarily? Many companies offer you an option to continue health insurance coverage at the same rate the company pays for a maximum of 18 months. After that, you're on your own.

What will happen to your pension or 401(k) benefits? When you're let go and have contributed to a 401(k) plan, you may have to take all of your contributions in a *lump sum distribution*. That's a wad of dough that you need to make some quick decisions about within the next 60 days. You can:

➤ Roll it over into a new IRA *deposited directly from your employer into an IRA* and keep up the tax-deferred savings you've established. By doing so, you won't get hit by Uncle Sam's 10-percent tax penalty, which is on top of the income tax penalty you'll pay if you keep the money—BUT if you take hold of the check, then the company must withhold 20 percent for income taxes. However, you're only allowed one IRA rollover per year.

➤ Roll it over into your *new* employer's plan, if you've secured another job. It's a simple transfer with no tax penalties.

➤ Keep the money growing tax-deferred in your company's 401(k) plan. While it may sound like a good choice because you can still take advantage of the tax-deferral feature, ask yourself this: Why keep your money with the company that just laid you off?

You don't have as much flexibility with your pension benefits, unless you're being offered early retirement. You will have to meet with your employee benefits department to determine what is allowed according to their plan. During this meeting, find out how much of your benefits you own, known as being *vested*. You can roll that money into an IRA, or you may have to leave it with the company until you retire. Get the specifics from the benefits department.

Do you have access to outplacement counselors through your company? If so, take them up on it!

Finally, are you going to receive any type of severance? Two weeks is pretty standard, and employers can pay you in a lump sum or over a period of a few weeks. You can take the lump sum, but know that you'll face a bigger tax bill next April if you receive the money at the end of the year. The decision is up to you. If you are going to receive a severance, why not lobby for more? The worst thing that could happen is that they say no.

Asset Advisory

You're better off rolling the money over into an IRA if you can, especially if the company's pension plan is not funded to full capacity—a problem many corporations have been facing over the past decade.

287

The Least You Need to Know

➤ Take advantage of your employer's retirement plan, whether it's a 401(k) or something else. It's one of the best investments you can make. If you're not sure how it works, sit down with your company's benefits specialist and get him or her to explain it to you.

➤ If you really need the money, you can borrow from your retirement fund. Although you'll get a lower interest rate than what you would at the bank, you're also costing yourself future earnings on the fund when you do this.

➤ If your company offers it, take the payroll deduction to invest in savings bonds. You'll thank yourself later. Also, have your paycheck directly deposited into your bank account. You'll save yourself some time and earn an extra day's worth of interest if you have it deposited in an interest-earning account.

➤ If the worst happens and you're fired or laid off, make sure you find out whether you can continue your health insurance, what happens with your 401(k) and pension, and if you will get any severance pay.

Chapter 25

Getting the Right Insurance Coverage for Your Needs

In This Chapter

➤ Why you need to protect yourself

➤ Insurance strategies that will save you a few bucks

➤ Assessing your life, health, and wealth

➤ Insurance you don't need

Many folks believe that paying a lot of money on insurance premiums is like flushing your money down the toilet—that is, until tragedy strikes. Then those expensive insurance premiums seem like the best thing since the invention of the paper clip.

You need to insure your health and protect your wealth. And the more you have to protect, the more you'll spend on insurance. Typical insurance policies include homeowner's insurance to protect your home, automobile insurance to help in case of an accident (whether or not it's your fault!), life insurance to help your loved ones financially when you die, and disability insurance to cover you if you aren't able to perform your current job.

This chapter defines the types of insurance you need. In addition, it will help you get the best buy for your insurance dollars and show you how to shield yourself from unexpected disasters.

Making Sense of Insurance Mumbo-Jumbo

Your insurance needs are determined by which of these categories you fall under: single, married couple with no kids, married couple with kids, or married couple with adult children (empty-nesters). The following list explains the insurance needs for each category:

➤ **Singles:** You can skip the life insurance, but you'll need auto insurance (make sure you get comprehensive coverage if you have an outstanding car loan) and renter's insurance (unless you own your home). Disability insurance is also a good idea; you can usually get this through your employer.

➤ **Married without children:** Look into term life insurance, particularly if one spouse does not work or you own a home. Auto insurance is a must, as is homeowner's or renter's insurance. Get disability insurance through your employer, but look into a supplemental policy if your employer's coverage is not enough.

➤ **Married with children:** When children enter the picture, the necessity for insurance coverage increases. For one thing, you definitely need life insurance. Term life insurance is the best bet if you are in this age range. As you get older, the premiums may rise, so you'll need to reevaluate your situation and perhaps choose another policy. Your car insurance coverage may remain the same, with one addition. If you have children who can drive, see how much a multi-car discount policy would be. You may be able to save as much as 25 percent on your total premiums.

Disability insurance is more important when you have children. Choose a policy that is guaranteed renewable, and lock into a guaranteed annual premium that cannot be increased and is non-cancelable until you turn 65. Add a cost-of-living adjustment clause to your policy for an extra premium. This will raise your disability payments based on an index tied to the Consumer Price Index (CPI).

Finally, get complete coverage on your homeowner's insurance. Make sure you know what your policy does and does not cover, and purchase additional coverage if necessary.

➤ **Empty nesters:** The kids are gone and you have the house back to yourselves—Hallelujah! All previous insurance needs remain the same, although you may need insurance to cover any debts—such as death/funeral expenses and estate taxes, which are usually cared for by a good life insurance policy. Keep in mind the following exceptions:

➤ **Automobile coverage:** Senior citizens usually get 20 percent discounts on auto insurance. Remember to get rid of your multi-car discount now that the children are on their own.

➤ **Homeowner's insurance:** Re-evaluate your existing policy and what it covers. If you've sold the house and moved into a smaller place, you'll need less coverage, which means lower annual premium costs.

➤ **Long-term care insurance:** People with substantial resources they don't want to lose need this type of coverage. Average annual premium costs are $1,100 a year. Make sure that there's an inflation-protection rider, that the policy is renewable for life, and that there is a short elimination period, such as 20 to 60 days. For more tips on shopping for long-term care insurance, contact the National Association of Insurance Commissioners, Attn: Publications Dept., 120 W. 12th Street, Suite 1100, Kansas City, MO 64105-1925. Ask for their free booklet, "A Shopper's Guide to Long-Term Care Insurance."

➤ **Life insurance:** Purchase a cash value life insurance policy to pay your estate taxes in the event of your death, especially if you have more than the $600,000 exemption that Uncle Sam allows. Why? Keeping term insurance becomes too expensive as you get older. Plus, in a cash value insurance policy, the cash inside the policy builds up and may be used in the future to pay premiums or help pay estate taxes. This isn't true of term insurance.

The rest of this chapter explains the ins and outs of the different types of insurance.

Insuring Home Sweet Home

No matter where you live, whether you rent or own, you need some sort of insurance to cover your belongings. The following paragraphs explain what kind of insurance you need based on your living arrangements.

If you rent your home, you need to have a renter's insurance policy. Renter's insurance is available through most insurance agents. The form, known as an HO-4 form, covers any damage to your personal property and any structural damage to the building caused by tenants.

The amount you will pay on your renter's insurance policy can be on a monthly, semi-annual, or annual basis. No matter what the term, the amount you pay is known as a premium, and the amount of your premium depends on where you live. Do you live in a good neighborhood or a bad one? Is there a 24-hour doorman? Is the apartment unoccupied for more than two hours per day? Another factor is whether you have taken out other insurance policies (such as car insurance) with the insurance agent. If you haven't, your premium will be higher. Typical premiums average around $150 per year.

If you are a condo or co-op owner, you will need an HO-6 policy. Similar to a renter's insurance policy, this policy covers risks and damage to your personal property. Building property is covered for 10 percent of contents (such as cabinets and wall fixtures). Make sure you check with your insurance agent about anything that is not covered.

If you own your home, you should already have homeowner's insurance. Mortgage lenders require that you have property insurance before you buy a new home. If you are in the market for a new home and are getting homeowner's insurance for the first time, you should understand the basic forms of homeowner's coverage.

Types of Coverage

If you want to get the right type of coverage for your home, compare the following types of homeowner's insurance. The items that are listed as types of coverage are known as *perils*, as in "all the things that could go wrong." In the industry, it is known as a *standard peril policy*. The more coverage you acquire, the higher your insurance premiums will be. It is up to you to decide if you want to pay more in insurance premiums and have more coverage. However, if you try to cut corners on your homeowner's insurance policy to save a few bucks and tragedy strikes, you will be sorry.

> **HO-1** covers the 11 most common perils: glass breakage, fire or lightning, smoke damage, explosion, riots, damage caused by vehicles, damage caused by aircraft, theft, property loss, vandalism, and weather, such as windstorms, hurricanes, and hail.

> **HO-2** covers HO-1 perils plus roof collapse from snow, heavy sleet, or ice; damage from hot or frozen water pipes; heat or air conditioning explosion; damage caused by falling objects; damage caused by electrical surges to appliances (except televisions); and collapse of any part of your home.

> **HO-3** is a special form that covers HO-1 and HO-2 and other risks to an older home, except floods, wars, and earthquakes. You do pay a premium for having replacement cost.

> **HO-4** is a policy that varies from insurance company to company; check with your insurance agent to see what an HO-4 homeowner's policy covers.

Watch Your Wallet

Earthquake insurance is expensive for Californians. It carries an extremely high deductible—between nine and 10 percent of the coverage. This means that if you are trying to insure a $250,000 home with a 10 percent deductible, you'll pay the first $25,000 of repairs before your insurance coverage kicks in.

> **HO-5** includes replacement cost, and personal property and is covered for 75 percent of the home—as opposed to HO-3, where 70 percent is covered. To qualify for this type of coverage, your home must have been built after 1950 and must be in decent condition. It's required that you have a smoke detector, a dead bolt lock, and a hand-held fire extinguisher. If you don't have these items, you *cannot* get an HO-5 policy. You will pay more in premiums for this type of policy, but it does provide the most extensive coverage (including HO-1 and HO-2 disasters).

> **HO-6** policies, as previously described, are for condo and co-op owners only.

Now that you know what is covered, let's find out what is not covered. For example, the HO-3 policy does not cover flood damage, but you can purchase separate flood insurance. However, you do have to qualify for this insurance by meeting the federal zoning standards, so check with your insurance agent to determine if you even need this type of coverage. The National Flood Insurance Program "backs" this type of insurance, but be aware that flood coverage is limited. It does not provide coverage for valuables stored below the ground level in your basement—except for major appliances, such as a freezer or washer and dryer.

Saving Money on Homeowner's Insurance

There's no escaping it—you must have homeowners insurance to buy a house. What you can escape are the extra costs that most folks end up paying because they haven't done their homework. Here are a few financial secrets that will help trim the fat:

➤ **Raise your deductible amounts.** If you're willing to accept a $1,000 deductible, you can save almost 15 percent on your premiums.

➤ **Take protective measures.** Installing a burglar alarm, dead bolts, or a smoke detector, purchasing a hand-held fire extinguisher, and/or having a non-smoking household protects your home and lowers your premiums.

➤ **Get replacement cost insurance.** Most insurance policies plan to give you the *actual cash value* of your personal property in the event of loss or damage. Folks, it's not worth it. If you buy a $3,500 leather couch today, five years from now it will be worth only $1,500 (because it's used). If you have a fire when that couch is five years old, the insurance company will pay you $1,500. Just try to find the same type of couch for $1,500. It's not likely. However, if you have replacement cost insurance, the insurance company is required to pay you whatever it costs to purchase a new replacement item.

➤ **Purchase your homeowner's insurance from the same insurance company that insures your automobile.** Purchasing both policies from the same agent or company may qualify you for a discount.

➤ **Pay your homeowner's insurance annually.** Although most insurance policies have annual, semi-annual, and monthly terms, you will save a few dollars if you pay it on an annual basis. For example, a renter's insurance policy with a $160 per year annual premium may cost you $87 on a semi-annual basis. This comes out to be an extra $14 out of your pocket.

➤ **Make a home video of your property and all of its contents.** By doing so, you ensure—and insure—that your claims will be paid.

➤ **Familiarize yourself with the additional coverages and exceptions noted on your policy.** For example, if your policy allows you to have additional coverage on credit card losses, don't take it. Why? Because most standard credit card companies limit you to a $50 loss per card. That's just wasting money. Read the fine print!

Car Coverage

The liability involved when you are in a car accident is phenomenal, which is why automobile insurance costs so much. You need to know what is required in your state and what's worth paying for. Comparing the differences between the two can save you a few dollars. The following sections cover the types of coverage available and give you some money saving strategies.

Types of Coverage

Liability coverage is required in almost every state and is split into two parts: bodily injury liability and property damage liability. Bodily injury liability provides insurance against lawsuits. Most states require a minimum of $25,000 per person and $50,000 per accident. If you want to protect your assets in the event of a lawsuit, you'll need as much as $300,000 worth of coverage. Property damage liability covers damage done by your car to other people's cars and property. The standard minimum for this is $10,000.

If you're a victim of a hit-and-run accident, you'll need uninsured motorist coverage. Uninsured motorist coverage allows you to collect lost wages and payments for any medical expenses that result from an accident with an uninsured motorist. Do *not* skip over this type of insurance, especially since an increasingly high number of drivers have dropped their insurance coverage because of high premiums. And you should especially include this if you don't already have a comprehensive medical plan and long-term disability insurance.

You must also have comprehensive coverage if you have an outstanding car loan (which many of us do). Comprehensive coverage covers theft and damage to the car from riots, fire, flood, falling trees, and theft.

Watch Your Wallet

Uninsured motorist coverage should not be confused with underinsured motorist coverage, which is the part of your policy that pays after the other driver's coverage has been used up.

Collision coverage, which pays for damage to your car if you're in an accident or replaces a vehicle that is a total loss, is optional unless you have a loan on your car. If you do have a loan, this type of coverage is usually required by the lender.

Medical payments coverage and personal injury protection (PIP) covers medical, hospital, and funeral bills that result from an automobile accident—no matter who is at fault. PIP goes one step further and covers any lost wages. If you have a good medical plan and/or disability insurance policy, you may want to pass on these types of coverages, since they can be expensive.

Saving Some Moolah

When you apply for automobile insurance, you always want to look for the best rate possible, but that's not always so easy. Insurers take into account certain considerations when they give you quotes on auto insurance. Keep these financial tidbits in mind to help cut costs on auto insurance:

➤ **Comparison shop.** You don't always have to go to your friendly insurance agent down the street. In fact, if you do your homework, you'll find that the price of similar auto coverage can vary as much as 80 percent from insurer to insurer. Check with the largest national insurers, which could potentially save you a few bucks if you buy directly from them.

➤ **Drive safely and defensively.** This tip is just common sense, but the fewer traffic violations and accidents you have under your belt, the lower your premiums will be. Maintain a good driving record!

➤ **Don't buy the latest "fad" or "hot" car.** In 1997, the vehicles stolen most often were sport utility vehicles, which is why the average annual premium to insure this type of automobile is higher than the average premium for a not-so-trendy car.

➤ **Buy a car that will handle well if you are ever in an accident.** Ask the car sales rep how much of the car is damaged during an accident and whether or not it holds up well in an accident. For example, if you buy a car that falls apart in a fender bender, your insurance premiums will be much higher than if you buy a car that is a bit more resilient in an accident. In addition, find out how expensive any repairs may be. The more expensive it is to repair, the higher your premiums will be.

➤ **Raise your deductible and pay premiums annually.** Carrying a higher deductible will decrease your insurance premiums. For example, say you're a 30-year-old single female living in Chicago, driving a 1998 Pontiac Grand Am, and carrying full coverage on your car. You could pay $760 in semi-annual (every six months) premiums on a $250 deductible, or you could pay $589 in semi-annual premiums with a $500 deductible. You can reduce your premiums even further by paying on an annual basis.

The DOs and DON'Ts of Buying Life Insurance

Life insurance is a bugaboo in mainstream America because not many people understand it. However, it's really quite simple. Most folks buy life insurance to provide benefits for their survivors in case they die before "their time."

As you do for car insurance, you pay premiums when you buy life insurance. Your annual premiums are based on your age, your health, how much money your insurance company can earn by investing the money you give them (your premiums) until you die, and the expenses the insurance company incurs for mailings and commissions for its agents. Whew!

What makes life insurance a difficult concept to grasp is choosing which kind will best suit your personal needs. The most common reason to purchase life insurance is to support your family members who depend on your income in the event that you die prematurely. Life insurance can also prove helpful by providing immediate cash to pay estate taxes when you die or to repay business loans (if you are an owner of a business and you die prematurely).

Although life insurance can be confusing, figuring out the differences in insurance policies doesn't require a secret decoder ring. You just need to find out if you need life insurance and, if so, how much you need.

Do you need life insurance? The rule of thumb is that if you're young and single and have no one else depending on your income, you don't need it. Even if you're married, if both of you are working, you probably don't need life insurance. But if there are family members who depend upon your income, you definitely do.

How much insurance you need depends on how old you are and how well your family can live without your income. To determine this, consider the following factors:

➤ Your family would need immediate cash to cover death-related expenses. This would cover uninsured medical costs, funeral expenses, debts, taxes, and estate-settlement fees. Many insurance agents recommend at least $5,000.

➤ Tack on six to 12 months of your family's lost net income because of your death (to take immediate economic pressure off of your family).

➤ Calculate your family's expenses on an annual basis (you learned how to do this on a monthly basis in Chapter 2). What percent of these expenses are covered by your income? The mortgage still has to be paid and Junior's college tuition bill is still due. Also, how much will these expenses grow over the next five to eight years?

➤ Contact the Social Security Administration at (800) 772-1213 to see if your spouse and children are entitled to *survivors' benefits*. However, if your surviving spouse earns more than $20,000 a year, he or she is not entitled to any survivors' benefits coverage. If your family is eligible, have them determine what percentage of your current income the benefits cover. Why? Because if the survivors' benefits replace 30 percent of your income, you would have to purchase 30 percent less in life insurance benefits. Got it?

Without any mind-bending calculations, here's a basic rule of thumb for purchasing life insurance, according to a Citibank report. After the death of its principal income producer, a family requires 75 percent of its former after-tax income to maintain its standard of living. It must have at least 60 percent to get along at all. If you want to figure out your after-tax income without the help of a CPA, simply multiply your gross income by 60 percent if you earn a high income, 70 percent if you earn a moderate living, and 80 percent if you have a low income. Otherwise, if you want to simply figure out a rough estimate, just make it five to eight times your current wages. It comes out to about the same amount as Citibank's calculation.

Finally, you need to decide what kind of life insurance you need. Yuck! Because this could be the American public's most-despised question, we're going to make it easy on you and help you save a few bucks along the way. There are two very basic types of life insurance coverage: term insurance and cash value insurance. Term insurance is usually the best bet for all but the very wealthy. Whichever type of life insurance you decide to buy, keep the following things in mind:

➤ **Check out the insurance company's financial stability.** Even though term insurance policies always get paid—even if the insurance company goes belly up—those of you who are weak-kneed when it comes to your money should check on the health of the insurance company. Contact Weiss Research at (800) 289-9222 for more information. Other sources are A.M. Best (908/439-2200); Duff & Phelp's (312/368-3157); Moody's Investor Service (212/553-0300); and Standard & Poor (212/208-1527). These services will provide you with the financial strength of the insurance company and give you an explanation of how it grades each company. Of course, you want the highest rated companies possible, with grades of A++ and A+.

➤ **Buy your life insurance from a fee-only financial planner or a "direct-purchase."** You can save up to 40—sometimes 50—percent on an insurance agent's commissions if you go to a discount insurance broker. Better yet, if you purchase a policy directly from an insurance company, you can avoid the middleman altogether. Whichever type of life insurance you're purchasing, contact USAA at (800) 531-8000 for more information. Ameritas also provides low-cost cash value insurance policies to the public. Contact them toll-free at (800) 552-3553.

   In addition, if you're not sure about your policy, contact the National Insurance Consumer Organization (NICO) for information about how they can evaluate your proposed insurance policy (typically, the performance per $1,000 of coverage). Write to them at 121 N. Payne Street, Alexandria, VA 22314.

➤ **If you build up a sizeable net worth, consider life insurance as an option to pay estate taxes.** As you'll see in Chapter 26 about estate planning, life insurance can help alleviate the sting for wealthy people who owe Uncle Sam a lot in estate taxes. Make sure you review your situation with an estate-planning attorney (not your insurance agent) to figure out what options are available to you.

Term Insurance 101

Term insurance is usually the least expensive form of insurance coverage and is very affordable when you're young. As you get older, your risk of dying increases, so the cost of term insurance goes up. This risk is known as the *mortality rate*.

As with most other insurance coverages, you pay premiums annually, semiannually, or quarterly for term insurance. For this premium, you receive a predetermined amount of life insurance protection. If you are the insured spouse and you die during the term you are insured, your beneficiaries will collect. If not, all of the premiums are gone, since there is no cash buildup in the policy, as there is in other types of life insurance policies that promote savings features (and hefty commissions). You will probably be required to take a physical examination to qualify for term insurance.

Term insurance is very inexpensive, which is why it's a popular life insurance policy. However, it only provides for death protection—there's no build-up of the money you pay in premiums.

When you buy term insurance, you can buy it with level (same) premiums for one year, called *annual renewable term* (ART), and renewable until age 90. Other term policies and specified time periods are typically five, 10, 15, or 20 years. At the end of these time periods, the term insurance is renewable at sharply higher premium levels because you are older and statistically more likely to die during this time period.

Some people refer to term insurance as "renting coverage" because the only way your insurance policy pays out is if you die during this period. The payouts are offered in a lump sum payment or a steady stream of payments to your beneficiaries.

Asset Advisory

Young women who are non-smokers tend to pay the least amount in premiums for term insurance. Because the cost of term insurance does not depend solely on age (where the younger you are, the lower your premiums are), and women live longer than men, women will pay less—especially if they don't light up.

Make sure your policy offers a *guaranteed renewability feature*, so you don't have to take a medical test to continue coverage for another term, especially as you get older. Also, if you have an annual renewable term policy, you can convert it to a whole-life policy—without a medical exam. This is called *guaranteed conversion*, and allows you to convert from rising-premium term insurance to a fixed-premium whole life (cash value policy, which you'll learn about later in this chapter) policy. Here's a tip: If you think you may do this sometime down the road, make sure your term insurance policy is convertible into a whole life policy without another medical examination. There's an additional cost for this provision, but as you get older you'll end up saving more in premiums by doing so and avoiding the medical examination.

Here are some things to keep in mind when looking at a term insurance policy.

➤ **Make sure the illustrations that your insurance agent gives you show the rates you will pay and the maximum guaranteed rate they can require you to pay.** There is a state law that regulates the maximum guarantees. But remember, policy illustrations are not guarantees—even if they're in black and white. Term premiums are subject to change based on mortality and the insurance company's finances.

➤ **Compare a *level premium term* policy to an annual renewable term (which increases after each term).** You know that premiums on ordinary ART policies increase in cost every year, right? Well, some companies offer a form of *level premium term*, in which they project that the annual premium will remain the same for 5, 10, or 20 years. At the end of the specified time period, your policy may kick back into a policy that has increasing premiums every year, or remain level for five years and *then* kick back into increasing premiums. Ask your agent if the premiums are projected or guaranteed. Insurance companies are not obligated to meet projected premiums—even if they are in the illustrations they give you.

➤ **Don't always settle for a short-term level premium policy.** Why? Because the premiums may skyrocket after the short-term is over. Again, because this is the life insurance industry, it depends on the policy. Make sure the agent explains all details in black and white.

➤ **Choose a guaranteed annual renewable term to avoid medical exams.** This ensures that you do not have to have a new medical exam every year to renew your term policy. Avoid those policies, which are known as *reentry term*.

If you would like quotes on term insurance, contact one of the following quote services. There is no obligation to purchase term insurance, but make sure they can handle the transaction in your state if you do buy a policy.

TermQuote (800/444-8376) maintains a database of 70 companies and will search to find the lowest cost term insurance policy based on your specifications, your age, and health condition.

SelectQuote (800/343-1985) tracks term insurance prices nationwide.

INSurance INFOrmation (800/472-5800) provides only advice—they do not sell insurance—but will find the lowest cost term insurance policy for you and can even reevaluate your existing policy.

Insurance Quote Services (800/972-1104) sends a free booklet "Simple Guide to Insurance Savings," in addition to providing a quote service on low-cost term insurance. They will do a simple analysis on your life insurance needs based on your criteria and personal situation.

Cash Value Insurance

Sometimes known as *permanent insurance*, cash value insurance generally covers longer-term needs because term insurance becomes too expensive as you get older. But beware: Cash value insurance only makes sense for a few people and generates a lot of commissions for the insurance agent (unless you buy low-load or no-load insurance).

Cash value insurance combines life insurance and a savings "account." Most of the money you pay in premiums goes toward life insurance, and a few bucks are deposited into this "account" that is supposed to grow in value over time. Sounds like a winner, huh?

Wrong. The biggest hit your account takes in the early years you're building it is the commission that your insurance agent earns, which is shown to you in the illustration he or she shows you. What most folks don't know is that the commission is built right into the premium you pay for the insurance. It may take years until the true return (what the insurance company promised you) on your account is equal to what it's supposed to be. To find out how much and what portion of your premium is going into your account, ask your insurance agent to show you the *surrender value* on the piece of paper (usually a ledger) he has. If the amount in the first few years is ZILCH, that's what your little account is getting.

All of the cash value insurance policies offer a tax-deferred savings feature to the insurance protection component of the policy. It is merely a death benefit plus an investment fund.

Interestingly enough, both term and cash value policies come in two varieties: participating and nonparticipating. Why all this gobbledygook? It seems confusing, but pay attention and you'll know more about how to make life insurance *work for you* than anyone you know!

Participating insurance entitles you to receive dividends (kind of like stock dividends) from the policy. These dividends are considered a refund of the portion of the premium that the insurance company did not pay in death benefits or administrative expenses over the previous year. This means that if the insurance company is collecting all of these premiums and no one died or administrative costs for the year were low, all the policy holders would get a "refund" in the form of dividends.

So what do you do with these dividends? You can take them as cash—and, of course, pay taxes to the IRS because the dividends are considered income. You can reinvest your dividends and *reduce* the future premiums you have to pay. Or, you can buy additional "paid-up" (more) insurance. The choice is yours.

Non-participating policies pay no dividends, so there's nothing to reinvest. Instead, your premiums are fixed when you buy a policy at a set amount. True, these premiums on a non-participating policy will be less than those on a participating policy, but non-participating policies *do not* offer the perks of reinvesting your dividends for future growth or whatever you choose to do with the money.

Be careful; some insurance company illustrations show that dividends from a paid-up policy can cover the premiums for a new policy when they *don't*. Instead, the new policies will really borrow against the death benefit (like a loan) in order to pay the premiums. Watch out for the fine print!

Because cash value insurance policies are not straightforward (it would make life too easy if they were), here's a rundown of the terms you can expect to hear about from an insurance agent:

➤ **Whole Life:** Your premium stays the same every year, and your death benefit is fixed. Since the amount of the premium is much more than what you would need to pay death benefits in the early years, the extra money is "deposited" into your "account" (inside the policy), which earns interest and grows tax-deferred. You can choose from two types of whole life policies. In the first, you pay the same level premiums into your old age—where you can borrow against the policy to get some extra cash in your retirement years. In the second, you pay premiums for a fixed number of years only; after that, the cash value in your "account" pays for the premiums. This is known as *vanishing premiums*. But be careful. If you don't have enough cash value built up to pay for those future premiums, your policy will be the thing that vanishes! And then you're stuck with kicking in more money. Whole life premiums are often invested in long-term bonds and mortgages.

➤ **Universal Life:** Unlike a standard whole life insurance policy, universal life offers you flexibility because it allows you the decision of changing the premium payments or the amount of the death benefit, as long as certain minimum requirements are met. (Sometimes, if you don't meet the minimum requirements or you violate the rules, your tax liability may skyrocket if you borrow or withdraw the money.) *You* decide how to design your policy. You can pay hefty premiums, build up a lot of tax-deferred cash value in your account, and then later change your mind that you want your cash value to pay for your premiums. Or, you can opt for lower death benefits and a larger cash buildup or a smaller cash buildup and higher death benefits. It's up to you. You can even take a cash withdrawal and lower the death benefit. There's no interest expense if you do this, but even if you pay back the withdrawal, this permanently lowers the death benefit. Typically, there's enough cash value earnings to cover the cost of the insurance. Universal life premiums are invested in and reflect the current short-term rates available in the money market.

➤ **Variable Life:** Even though the annual premiums are fixed, the cash value of your account doesn't earn a fixed rate of return. The growth of your account in the policy depends on what investment choices you make. Generally, the investment choices are mutual funds managed by the insurance company. You have the option of shifting your money around. Note that the death benefit also rises and falls based on the performance, but it will never drop below the original amount of insurance coverage you specified on your contract.

➤ **Single-Premium Life:** The person who would benefit from this type of policy is someone who is older, has a lump sum of cash to invest on a tax-deferred basis that meets with IRS guidelines, and wants insurance benefits for his or her beneficiaries. These policies can earn a fixed rate of interest (like those in a whole life or universal life), or you can choose your own investment (as in a variable life policy).

Whatever you do, don't look upon a cash value insurance policy as retirement savings or your first means to accumulate growth on a tax-deferred basis. Even if your insurance agent tells you that your cash value account is compounding on a tax-deferred basis, that shouldn't be the reason to buy a cash value policy. If you're seeking tax-deferred growth, you should be participating in a company's 401(k) or an individual retirement account.

Insure Your Paycheck!

Have you ever thought about what would happen if you were suddenly unable to perform the work that provides your income? You should. According to the Health Insurance Association of America, if you are between the ages of 35 and 65, your chances of dying are equal to your chances of being unable to work for three months or more because of a disability through illness or injury. It is stressful enough trying to deal with an injury or illness that you don't want to have to worry about whether or not you're going to receive your salary while you're off work.

The Money Line

Some disability factoids:

One year of disability can wipe out 10 years' worth of savings.

Forty-three percent of all foreclosures result from a disability in the family.

Less than 50 percent of the labor force is covered by disability insurance.

Your earning power is the most valuable asset that you will ever own—not your home, your car, or even your antique furniture. If you own your home, you probably have homeowner's insurance in case of loss or damage, and automobile insurance protects you and your family in case of a car accident. So why not insure your paycheck, too?

If you're like most folks, you probably have some type of access to a company-sponsored disability plan. Under the plan, most companies extend a form of paid sick leave or actual disability payments in case you are unable to work for a long time period. According to these plans, in order for you to receive benefits, many companies require you to be totally disabled. Other companies have both short-term and long-term disability plans. Ask your employer what provisions the company provides for both short and long-term disability. The industry standard is 26 weeks for short-term disability, and you must qualify for most long-term disability plans. On average, an employer will pay the premiums for its employees' short-term disability insurance policy. For a long-term disability policy, it is standard for the employer and the employee to split the cost of the premium.

If you are paying part of the premium on disability insurance and your employer is paying the remainder, the benefits you receive are taxable equal to the amount of the premium your employer pays. For example, let's say your annual premium on your disability insurance policy is $1,200. You pay a third of your annual premium ($400), and your employer pays the other two-thirds ($800). If you were to become disabled and start collecting benefits, the portion of the premium that your employer paid would be considered taxable income. You would owe ordinary income taxes on your monthly benefits check.

Make sure you find out as much as you can about your company's disability plan. One woman we know did her homework before she went in for surgery. She was able to take a short-term disability leave for eight weeks and received 60 percent of her salary while recuperating at home. Many folks who don't do their homework go back to work a lot sooner without recovering fully and risk injuring themselves further.

If your company does not sponsor a plan, you can purchase your own individual policy. However, you have to have a job to receive disability insurance—no ifs, ands, or buts. But only you can determine which type of disability policy is best. Your goal should be to maximize your coverage without paying for any unnecessary benefits.

Annual individual policy premiums range anywhere from $800 to $1,800, sometimes a lot more, depending on the bells and whistles you add to the policy. You will need enough coverage to provide between 60 and 70 percent of your gross earned income. Sit down and figure out what your living expenses would be if you were disabled for three to six months or more. Keep in mind you'll have to cover the mortgage or rent, automobile expenses, food, clothing, and utilities. Plus, you will incur additional expenses: medicine, doctor visits, and possibly nursing care.

Keep these other factors in mind if you're considering buying disability insurance:

➤ **If you have a risky job, you will pay a higher premium for disability insurance.** The cost of disability insurance is determined by your job and the amount of income you want. If you are in a hazardous occupation class (for example, if you are a firefighter, carpenter, or construction worker), you might not be able to receive long-term disability at any cost, unless it's through a company or a union.

➤ **Stay in good health and maintain a good credit report.** You will be required to take a medical exam to qualify for disability insurance. Plus, the insurance company looks into your credit history. If you have a poor credit history or have recently filed for bankruptcy, an insurance company might not cover you.

➤ **Start your policy as soon as you can.** Why? The younger you are, the less your annual premiums will be.

➤ **Set a long elimination period.** This is the period of time before the benefits start. What you can do is match your emergency fund to this time period. Your premiums may be reduced by nearly 10 percent.

➤ **Avoid policies that pay only if you are totally disabled.** Instead, look for a policy that covers the "own occupation." This guarantees that you will receive the full guaranteed disability payment, no matter what other work you do, as long as you are not able to return to your original occupation.

➤ **Make sure your policy is non-cancelable as long as you keep paying the premiums.** Also make sure it has a guaranteed annual premium that can never be increased. Also crucial is a waiver of premiums clause, which states that you don't have to pay any more premiums once you become disabled.

➤ **Shop around.** Want the best price? Get quotes from three different insurance agents. Then contact USAA Life Insurance Company (which sells directly to consumers) toll-free at (800) 531-8000 and compare prices.

➤ **See what Social Security has to offer.** Through Social Security you will receive disability income if you are completely disabled for five months and the disability is expected to last for at least one year or your lifetime.

Insurance Products You DON'T Need

You want to cover your life, health, and wealth, right? That's why you're reading this chapter: to protect yourself and your loved ones. Unfortunately, many companies are jumping on the insurance bandwagon to take advantage of consumers, making them think they need these superfluous policies. Not so. Here's a list of what to avoid.

Credit life and credit disability policies: Sold by credit card companies, such as VISA and MasterCard, these policies will pay a small monthly income in case of liability or a small benefit in case you die with an outstanding loan. Skip this coverage and purchase disability insurance instead.

Extended warranties: Never purchase an extended warranty on anything—a television, VCR, or even an automobile. If something breaks down, it's likely that it would cost less to pay for it out of your own pocket.

Flight insurance: This type of insurance is based on fears and misconceptions. Instead of protecting yourself with flight insurance, in case you die while flying, choose a good life insurance policy that protects you wherever you are—even if you're at 31,000 feet.

Dental insurance: Many employers offer this type of coverage through company-sponsored health insurance plans. Take advantage of it. If your employer does not offer this, the routine cleanings cost much less than your annual premiums would.

Life insurance for your children: Touted on late-night television, this form of insurance boasts inexpensive monthly premiums to provide coverage for your children. It's not necessary at all, and it can be quite expensive. Besides, what parents would spend the benefits from a life insurance policy on their children if something terrible happened?

The Least You Need to Know

➤ Renter's insurance is inexpensive and can help you replace your belongings in case of fire, theft, or other disaster.

➤ Homeowner's insurance is required by mortgage lenders. It's usually best to get as much coverage as you can afford. You can save money on premiums by raising your deductible, paying your premium annually, and using the same insurance company for your home and car.

➤ Car insurance is required by law in most states. You can save money on your premiums by being a safe driver, driving a reliable car, and shopping around.

➤ There are two types of life insurance: term and cash-value. Term insurance is a better deal unless you're older or wealthy.

➤ Long-term disabilities that leave you unable to work can result in financial disaster. Take advantage of any disability insurance available through your employer and consider buying supplemental insurance if necessary.

Chapter 26

Tackling Your Taxes

In This Chapter

➤ The basics on the latest tax law changes

➤ Avoiding common tax mistakes

➤ Strategies to keep tax liabilities to a (legal) minimum

➤ Finding a good tax pro

Being smart about your taxes is more than just correctly using a black pen instead of a pencil on your tax return. Your investment and retirement planning strategies, marital status, and, if you're self-employed, business decisions, affect your tax situation—especially with the changes that have taken place in the last couple of years, providing taxpayer relief in the Taxpayer Relief Act of 1997 and the IRS Restructuring and Reform Act of 1998.

That's right, taxpayers. Tax planning doesn't just concern the wealthy. The money you save in taxes creates more investment dollars that can be put to work for you and your family if you start your tax planning now. Plus, preparing for April's tax season ahead of the typical last-minute schedule will help you get your records in order for when you really need them.

We don't expect you to leisurely read the U.S. tax code, but if you want to make sure you're doing all that you can to keep the money you work so hard for, then let's see how you can avoid common problems people make when it comes to tax planning. Of course, since tax planning isn't always the easiest task to complete, this chapter also reviews the best ways to find a competent tax professional who can help you.

Change Is Good

Congress is looking out for you, Mr. and Mrs. Taxpayer. In 1998, the IRS Restructuring and Reform Act was passed into law in an effort to give taxpayers more protection in disputes with the IRS. In the past, taxpayers would have to prove that the IRS determination was incorrect; today, it's the other way around.

Aside from being able to flex a bit more muscle in tax court, taxpayers can also enjoy the single largest tax planning opportunity from the new law. The capital gains rate, which is now a maximum of 20 percent, is applied to sales and exchanges of assets held more than 12 months, instead of the 18 months that was enacted in the 1997 Act. This change is retroactive to January 1, 1998.

If you invest in mutual funds, as many Americans do, this change is a big plus. Here's why. Growth of mutual funds usually comes in the form of capital gains and dividends. The tax savings under the new approach is substantial, as dividends are taxed at up to approximately 40 percent and capital gains are taxed at a maximum of 20 percent—rather than the traditional 28 percent.

The IRS dubs it only as a work in progress to modernize the IRS, but no matter what it's slugged, taxpayers will now know who they're dealing with. Case in point. Let's say you filed your taxes and you expect a refund, only to find out that the IRS is denying you the monies. Under the new law, the agency is required to explain why it denies you your refund and—get this—provide you with the phone number of the IRS worker handling your case. Hello, carrot, meet Mr. Rabbit.

What if you have interest and penalties to pay? Expect changes, too, because under prior law, the IRS did not have to show how penalties are computed on the Notice of Penalty, and in some cases, without supervisory approval. Now, however, after December 31, 2000, each penalty notice must include the name of the penalty, the code section imposing it, and the computation of it. Supervisory approval must also be assessed.

For many taxpayers, some of these changes may result in substantial tax savings, as long as proper planning is done in advance. Check with your tax professional to review your individual and/or business situation.

In the meantime, know that progress can only be made as long as you're not making mistakes on basic tax planning issues along the way.

Ten Most Common Tax Mistakes

Mistake 1: Failing to keep good records. Getting organized is imperative. At some point, most people have the motivation to sort out their tax records, but they seem to drop the ball several months later. If you are one of those consumers whose sock drawer is stuffed with unopened envelopes holding your mutual fund statements and past IRS tax returns, kick the habit. It's time to clean house.

You have several options for maintaining good records, including tax software programs for your computer and your basic file folder for file statements. Tax preparation software packages for your computer can save you time and money. You just have to answer a few questions, and the software program plugs the information into the appropriate tax form. In addition, most tax-software packages print and file your returns automatically.

Mistake 2: Not withholding the right amount of taxes. Estimated tax payment and underpayment penalty rules have eased somewhat for Americans, but that does not give you the green light to ignore the rules. On the other hand, if you're anticipating a tax refund, all that means is that you've overpaid the government. You could have put that "extra" money to work for you in an investment instead of loaning it to Uncle Sam.

If you make estimated tax payments (as do many self-employed individuals or people who earn a whopping taxable income from investments outside a tax-deferred account), you should constantly monitor your tax-paying situation. The best way is to get Form 1040-ES, Estimated Tax for Individuals, from the Internal Revenue Service by calling (800) TAX-FORM. Your goal should be to not overpay but not underpay; try to get as close to the mark as possible.

Mistake 3: Getting help when it's too late. This mistake is so common it's not even funny. It's like trying to prevent a cavity that has already made its way into your molar—there's no way to do it. Because many of your personal finance and investment decisions will affect your tax plan, get *preventive* help before it's too late.

Once you assess your personal financial picture and investment game plan, you'll need to monitor it consistently, especially as you build your wealth and accumulate a higher net worth. In the section "Finding a Tax Pro" later in this chapter, you'll read which types of tax pros can help you, no matter what your circumstances are.

Mistake 4: Not contributing to a tax-deferred investment program. Up to certain limits, Individual Retirement Accounts (IRAs), 401(k)s, and other popular tax-deferred retirement plans allow you to reduce your taxable income by the amount of your contribution. Even if you only receive a partial or no tax deduction, investing your money in a mutual fund within your IRA takes advantage of the power of tax-deferred compounding.

Here's the magic of tax-deferred compounding at work. If for 30 years you invest $2,000 a year in a mutual fund in your IRA instead of in a taxable account, assuming a nine-percent annual return, you will have accumulated almost $300,000 in your IRA. In contrast, you would have accumulated only $184,000 in a taxable account in the same amount of time. The capital gains and dividend distributions made would be tax-deferred for the entire 30 years. So just do it!

Mistake 5: Not replacing personal debt with mortgage debt to the extent possible. It's a smart tax planning strategy if you do this, especially since interest expense on mortgage loans is 100 percent tax-deductible. Interest expense on personal debt, such as credit cards or personal loans, is *not* tax deductible at all. If possible, and where applicable, you may wish to consider a home equity loan to pay off your personal debt. The interest on a home equity loan is 100 percent tax deductible, and you can get rid of your personal debt, too!

Mistake 6: Forgetting to check last year's income tax return for important items. For example, if you have $10,000 worth of gains and $10,000 worth of losses in one tax year, you can net the losses against the gains, and not have any taxable income from your investments. However, if your ordinary income (from your wages or salary) is $30,000 and you had $10,000 worth of losses (and no gains), you could only apply a total of $3,000 to your ordinary income to reduce your taxable income. The mistake people make is forgetting to carry forward the remaining loss amount on next year's return. Under current IRS rules, the remaining amount over $3,000 (in $3,000 increments) can be applied to the *following year's* tax bill.

Mistake 7: Not taking a profit because you're afraid to have a capital gain. When you buy low and sell high, you earn a profit, which is a capital gain. And, depending on your income tax bracket, you are subject to pay capital gains of 15 percent or 28 percent under current IRS law. Of course, review the tax implications a capital gain will have on your investment portfolio—and tax return—with your tax professional, but don't shy away from taking a gain. After all, why are you investing in the first place? To *lose* money? We hope not.

Mistake 8: Choosing the wrong filing status. Usually newly married couples have this problem—not knowing which filing status to choose. They have two options: married filing jointly and married filing singly. The IRS advises confused newlyweds (and other married folks) to complete returns based on both situations and, based on the bottom-line outcome (whether you owe a little, a lot, or expect a refund), make your decision then. Nine times out of ten you'll "save" more in taxes by filing jointly.

Mistake 9: Anticipating a large refund. If you regularly look forward to receiving a huge income tax refund, know this: You're having too much in taxes withheld from your paycheck and, in effect, giving an interest-free loan to the IRS. Changing the number of allowances you claim on a W-4 form will increase your take-home pay.

Mistake 10: Forgetting to attach the right copy to your tax returns. Sounds silly, but it happens. Attach all the "Copy Bs" of your W-2 forms to your return in order to avoid future correspondence with the IRS. And, above all, make copies of all your returns and correspondence…just in case!

Investments and Taxes

Whenever you invest your moolah, you have tax consequences to consider. For example, when you buy low and sell high, you earn a profit, which is a capital gain. And, depending on your income tax bracket, if it's a sizeable gain, it can really make a difference in your bottom-line return figures.

The government did Americans a favor in the Taxpayer Relief Act of 1997 when it announced that the maximum capital gains rate was reduced to 20 percent, down from 28 percent in the past. In fact, subsequently, the IRS Reform Act of 1998 added another benefit: Any asset held for more than 12 months—not the traditional 18 months—will be applied to the 20 percent rate, retroactive to January 1, 1998.

Fiscal Facts

Capital gains are profit, expressed as the difference in purchase price and selling price, when the difference is positive.

So, how can you determine if you should invest your money in an investment vehicle that stresses capital gains or income (usually in the form of interest payments or dividends that are taxed at your income tax rate)? The decision depends on your investment objective, but also creates different tax consequences.

Here's an example. Let's say you are in a higher tax bracket and invest more of your money in taxable bond funds. You get a pretty steady income stream through interest payments. These interest payments are taxed at *your* income tax rate. If you are taking out any cash distributions, that is a taxable event and subject to your tax bracket.

On the other hand, if you are investing in an investment that stresses capital gains (profit), it's a different story. For example, if you are investing in growth funds (no dividend income, rather long-term appreciation), any capital gains you realize are taxed at a maximum rate of 20 percent—a rate much less than taxable income brackets for high-income individuals.

The general rule of thumb is not to necessarily base your investment decisions solely on tax implications. If that were the case, many investors would never sell their investments! Your investment strategy is more important than a tax strategy. If you think market prices are dropping, you should take your profits and pay your taxes. A capital gain is always better than a capital loss!

Two of the Biggest Tax Blunders Ever

When folks hear "tax-free" or "tax-exempt," they jump for joy. The allure of tax-free investing is appealing, but it's not for everybody.

Many times, investors put their money in tax-exempt investments, such as municipal bonds, for the wrong reasons. Investors jump at the chance to boast of receiving tax-free income. But many of these municipal-bond funds tend to have lower yields than comparable taxable mutual funds for investors in lower tax brackets. If you are in a higher tax bracket, investing in municipal-bond funds is worth checking out because the income distributions you receive are exempt from federal tax. (Remember that the capital gains payouts are taxed.)

The best way to determine whether a fund's tax-free yield is competitive with the yield of a similar taxable fund is to find your taxable equivalent yield. If you want to calculate your taxable equivalent yield, take your marginal tax rate (your tax bracket) and subtract it from 100. For example, if you were in the 28 percent tax bracket, subtract 28 from 100 to get your denominator, which is 72. Therefore, if you were deciding whether to invest in a tax-exempt or a taxable fund, you would take 5.25 percent (the tax-exempt municipal bond return rate) and divide it by 72 to get your taxable equivalent yield, which is 7.29 percent. That means you would have to earn at least 7.29 percent on a taxable bond fund to end up with the same amount you would have left over after taxes if you were to invest in a tax-exempt bond fund.

Table 26.1 does the math for you so you can easily determine whether a municipal-bond fund is a worthwhile investment for you. Compare the taxable equivalent yield for municipal bonds listed under your tax bracket with the rates listed for non tax-exempt treasury-only and corporate-bond funds to see which provides the highest yield. As you can see in Table 26.1, the lower the tax bracket, the less incentive there is to invest in tax-exempt mutual funds.

Table 26.1   Tax-Free or Not Tax-Free?

Investment	Return	Your Tax Bracket			
		39.6%	33%	28%	15%
Municipal-Bond Fund	5.25%	8.69%	7.83%	7.29%	6.17%
Treasury-Only Bond Fund	6.00%	6.00%	6.00%	6.00%	6.00%
Corporate-Bond Fund	7.50%	7.50%	7.50%	7.50%	7.50%

Another blunder is when folks forget to swap or exchange investments to take a tax-loss and offset any other capital gains. If you sell an investment for a profit, you must pay capital gains tax on that profit. Depending on your level of income, you are taxed on the gain at either 15 percent or 20 percent, which is the maximum tax rate on capital gains.

Asset Advisory

You can deduct up to $3,000 in losses from capital gains, thereby reducing your capital gains taxes. If you have no gains to offset your losses, you can deduct up to $3,000 from your ordinary income. Any additional amount can be carried forward to future years.

If you sell an investment at a loss, you can get a tax benefit, too. For example, if you have exchange privileges with your mutual fund family, consider using it in the event you are going to take a loss. Why? First, if you exchange shares of one mutual fund for shares of another mutual fund, it is considered a sale and a new purchase. If the sale of the first mutual fund constitutes a loss, you can use that amount to offset any other capital gains you have realized. This is considered a tax swap. Although your investment position is the same, you've saved on taxes. If you want to repurchase the shares in the same fund, you must wait 31 days before doing so according to IRS rules, in order to take the tax loss on the initial sale. If you don't wait the 31 days, it is known as a "wash sale," and you don't get to claim the loss. All capital gains and losses are reported on Schedule D of your tax return.

Finding a Tax Pro

Congress keeps talking about simplifying the tax code, yet it doesn't seem to get any easier. If you don't understand the tax system, you probably pay more in taxes than necessary. A good tax professional will cut through the muck and identify tax-reduction strategies that will help reduce your tax bill, possibly increase your deductions, and decrease the likelihood of an audit (which can be triggered by any mistakes you make).

Hiring a professional isn't cheap, but you can save a few bucks if you know what to look for. Keep the following tips in mind before you hire anybody:

➤ **Don't hire the first tax adviser you find.** You don't buy the first house you look at, so apply the same theory here. You will be telling this person the most intimate financial details of your life. Make sure you interview at least five tax professionals face-to-face before you make your final decision. If the person is a true professional, he or she should spend quality time with you, ask a lot of questions, and above all, listen to you.

➤ **Ask the tax adviser about his or her credentials.** A continuing crackdown on unscrupulous tax preparers in the past five years has created stricter guidelines for tax preparers who file electronically. This effort screened out preparers with criminal records and severe financial problems who were claiming false refunds on clients' electronic returns. Preparers with access to IRS computers must be at least 21 years old and be a U.S. citizen or permanent resident alien. Credentials for all other types of tax preparers are listed in the appropriate section below.

➤ **Understand how the adviser gets paid.** There are flat fees, hourly fees, and fees based on a percentage of your return. The method of compensation is important because it can sway an adviser to recommend one course of action over another. By knowing the adviser's motivation, you can guard against any self-serving advice.

The Lowdown on CPAs

You will need a CPA if your tax situation is complex. For example, if you are self-employed, run a small business, or have a high salary and claim many deductions, a CPA can not only help you prepare your return but help you plan your taxes throughout the year. She looks at your entire financial picture and how each of your financial

Watch Your Wallet

Just because a CPA specializes in accounting issues doesn't mean he or she files tax returns. Make sure you find out if the CPA does before you shell out any dough.

decisions (whether it's unloading a poor-performing stock or buying real estate for income) will impact your tax situation over the long haul. In addition, she can save you thousands of dollars in taxes by helping you conduct your financial affairs in a way that minimizes the government's tax bite.

Follow these guidelines when using a CPA:

➤ **Get a letter of engagement from the CPA.** This will list in detail what the CPA will do for you and what she will charge. Since a CPA charges more than any other tax preparer, the letter should state whether you are charged on an hourly basis or as a flat fee per return. You should also get an estimate of the time the CPA will spend on your return. If the CPA works on an hourly basis, ask her to guess how long it will take to do your tax preparations and complete your returns. However, if your CPA gives you a flat fee, see what other types of services are included in this fee, such as tax planning advice or whether she will attend an audit.

➤ **Don't simply dump your box of receipts and tell the CPA, "It's up to you to figure this all out."** One way to minimize their fees is to provide accurate records. You'll end up paying bucks deluxe if you're disorganized.

➤ **Find out how many tax returns the CPA works on each year.** If it's fewer than 300, consider him a candidate. If he prepares any more than that, he's probably sacrificing quality. Also, see what percentage of your CPA's clients had to file extensions last year. If it's more than 20 percent, the CPA is probably swimming in (and behind on) paperwork.

➤ **Find a CPA in your area by contacting the AICPA.** This is the professional organization for CPAs, and you can reach it at (800) 862-4272.

Try an Enrolled Agent

Enrolled agents are the biggest secret in the world of tax preparation. They are tax experts who worked for the IRS at least five years as auditors or who have passed a strict two-day test of federal tax law. If you don't mind that an enrolled agent doesn't have "CPA" listed after his name on the letterhead, an enrolled agent can be just as good—for much less money. Enrolled agents are experts in all areas of tax preparation; some even specialize in a few areas of the law. Make sure you determine an agent's specialty before you hire him. The best way to find an enrolled agent near you is to contact the National Association of Enrolled Agents (NAEA) at (800) 424-4339. They will send you a list of three agents in your area.

The Truth About Tax Attorneys

Tax attorneys know the ins and outs of federal tax law, but they do not prepare tax returns. Their role is to offer tax advice to your CPA or enrolled agent if you are in a complicated legal tax jam.

Hire a tax attorney if—and only if—you find yourself in a major legal jam resolving tax issues, such as a serious tax dispute with the IRS that can only be resolved in Tax Court. You may also need a tax attorney when you are working on the details of your estate plan and how it will affect your tax situation. Keep in mind, however, that these professionals are expensive! You will pay a price for their legal advice. Tax attorneys charge as much as several hundred dollars per hour, sometimes more if they represent you in court. Their fees may be deductible, but it's not guaranteed.

If a legal problem arises and your CPA cannot recommend a competent tax attorney, call the American Bar Association at (312) 988-5000 or find one listed in the *Martindale-Hubbell Law Directory*, which lists lawyers by state and specialty.

Certified Financial Planner: Jack-of-All-Trades

Imagine someone who knows your entire financial picture *and* can prepare your tax return. Sound like a financial dream come true? A certified financial planner (CFP) can create a budget for you, help you build an investment portfolio, and assist you with retirement and estate planning and tax preparation. Since CFPs must be licensed by the International Boards of Standards and Practices for Certified Financial Planners (IBCFP), look for their accreditation. There are a lot of financial planners out there masquerading as professionals; unless they have the acronym, don't deal with them.

CFPs do *not* have the same credentials as a CPA. People who choose CFPs to help with their tax preparation often do so because they know their whole financial picture.

CFPs are compensated in one of three ways: on a commission-only, fee-only, or commission and fee basis. The least expensive of the three for you (if you plan to maintain a working relationship with this person) is fee-only. For tax preparation, the most common form of payment will be fee-only. Fee-only planners do not get a dime for any type of investment recommendations they make, which is one of the reasons this condition works out best for most folks. When you find a fee-only planner, she should give you a no-cost, no-frills initial consultation to assess your financial condition. Based on this information, the CFP will give you an estimated fee that is set in advance. Typical rates average $75 an hour, depending on the complexities involved.

Watch Your Wallet

You do not want to be troubled by a nagging concern that your CFP is recommending products because of the commissions they generate instead of for their appropriateness of your situation. Make sure you get a written estimate of any fees you must pay, and make sure he or she is certified by the IRS to help you with your tax returns.

Watch Your Wallet

Fees for instant refunds are costly because they're based on an interest rate on this short-term "loan" that can run as high as 20 to 30 percent on an annual basis.

To find a qualified CFP in your area, contact the Institute of Certified Financial Planners (ICFP) at (800) 282-7526.

H&R Block and the Like

Places like H&R Block or Jackson Hewitt Associates process millions of tax returns each year and file electronically, which speeds up your refund if you are expecting one. In addition, some chains offer an instant refund, which is actually a loan that is paid back when your refund arrives from the IRS.

If you don't have a complicated tax situation, check out a national tax preparation chain. They are convenient, and they help you on a first-come, first-serve basis. However, keep in mind that you probably won't establish a long-term relationship with your tax preparer as you would with other tax professionals. The best way to find a national chain near you is to look in the Yellow Pages.

Going It Alone

Even if you have a CPA do your taxes, you should know *every* single detail that goes into your income tax return! If you prepare your own tax return, you know the ins and outs and can monitor your tax situation. Just make sure you keep up with any major changes in federal tax laws.

If you do go it alone, the IRS can actually help you. Although the IRS won't fill out your return, it will help you do so free of charge. All IRS offices hold tax preparation clinics, distribute free IRS publications, and answer tax questions over the phone. To contact them toll-free, call (800) 829-1040. There are some free books and publications that can help you, such as Publication 17, *Your Federal Income Tax*, which is published by the IRS to help individual tax-return preparation.

> ### The Least You Need to Know
>
> ➤ The key to having a less stressful tax time is to keep your tax-related documents organized. Tax-preparation software can help you do this.
>
> ➤ Investing in IRAs and 401(k)s is a great way to reduce your tax liability.
>
> ➤ Before you invest in stocks, bonds, or mutual funds, make sure you assess what effect those investments will have on your tax situation. However, don't base your decision solely on the tax consequence.
>
> ➤ Tax attorneys and CPAs are only necessary if your tax situation is complex. Less expensive sources of help include enrolled agents, certified financial planners, and tax preparation chains such as H & R Block.
>
> ➤ The cheapest way to handle your taxes is to do them yourself. The IRS can help; they provide tax booklets, clinics, and over-the-phone advice. Call (800) 829-1040 for more information.

Index

Y-Z